2002

The Idea of a Catholic **University**

The Idea of a Catholic **University**

George Dennis O'Brien

The University of Chicago Press . Chicago and London

George Dennis O'Brien is president emeritus of the University of Rochester
and former president of Bucknell University. He is the author of *Hegel on Reason
and History* (1975), *God and the New Haven Railroad* (1986), *What to Expect from
College* (1991), and *All the Essential Half-Truths about Higher Education* (1997).

The University of Chicago Press, Chicago 60637
The University of Chicago Press, Ltd., London
© 2002 by The University of Chicago
All rights reserved. Published 2002
Printed in the United States of America
11 10 09 08 07 06 05 04 03 02   1 2 3 4 5

ISBN: 0-226-61661-4 (cloth)

Library of Congress Cataloging-in-Publication Data

O'Brien, Dennis, 1931–
   The idea of a Catholic university / George Dennis O'Brien.
      p.   cm.
   Includes bibliographical references and index.
   ISBN 0-226-61661-4 (alk. paper)
   1. Catholic universities and colleges.   2. Education, Higher—Aims and
objectives.   I. Title.

LC487 .O23 2002
378'.0712'73—dc21

                                                   2001051051

♾ The paper used in this publication meets the minimum requirements of the
American National Standard for Information Sciences—Permanence of Paper
for Printed Library Materials, ANSI Z39.48-1992.

To my religious teachers, mentors, and friends
            the Sisters of St. Dominic
            the Christian Brothers of Ireland
            the Norbertines
            the Brothers of the Christian Schools

To the Sisters of Holy Names College
            opening Catholicism to Judith

... surely it is high time to utter a warning against the great-hearted, heroic objectivity with which many thinkers think on behalf of others and not on their own behalf.

SØREN KIERKEGAARD, *Either/Or*

Contents

Introduction

It was George Bernard Shaw who pronounced that "Catholic University" was a contradiction. Catholicism is committed to dogmatic authoritarianism, Shaw felt, whereas universities are committed to intellectual freedom and methodological skepticism—an opinion widely shared in the academic establishment. Whatever Catholic institutions may *say* about their commitment to academic freedom, critics need only point to such recent cases as the banishment of Fr. Charles Curran from the theological faculty of Catholic University of America to confirm their doubts about the intrusion of dogma into free discourse. The institution remains on the censure list of the official guardian of academic freedom, the American Association of University Professors (AAUP). The judge in the Curran case simply underlined the suspicions when he ruled that Catholic University was within its rights to dismiss Curran: it could chose to be an instrument of the Catholic Church or a "real" university (with academic freedom).[1]

If Catholic universities are not simply banned from the company of the intellectually respectable, they are nevertheless viewed with continuing suspicion, accepted only as they seem to approach the value-neutral open market of ideas espoused by the great secular institutions. In a recent statement, Mary Brugan, general secretary of the AAUP, noted that since the AAUP's declaration on academic freedom in 1940 (in which a reluctant acceptance of faith restriction on open inquiry was permitted), Catholic institutions had become so "open" that this qualification may no longer be needed.[2] If a *Catholic* university has traditionally been a suspicious character from the side of the academic establishment, Ms. Brugan's comments may well alarm the Catholic establishment. Such alarm presumably underlies Pope John Paul II's Apostolic Constitution of 1990 entitled *Ex Corde Ecclesiae* (*From the Heart of the Church*), which raises significant concerns about whether Catholic colleges and universities today are truly *Catholic*. While affirming the importance of academic freedom, the Pope insists that the Faith must remain the guiding principle of any institution claiming a Catholic identity. In November of 1999, the National Council of Catholic Bishops approved by an overwhelming vote a "juridical" interpretation of *Ex Corde*, directing that at putatively Catholic institutions the president should be a Catholic, the majority of the board of trustees should be Catholic, faculty appointments should go to Catholics, and that there should be a theology department and those who teach therein should seek an official *mandatum*[3] from church authorities to ensure their conformity to the official *magisterium* (the teaching office of the church). This sounded ominous to the defenders of open inquiry, and so it seemed to distinguished Catholic educators. President Edmund Malloy, C.S.C. of Notre Dame and Chancellor Donald Monan, S.J. of Boston College published[4] a sustained critique of the earlier draft of the juridical document, complaining among other things about the threat to academic freedom.

The pope was not the only one who seemed to worry about the Catholicity of Catholic colleges. The Vatican's concerns expressed the conservative stance of this papacy against what it regards as a type of freewheeling Vatican II Catholicism that emerged among Catholic liberals and "leftists" after the Council. But Catholic "liberals" have expressed their own concerns about the Catholicity of Catholic colleges. Peter Steinfels, a former editor in chief of *the* Catholic liberal journal, *Commonweal*, while sharply critical of the juridical interpretation of *Ex Corde* and the general minatory attitude of Rome, is equally uneasy about the loss of Catholic identity: "In questioning the wisdom of Rome's attitude . . . it is easy . . . to skirt the fact that the threat to Catholic identity of Catholic colleges and universities is very real. For altogether too long, many leading Catholic educators chose to minimize the dangers, and a few still do.[5]

One might very well conclude from the doubts, dangers, and dilemmas that seem to surround "Catholic" when joined with "university" that there really is something about this marriage that doesn't work. If it is university enough to satisfy the academic establishment, it is not churchy enough to satisfy Rome. Liberals would like to believe that the conjunction can be effected, but that may seem to be a wish refuted by long history and present circumstance. Catholic universities, if they want to be "real" universities, will have to follow the path of the great Protestant universities—Chicago (Baptist), Princeton (Presbyterian), Vanderbilt (Methodist), and so on—that have long since abandoned all sense of denominational commitment.[6]

The thesis of this book is that there is a *fundamental* clash between Catholic faith and the modern university. I say "Catholic" faith, but I really mean this treatment to deal more generally with the relation between the modern university and Christianity as well as the whole biblical tradition (Douglas John Hall calls the amalgam of Judaism and Christianity the "Jerusalem Tradition"). Because there are many Catholic colleges and because of the centralized and dogmatic teaching of the Roman Church, the problems of relating faith and learning are particularly acute and visible within the Catholic sector. Yet the essential issue of "faith and reason" is (or should be) common to all the biblical faiths. Thus, when I talk about problems of Catholic higher education, I do not in any way wish to exclude other Christian institutions of higher learning.

If the relation of the Jerusalem Tradition to the university raises problems, one should not think that the modern university is without its own set of philosophical assumptions or presumptions. Given the ideological assumptions of the modern research university, Catholic faith may well find it is not welcome there.[7] Shaw was correct: a contradiction. It is not clear, however, that the ideology of the modern university is the *only* possible ground, a sufficient ground, or the proper ground for what is (or should be) "higher" in higher education. There is enough denunciation of the modern university from the ideological/ political Right and Left to at least raise the suspicion that the problem with Catholic + university may be as much a problem for the academic establishment as for the Roman *magisterium*.

The modern conflict of church and university culture must seem, however, something of a paradox in the longer historical perspective. Universities were, after all, founded and sustained in the Middle Ages by the church. Although there were bitter critics of the new university movement in the older monastic schools, the universities nevertheless prospered and became the center of extraordinarily important theological and philosophical work. There were rumbles about heresy from time to time, but church officials did not seem to think that there was something fundamentally risky about the university. That a measure of assumed harmony existed was not an accident or oversight: the very notion of the university was subtly and importantly different. The university way and the church way were not regarded as divergent. How the notion of university has changed will be a theme of this book.

If there has been a significant shift in the understanding of the university, I would argue that there has been a concomitant shift in the understanding of Catholic *faith*, which is an even more tangled story than that of the university and one I will not even attempt to trace here. What seems to have happened, however, is that the Catholic Church (and mainline Protestant denominations)—as they sought to present Christianity to the modern world, particularly after the growth of science and the emergence of Enlightenment ideas—made the common but profound mistake of trying to refute their modernistic opponents while unconsciously accepting their basic assumptions.

To cite but one consequence of this mistake—the most crucial consequence for my present purposes and one on which I expand at length—there is great confusion between church and academy about the notion of "truth." In the clash between the modern university and Catholic faith, the university seems to hold the upper hand as the guardian of the best if not the only method of arriving at the truth. Something like scientific appraisal and scholarly research seem to capture the field when it comes to truth assessment. Insofar as this is the case, biblical testimony, Papal pronouncements, and the rulings of the *magisterium* just have no weight at all. But what is the "truth" that the church "teaches"? All I would say here is that it is downright odd, if not nonsensical. Not because it may be false but because it seems to be what philosophers call a "category mistake." What is the Christian truth? Jesus said, "*I* am the Truth." But that is absurd! Individuals aren't truths or the Truth—or if they are it must be in a sense quite different from the truth of well-established facts and theories of science. The clash between Catholic faith and scientific truth is not a clash between some Christian facts and some scientific facts, a competition over "the truth of *x*." If there is "contradiction" at all it does not lie simply and directly on the plane of our Christian truths versus their scientific (university) truths. Thus, in the course of this book, I want to question not only the ideology of the modern university, but also the way in which Catholic defenders of the truth of the Catholic faith construe "truth."

A Catholic university may not be a Shavian contradiction but I think there is a fully legitimate university endeavor that is both "Catholic" and "contrarian" to the prevailing ideology of the modern research university. In order to delineate such a possibility it is necessary to discuss the power and importance of the modern university—but also its significant limitations. A Catholic university properly understood as contrarian could play a significant role as a counterweight to the prevailing university ideology. Not only that, I believe it could be more fully an instrument of "higher learning" than the admittedly splendid universities of the present day. Having said that, I would be the first to acknowledge that the Catholic institutions in the United States today often express this contrarian position at best partially, usually defensively and apologetically, and in only the vaguest and often muddled ways.

Alisdair MacIntyre—no fan of the modern university—characterized the defense of secular universities (during the turbulent 1960s) by their presidents as "stuttering ineptitudes."[8] I won't comment on the "epitude" of Catholic defenders, but there has certainly been a surfeit of stuttering in the discussion of Catholicity and the university. If there is a common failure in the apologetics for Catholic higher education, I would say that it is excessive piety toward "the unity of truth." Of course, Catholic apologists often say, one can proceed with all the trappings of the modern scholarly establishment and yet hold to the truths of faith. There is no way that they could finally be in conflict. When that seems to be the case, a twist or tweak of faith or scientific theory will suffice to recreate harmony. This tactic is like pious solutions to the problem of suffering: somehow it will all work out in the end. One fails to appreciate the stark challenge of scientific truth—or science fails to appreciate the stark challenge of faith—in the bland belief that truth is truth is truth after all. My own treatment of faith and reason, however "ept," will at least present the problematic of faith and reason as difficult and deep. Whether I can illuminate from the deep is for the reader to judge.

A justification of and argument for a Catholic or, more generally, a Christian institution of higher learning must ask some deep questions about contemporary higher education. Because we so easily accept the facts on the ground of the modern university, the questions raised might often seem strained. Ideological possession of the curriculum is nine points of the law, so why dispute the current academic configuration? But a mere glance at history should raise some puzzles about present academic reality. For instance, nothing would seem to mark the character of the present-day university more than the role and influence of natural science. One can make a plausible case that the "scientific method" broadly defined is the essential commitment of the modern university. Given the present prominence of science, it is at least a wonder that the great developments of modern science from Newton to almost the end of the nineteenth century occurred outside the universities. As one educational historian has noted, "Experimental science . . . evolved basically outside and in opposition to the traditional universities."[9] Science was an activity of individuals and groups like the Royal Academy, not of the universities.

A similar puzzle can be constructed about the place of the arts in the academy. Academic departments of art and music are largely twentieth-century incursions. Training in art was traditionally in someone's studio or *atelier*; history of art was the activity of enthusiasts like Vasari and Ruskin or groups like the *Societa de Dilletanti*, which carried on the earliest excavations of ancient artifacts. Universities up until the twentieth century paid little attention to literature other than Latin models of composition. Departments of English are scarcely a century old. What exactly are the fine arts and the study of novels supposed to convey in the modern curriculum? As I say, it may seem odd to us today to ask why universities teach science and the arts, but there is no way to understand some of the most important fundamental assumptions of higher education without raising the question. It may be that universities of the past were just too dull or obstinate to include these stars of the current curricular constellation, but it may also be that earlier institutions were understood by themselves and their societies as having quite different needs and aims. I do not mean to denigrate the importance of the current higher educational establishment. No one who has considered the lazy world of eighteenth-century Oxford or the wooden denominationalism of much of nineteenth-century American higher education would advocate a return to some imagined golden age of higher education. On the other hand, there may have been something important in those earlier days that has been lost—lost, perhaps, by the colleges' own feeble attention to assumed goals, but lost nonetheless.

Among the "lost" interests of higher education, when one compares past—even the recent past—and present, is theological instruction and commitment. There was a day when theology was "the queen of the sciences." In his classic *The Idea of a University*, published in 1854, Cardinal Newman insisted that no place could call itself a university that did not teach theology. When modern university presidents piously cite Newman's elevated rhetoric as they often do, they do *not* cite his defense of theology. The queen of the sciences seems to have gone the way of other monarchs in our modern democratic age. Since the theme of this book is the idea of a Catholic university, one of the issues that must be addressed is what loss (or gain) has come to contemporary higher education from the marginalization, if not utter exclusion, of theology from the curricular requirements. If it seems *prima facie* odd to ask why science and art, it will no doubt seem even stranger to ask why not theology—and theology as the queen of the sciences!

Asking the "deep" questions about the modern university will necessarily lead to considerations about academic life that in one sense seem to have nothing at all to do with the ongoing research and teaching at our institutions. For instance, I will discuss the importance of the Creation story in Genesis for scientific research. I am certain that one can be a brilliantly productive quantum physicist without believing in Genesis or, in fact, even knowing that there is such a book in the Bible. The researcher might, given several religious options, choose the Creation story as fitting for his physics, but that recognition will not produce even a footnote for the *American Physical Review*. Creation may fit the *spirit* of the enterprise, but the spirit is not an item of experimental data. The deeper, "spirit-of-the-enterprise" assumptions often go without saying. But, for all that, it may be important to coax them out into verbal recognition. It is possible, after all, to misconstrue the spirit in its substance and range. The result can be destructive to the academic enterprise or to other areas upon which the academic world might seek to comment. The acknowledged importance and status of the modern university gives it an authority to either reinforce or subtly undermine other areas of human endeavor. Thus it has been argued that the fundamental methodological assumptions of the academic enterprise constitute a form of "methodological atheism." Not only is theology no longer queen of the sciences, she has been methodologically exiled. Being exiled from the place of prestige as authority on truth hardly commends faith to the common lot.

Finally, because the issues I wish to address are in the deep background, there is some relatively challenging philosophical and theological reading involved in the text.[10] I have tried to keep this to a minimum, however, since I do not wish this book to be a treatise only for professional scholars. My hope is that anyone interested in higher education, and Catholic higher education in particular, will be able to understand the basic lines of the argument. As the book developed, it turned in two directions that I had not initially planned or expected. In reflecting on the completed work, I was surprised to discover that I had devoted as much attention to the problem of "church" as I had to "university." I suppose that should not have been a surprise. Insofar as the spur for this investigation was the claim by John Paul II that universities were "from the heart of the church," I could hardly discuss Catholic (church) universities without extended discussion of the church and the meaning of its faith. The second and less pleasant surprise is that the book has turned out to be more theoretical than I had first intended. Although I conclude with a "practical postscript" in chapter 12, the bulk of the text concentrates on what the title promises: the *idea* of a Catholic university. Unless one gets the theory straight, practical application will seem arbitrary.

The central term of the discussion—namely, "truth"—lies at the heart of the problems surrounding the relation between university study and religious belief. Nothing much less than the vast history of philosophy could be an adequate treatment of this elusive notion. But I have sought to simplify matters by focusing on three areas in which truth may be thought to play a part: science, art, and religion. My intent is to demonstrate the important connections, and even more important differentiations, among the "truths" of these three.

The views of science, art, and religion I offer are current but not beyond dispute. For instance, I make a case for the *individuality* of the work of art. That is not how art has always been viewed. Rather than valuing individuality, deviation from traditional forms was regarded as problematic in Byzantine icons and Chinese scroll painting. That *we* now assign individual nuance to icons and scrolls reflects our view of art. I think it is an important and salient method of appropriation, but there have been other times and other ways. Similarly, my view of science as "transcendent truth" might be disputed by radical pluralists, but I believe my analysis is plausible and widely shared. Finally, it is impossible to talk about Catholic higher education without doing some theology, and that presented here is orthodox, I think, though I am quite conscious of the fact that it does not always read like traditional Catholic apologetics. I am specifically critical of much that issues from Rome as definitive of the Faith, particularly its interpretation of the "form" of faith statements.

I leave it to experts to ascertain the final adequacy of the theology, but I do need to assert straight off that what is offered is a "high Christology." Whether one starts with the so-called low Christology of the Gospel of Mark or the high Christology of John, I think that one has to end up with claims about Jesus that go beyond our best human categories. At least one has to end up there if there is to be any connection between the Christology offered and what has been the substance of both popular and learned Christianity since the proclamation by the apostles of the Resurrection. A low Christology shaped to Jesus as a moral ideal is a worthy enough notion, but it offers a painless solution to the relation of church and university. I think the relation of religion and higher learning, church and university, is more difficult, complex, and important.

I am uncertain that I could manage the depth of argument necessary to sub-stantiate all the views of science, art, and religion suggested in this text. I know that even attempting such a task would make the book impossibly long and convoluted. My aim is more modest. Because I believe that arguments about the aims of higher education and Catholic higher education tend toward the pietistic, my hope is not to be pious but provocative. I do not think that my views are particularly original—at least in the area of theology. The value I hope for is clarity. A great deal of the best theology is so directed at other schol-ars or so arcanely stated (either in technical language or approved "church speak") that it is often impossible to decide just what is being asserted. I hope to decipher some of that theological talk and to reset it in active dialogue with the assumptions of the university. This is not, therefore, a technical philosophical treatise on faith and reason. My intent is to make that conflict alive in the real interchange of church and academy. I have tried to make my argument clear not only by avoiding technical talk but by offering many examples. I would be very happy if what I say is clear enough and provocative enough to invite con-vincing refutation or counter constructions. Stirring up an argument in an area so coated with platitude would be itself of significant value.

Many of the arguments and suggested lines of interpretation are ones that I have offered in other contexts (as noted below). I have not, then, avoided a certain amount of repetition, which I have hesitated to excise for two reasons. First, if readers have as hard a time as I have had maintaining the main line of the argument, they may be assisted by the reiteration of central concepts. Second, I hope (and actually believe) that as the text progresses some of the puzzling turns of the argument are enriched. One might regard the overall structure of the text as circular. With luck, each return to the same points and turns is accompanied by a deepening sense of the argument.

My personal history with Catholic education and higher education should be noted. My elementary and secondary education was in Catholic schools of the "old school," pre–Vatican II, "ghetto Catholicism" as it has been pejoratively characterized. I have no negative feelings toward those early years. I have only fond memories of the Dominican sisters at St. Phillip Neri Grade School and the Christian Brothers of Ireland at Leo High School in Chicago. (The latter gave me an early appreciation of the Irish taste for terrorism.) After that, however, my education and career have all been as secular as one might wish: Yale (undergraduate), University of Chicago (Ph.D. in philosophy), teaching and administrative positions at Princeton, Middlebury College, Bucknell University, and the University of Rochester. (I served as president at the latter two.) In short, I have no career experience with Catholic institutions and so speak as something of an outsider.

As a Catholic in great secular institutions, however, I have had the interesting experience of being an outsider of a different sort. Looking back on it, it hardly seems coincidental that when I arrived at Yale as a freshman all three of my assigned roommates were Roman Catholics. (I do believe that they segregated us lest faith be polluted—whether ours or theirs I am not sure.) While at Middlebury serving as dean of the college, I was interviewed for the presidency of one of the country's most distinguished colleges. A member of the search committee asked a colleague at Middlebury, "Has the fact that Mr. O'Brien is a Catholic interfered with the performance of his duties?" Of all the nerve! (I did not get that presidency.) I am told that there was a minor skirmish at the Bucknell board when it was proposed that there might be a Catholic president of that fine old Baptist institution. (I did get that presidency—good for the Baptists. And, since the University of Rochester was also Baptist founded, I offer a second thanks to that enthusiastic church community for my achieving a second presidency.)

So, while my career has been almost wholly within secular institutions, the fact of my Catholic commitment has made me more than a little curious about what *I* was doing *there*, giving me an outsider's perspective on secular university culture. At the same time, I have had a continuing practical and professional interest in Catholic higher education and the relation between the church and the university. While at Princeton, I had several long discussions with John Noonan (now a federal judge on the Ninth Circuit) regarding plans for a Catholic college to be created in connection with a major research university. Noonan's view, quite accurate in the 1960s, was that there were no truly distinguished Catholic universities. To remedy that fault, it was proposed to create a college along the lines of St. Michael's at the University of Toronto: a Catholic college within the ambience of the larger university. The University of Chicago was the designated site; the then archbishop of Chicago, Cardinal Meyer, at first agreed but then backed down because of opposition from the local men's universities in the area. (The nuns were supportive.) I have served on the board of a Catholic college (now university)—LaSalle in Philadelphia—for almost thirty years, so I have had to watch the continuing struggle of an urban institution of modest means to establish its position in academia. How can one be Catholic and at the same time offer all those practical courses in accounting, television production, and journalism that attract an ever more choosy, consumer-oriented student clientele?

On the scholarly side, my first published article was entitled "State, Academy, and Church" (*Journal of Religion*, 1962), and my most recent article is on *Ex Corde Ecclesiae*.[11] In between, I have a book on theology (more or less)[12] and my more recent book on the philosophical foundations of the university (see note 7). In other words and in short, I have been mulling over this problem of a Catholic university for long enough to justify a full-length treatment. It also means that some of the material in this book has appeared in somewhat different form in a variety of articles and speeches. As noted above, because of earlier excursions, but also because of the nature of the subject matter, there will be inevitable repetition of certain turns of argument. I plead a Wittgensteinian indulgence: one sketches the landscape from different perspectives with the hope of capturing the whole.

Finally, I have chosen a title that no doubt displays Catholic *chutzpah* (perhaps itself a contradiction) since it obviously echoes the title of Cardinal Newman's classic work. However, the title seemed an accurate description and, anyhow, I share the same birthdate with the cardinal: February 21.

1

Biblical Foundations of the Modern University

The publication in 1990 of the papal document *Ex Corde Ecclesiae* and its subsequent interpretation by the U.S. National Conference of Catholic Bishops have raised fundamental questions about the "Catholicity" of American colleges and universities founded and sustained by various religious orders and church officials. It did not require papal intervention, however, to raise such questions. The flourishing of many major Catholic universities has seemed to many commentators to have occurred at the expense of visible Catholic heritage. Catholic universities increasingly have appeared to imitate their secular counterparts in faculty appointments, the shape of the curriculum, and the loosening of regulations governing student conduct and associations. Acute observers of Catholic institutions have prophesied that they will go the way of the great secular universities, which have long ago cast off their denominational roots and founding.[1]

Catholic institutions, caught between secular demands for intellectual openness and church demands for palpable Catholicity, have frequently defined themselves in terms of the founding ("St. Swithins is a college in the Jesuit tradition—founded by the Sisters of the Holy Names."). The claim of the founders may be augmented by alluding to the importance of social commitment as part of the extracurricular life of the institution. Peter Steinfels has likened "in the Jesuit tradition" to "taking off your wedding ring when traveling." As for good works: while these may well flow from Christian commitment, attention to social outreach is by no means confined to Catholic campuses. Indeed, since most American universities and colleges can fairly claim some degree of moral interest, social service urges can be thought to exist across the academic landscape.

Retreat from palpable Catholicity is understandable on many grounds, two of which bear special mention. In the American context, there is the simple reality of government funding. Because of the severe interpretation of the U.S. Constitution's First Amendment clause—the judicially constructed "wall of separation" between church and state—too much Catholicity (or Methodism) brands an institution as "sectarian" and prohibits federal and state financial assistance. No Catholic institution of any scope could exist without such funds. More important, of course, is the internal academic concern about conflict between Catholic dogmatism and the academic freedom essential to the modern university. As Catholic universities have sought a more prominent stature in the American higher education establishment, they have come to depend not only on government funds but on a firm commitment to academic freedom. The "Land O'Lakes" document produced under the leadership of Father Hesburgh of Notre Dame is the watershed document in the contemporary Catholic colleges' proclaimed allegiance to academic freedom.[2]

Government funding is a fact and there is no use "arguing with city hall" or the U.S. Supreme Court. Arguing with the pope is enough of a problem. Academic freedom, however, as a university invention invites intellectual critique; it is a term itself requiring interpretation. The reigning interpretation incorporates a special view of rationality derived from the scientific Enlightenment of the eighteenth century. A simplistic or "imperialistic" Enlightenment interpretation of academic freedom is inherently subversive to religious commitment and it is that interpretation that leads to the conclusion that a Catholic (or any religious) university is a contradiction. Enlightenment rationality may not be, however, the sole model of learning or the unique vehicle of "truth." Indicating the limitations of that form of rationality and the notion of academic freedom based upon it are main themes of this presentation.

But lest we too quickly succumb to the prevailing academic suspicion about mixing religion and higher learning, it is worth making a positive case for the biblical tradition as a supporter of the university project. There are aspects of biblical faith that are not only compatible with normal university assumptions but are in fact consonant with certain fundamental assumptions that legitimate university research and scholarship. Emphasizing them might make "Catholic university" seem less a contradiction than a tautology.

THE WORLD

Before relegating religion to the extracurricular good works and Sunday chapel, it is important to note that certain aspects of the Christian belief structure coincide with and support the basic "faith of universities," by which I mean the ultimate assumptions about the nature of cosmic reality and human beings that, if denied, would relegate the university to the same realm of fantasy to which the university often consigns the church. That Christian faith and university faith happen to coincide may suggest why universities rose and prospered under church sponsorship.

An argument for the compatibility of faith and learning can begin with appreciating the core belief of the biblical religions that the world at hand is a "Creation." The normative interpretation of Creation is intended to affirm the independent reality of the cosmos. The world is not an idea in the mind of God; it is a genuine reality that stands on its own. As Dominican theologian Herbert McCabe, claiming to be following Aquinas on this point, explained it, "Coming to know that the universe is dependent on God does not in fact tell us anything about the character of the universe."[3] The truth of science has full integrity; it is not a shadow of God's truth—a reality behind worldly appearance. Biblical affirmation of Creation denies those views that regard the world as illusion, as an unsatisfactory miasma from which we should escape in mystical transport or private fantasy. Asserting the independent reality of Creation checks any ultimate relativism or deconstructionism that roots all knowledge in social construction or individual need. Not only is the world real enough as it is, but humans in the world are understood to have real capacities to know that world. Human capacity and a world-for-knowledge are correlative concepts.

One of the earliest papal incursions into the independence of the university can be found in the Statutes of Paris of 1215, a document widely regarded as the Magna Carta of the university movement. But while that document may be seen as a charter for university independence (academic freedom), it contains conditions that today would bring censure by the American Association of Uni-

versity Professors (AAUP). It explicitly stated that the faculty at Paris was pro-
hibited from teaching the works of David of Dinent and Aumury of Bène.[4] As
best we can tell, David and Aumury were some species of pantheist. Pantheism
is not only a problem for Christianity; its view of the ultimate, the ultimate reality, proves very problematic for knowledge and the university. Pantheisms
come in different flavors and we do not know the exact doctrines of the two
philosophers in question. It is never clear in pantheism whether God is reduced
to the world, or the world is reduced to God. The first offends Christianity, the
second offends the university. If the world is reduced to God, nature becomes a
set of signs, metaphors, or mere appearances of God, the reality. That is a pious
thought, but for the researcher at the bench, "a rose is a rose is a rose" is not a
theological trope.

Pantheism is not much preached in church or the academy these days.
(Modern ecological enthusiasts might go for "pan" but not for "theism.") The
underlying intellectual problems of pantheism remain, however, so much so
that G. E. Moore found it important to reaffirm Bishop Butler's view that
"[e]verything is what it is and not another thing."[5] Moore's statement was, he
thought, a commonsense rejoinder to the idealism of F. H. Bradley, whose doctrine of internal relations (everything is related to and understood only through
something else) led him to assign the palpable world to "appearance" in contrast to the "reality" of the Absolute that summed all internal relations. Pantheism and Bradleyian idealism are fascinating speculative ideas, but they are not
philosophies for the university and its commonsense view that the reality out
there is just what it is and not another—even God or the Absolute. The biblical
doctrine of Creation may be "just" a belief, but it is a belief that gives full reality to the world. The university botanist pursuing research on roses need have
no religion; nor does he need to worry whether the floral display at hand is only
an appearance of something mightier, even Mother Nature.

At the initiation of the university movement in the Middle Ages, the influx
of Aristotelian writings created a scientific challenge to Christian faith that was
in its way equally as troubling as the Darwinian incursion of the nineteenth
century on the biblical account in Genesis. Theologians had found Plato's philosophy congenial to Christianity because of its sharp distinction between the
world of the senses and the world of Ideas, a distinction that seemed to fit the
emphasis in Christian spirituality of the otherworldliness of a Heavenly Kingdom. Aristotle, in contrast, rejected Plato's doctrine of transcendent ideas; he
held that the real was the conglomeration of substances—rocks and roses and

all the rest—which could be fully understood only as such. The "triumph" of Aristotelianism truly made Scholasticism "the philosophy of the schools." Aristotelian metaphysics may not have much to lend to a doctrine of Salvation, but it is a proper metaphysics of Creation and for this-worldly scientific research.

In citing the "heresies" of David of Dinant and Aumury as important considerations for *university* faith, it is important to make some distinction between what one might call ultimate or speculative heresy, and practical and operational heresy. Heaven forbid that one should cease to study F. H. Bradley or Amaury of Bène (if we could find any manuscripts). Perhaps they are correct that in the long run all this university knowledge is useless and irrelevant, a distraction from the real issues of human life. Certainly many great souls have judged that the ivory tower of knowledge is useless and distorting to ultimate human needs and concerns. Jesus thanks the Father for revealing himself to the children and not to the wise. The story is told that toward the end of his life, St. Thomas Aquinas, that paradigm of scholastic (university) philosophers, was granted a mystical vision that led him to judge his mighty intellectual labors to have been only "straw." All well and good, but one does not enter into the ongoing work of the university with the operational notion that argument and reason are only "straw." While I argue in the long run that Christian faith demands "transcendence" of the world-as-science, it does not operationally undermine the palpable reality of roses and rocks. Indeed, it is the palpable reality of the world that makes the Christian doctrine of historical Salvation comprehensible.

Modern deconstructionism resides in the same ambiguous position of the great sceptics, pantheists, and idealists: on the one hand it is an ultimate speculative view about the meaning and importance of knowledge; on the other it can be regarded, as it is by its academic establishment critics, as fundamental academic (operational) heresy. An operational deconstructionist who thought all argument was merely the struggle for political power would not receive academic appointment. Presumably even Foucault, who made such an assertion, thought better of his own arguments.[6] It is one thing to stake out by argument and assemblage of insight the view that university knowledge is on the far side of Salvation, but it is another to use this claim as an operational principle for the ongoing life of the academy. Nobel scientists who, in their philosophical moments, loftily express their modesty by asserting ultimate skepticism do not practice this virtue in the laboratory.

In sum: the biblical doctrine of Creation grounds a sort of commonsense reality about which true knowledge is possible against a host of idealisms, scepticisms, and even religious reductions of the real. Whatever the relation of the Creator God to the Creation, it is not reductionistic of world and human beings—they are as truly real as "the rose is a rose is a rose."

THE CREATOR

Having affirmed the reality of the world (and us in it), the biblical tradition also affirms it as Creation—that is, there is a Creator. Pantheism that reduces God to the world doesn't work any more than the opposite reduction. The world is not a "thing-in-itself," a brute fact that confronts us. Such an understanding— the world-as-brute-fact—can lead to the pretension of humankind as masters of the indifferent stuff of the world. Or it can lead to despair: humanity is a cosmic accident, a joke in the midst of "uncaring nature." If science is grounded on the reality of the world, the notion of Creation adds a moral dimension to scientific endeavor. The "morality" of science is as much a postulate of the university as "realism."

Insofar as we know the ways of the world, we also have been able to intervene in those ways. Science creates technologies. But even so, there is no necessary link between knowledge and technology. A pure scientist might well work on the physics that creates an atomic bomb as a strictly theoretical problem. Yet it is hard to argue with Robert Oppenheimer's assertion that when the bomb built at Los Alamos was dropped on Hiroshima, "for the first time physics knew sin." There is something eerie about the pure scientist who would stake a position of pure knower with no interest or care in the practical results that might emerge from such knowledge. The biblical doctrine of Creation raises the moral issue of knowledge. Yes, there is a world, a Creation, to be known. But this Creation is not our possession either as something merely to be scientifically described or technologically exploited. Biblical Creation holds that God is master of the world, not humanity; rather we are the stewards of Creation. Thus our responsibility not to despoil the world, other creatures, and especially other humans.

There are great and difficult issues in separating the need for so-called pure science, beneficent technology, and despoilation, but almost anyone will hold to these distinctions. Lose the distinctions and one gets the "mad scientist" of science fiction or the figure who "plays God" with an unbridled technological urge, indifferent to suffering and interested only in the knowledge to be gained. There has been a continuing controversy over whether the knowledge gained by Nazi doctors in their inhuman experiments on prisoners should be made available. Isn't the pursuit of knowledge a self-justifying good? Maybe not.

A serious question for the university is its practical position in regard to the world-as-known. Would it be acceptable to regard the university as simply and purely a citadel of knowledge? Does the university have some essential obligation to deal with the practical applications of knowledge? Does the university have inherent limitations on what can be allowed as means for attaining knowledge, as in the protocols governing the use of animal and human subjects in medical experimentation? Are these practical/moral concerns simply imposed by outside circumstance, the mores of the time, or is there some essential corruption of the university if it neglects the moral dimensions of knowledge and its pursuit? The biblical understanding of Creation, by positioning the world as the possession of a caring Creator, would certainly block despoliation and the inhumane treatment of the Creator's works. The world is not a plaything for knowledge.

Universities by and large do reject the unbridled pursuit of knowledge pure and simple. The question is on what basis? On what aspect of reality should such a restriction of university study be based? Presumably the biblical answer is not the only answer, but any attempt to found the moral responsibility surrounding knowledge will likely bear some kinship to the doctrine of Creation—for example, that the world of nature is our "inheritance," or that we have a duty to posterity (which didn't stop, however, a member of the Irish Dial from asking during debate, "What has posterity ever done for us?"). If one thinks that the doctrine of Creation is just too grandiose and murky, I suspect that these other appeals to our duty to nature, posterity, or solidarity with all life rest on equally lofty premises.

THE BOOKS

Judaism and Christianity are peculiarly religions of the Book, the Bible—more accurately *ta Biblia*, "the Books." Instead of reading religious lessons from nature, centuries of Jews and Christians have interpreted Scripture. The Jerusalem Tradition creates a "hermeneutic" people, interpreters of words, believing that in articulate speech there is a deep clue to human meaning. Humans do not act merely across a web of animate feeling and emotion; by means of articulate speech they create attitudes and emotions that are incommensurate with simple psychic urges. Roger Scruton has commented that animals cannot be angry. Anger is an emotion based on a sense of injustice, which like justice is a creation within the human world and as such it ultimately depends on speech, the ability to articulate ourselves in words and symbols. In that sense, the whole human world rests on "books."[7]

Reading books is an obvious university task to which and for which the tradition of *ta Biblia* is at least partly responsible and to which it is responsive. There are two alternatives to a hermeneutic tradition, neither of which would be acceptable to the Christian tradition or, I believe, to the university. One is to read the "book of Nature" as the sole guide to life and understanding: poetic pantheism. The other is to see the Bible as the *ipse dixit* of Deity itself.

It is difficult to know what to say about reading the book of Nature. Nature has had its ups and downs in human estimation. Disgusted with the banalities and cruelties of human society, romantics seek the beauty, tranquility, and steadiness of the natural order. "The world is too much with us; late and soon,/ Getting and spending we lay waste our powers: Little we see in Nature that is ours," says Wordsworth. But not everyone regards Nature with such benevolence. "So careful of the type she seems/So careless of the single life," says Tennyson, reflecting on Nature's indifference to the singularity of persons. My own take on Nature tends toward Tennyson's. Nature is not benevolent; post-Darwin it seems "red in tooth and claw"—awesome but not exactly friendly. Ultimately it does seem more interested in the type than the individual. Reading humans off the book of Nature deletes all the quirks, curiosities, and individualities that make human history different from natural history. Finally, the book of Nature lacks articulate speech.

There are sociobiologists within the university who prefer natural history over human history, dissolving all human idiosyncracies into twists of the DNA. Whatever the scientific merit of these views, departments of literature and the arts continue to believe in and be fascinated by the indissolubility of "the single life." This allegiance to particular histories is established in the modern curriculum, however shaky may be the philosophic justification for such a deviation from the sociobiologists' dream.

> Give me the splendid silent sun with all his beams full-dazzling,
> Give me juicy autumnal fruit ripe and red from the orchard
>
> .   .   .   .
> Give me solitude, give me Nature, give me again O Nature your
>   primal sanities!
>
> .   .   .   .

> I see my own soul trampling down what I have asked for.
> Keep your splendid silent sun,
> Keep your woods O Nature, and the quiet places by the woods
>
> . . . .
>
> Give me faces and streets—give me these phantoms incessant and
>   endless along the trottoirs!
> Give me interminable eyes—give me women—give me comrades
>   and lovers by the thousand!

Whitman's allegiance to "interminable eyes," the wash and variety of Broadway, is in its own way biblical. The God in question in the Books is the God of Abraham, Isaac, and Jacob—and then of Saul and David and Solomon, Isaiah, Jeremiah, Amos, and Jesus, but then of Paul, Mark, John. Later I discuss in some depth the importance of historical revelation for this tradition as against more universalist, "natural" theologies. For now, one can make a *prima facie* case that the Bible, this dominating collection of books, presents us with a problem of historical hermeneutics, interpretation of the insights or revelations to a specific people, Israel, and named individuals. If God reveals himself in the Books, that is quite different than spying him out in the verdant field, the looming mountain, or the surging sea.

If there is a biblical justification for the validity of science based on the doctrine that Creation is an independent reality, there is also a support for the humanities (*contra* the sociobiologists) in the Creation story. One of the effects of a doctrine of Creation is that in a sense humanity is "on its own." Humanity and the world are not reducible to some otherworldly reality. They are not reducible to a phenomenon of God. Furthermore, the progressive story of God's creating first the sun and moon, then the plants, then the animals, then man and woman—and declaring each day to be "good!"—expresses the understanding that humankind is not merely the phenomena of atoms, molecules, genes, or the animal pack. The biblical account stands firmly against reducing humanity to something higher—and also to something lower. Each day of Creation affirms an integrity within that order of nature. Reduction of later days to earlier days is out of order, as is mixing the orders created on the separate days. Mary Douglas's powerful reading of the odd dietary prescriptions in Leviticus confirms the integrity of the separate orders of Creation. "Birds gotta fly, fish gotta swim." Thus, if there is a bird that doesn't fly, it is out of order and to be avoided. As she says, had there been penguins in ancient Israel, they would have been a forbidden food.[8]

Having allowed the Creator to be a helping hand in legitimating science and the humanities, one must then guard against reducing science and the arts to an exegesis of Genesis. If one were to regard the Bible as God's literal word, *ipse dixit*, in the manner of fundamentalist biblicists, then the Bible would not be a plausible foundation or precursor for academic hermeneutics. One need only contrast in this respect one of the more pious Muslim views of the Koran with the Jewish or Christian view of the Bible to understand the difference. Ultra-pious Muslims regard the Koran as God's direct speech and may even hold that the Prophet was illiterate, that he was a "writing instrument." One need not delve deeply into modern biblical scholarship to see that the Christian tradition has always taken a critical or quizzical attitude toward the received texts. Modern redaction criticism of the New Testament, for example, clearly relies on parsing out the Marcan community's views as against the later Johannine. As for the rabbinic tradition: while there is, of course, great reverence for the text, it is hard to imagine a more quarrelsome tradition about the meaning and import of the biblical documents. The rabbis can be positively angry with the patriarchs. Why did Joseph sit there for all those years in Egypt without ever letting his grieving father know that he was alive?! In a famous rabbinical debate, Rabbi Eliezer appeals to heaven to confirm his interpretation of Scripture. There is a great voice from heaven, to which Rabbi Joshua replies, "The Law is not in heaven! It was given on Mt. Sinai. We pay no attention to a Heavenly Voice." In the tale, God laughs and admits, "My sons have defeated me."[9]

As Raymond Brown, the distinguished Catholic biblical scholar, has suggested, when people say "the Bible says" they might as well be saying "the Public Library says."[10] The Bible is not "the Book"; it is *ta Biblia*, the Books.

There is no mystery, then, to the fact that universities were creatures of the Christian Middle Ages. Belief in a common reality and a history of interpretative speech are fundamental to the life of the university. But while Catholic Christianity may have founded universities and fostered them out of its deepest beliefs, the Gospels stand as a check upon what can become the arrogance of isolating intellect. While scientific investigation and interpretation of texts (sacred and secular) are legitimated by the Christian tradition, reason and scholarship are not salvational. Strictly speaking, for Christianity all human endeavor—including even great accomplishments like the university—stand under the shadow of the Cross. Failure in academic pursuit is not a failure at life, nor is academic excellence identical to final human excellence. In the last analysis, it is the story of the person as one who lives a life of care and grace, of hope and love, that counts.

A Catholic university, without compromising the strict demands of intellectual pursuit, frames the academic life in terms of ultimate value. Salvation is a *life* issue, and the cliché can't be avoided: "What is the meaning of life?" One way in which the problematic of a Catholic university can be stated is to ask about the relation of the *life* of the university—for example, the life of the mind—to Life, assuming it is out there somewhere, beyond the quad. Is Salvation another issue out there, separate from the intellectual concerns of the university, like the private lives of the faculty or the success of the football team? Or do "Salvation issues" inherently command university recognition? The answer to this query will turn not on some intrusion of faith into the specific skills of the university, it will be a question of the "spirit" of the university enterprise. Is the academy a retreat from life or is the university a form of intellectual salvation? Should the university address such questions and if so how and where in the curriculum and the community?

This positive case for the relation of biblical religion and the university is, in a sense, a précis of this book as a whole. As stated, however, it has an air of easy piety about both church and university as if they were the most natural partners imaginable. Actual history belies such benign conclusions. I want to explore in greater depth, therefore, the suppositions of university work and Christian faith. There are points of distinct conflict and tension that are not at all easily resolved. As suggested earlier, defenders of Catholic higher education, beleaguered by their secular foes, often seem to misunderstand the heart of their own Catholic enterprise by offering simple assimilation to current university modes and fashions. I think that a truly Catholic university should be a serious critic of certain aspects of modernity and, perforce, of one of modernity's greatest if flawed (or limited) inventions: the university.

2

Science: The Truth of Universities

The simplest way to link Christian faith with university work would be to affirm the university commitment to the Truth, the whole Truth, and nothing but. The university's special commitment may be to the "truths of reason," but in addition to those that reason can ascertain there are truths *revealed*. Revealed truths are such as God might know but are beyond humanity's capacity—that is, their rational capacity—to come to on their own. Ideally there will be no conflict between the truths of human reason and the truths of Revelation. Seeming conflicts (the Galileo affair) can be resolved and are later seen as embarrassments caused by excessive biblical literalism. In sum, a properly *universal* university should encompass *all* the truth there is hither and thither: what we discover by reason and what we are given by Revelation.

This simple argument—that the whole Truth is arrived at by addition (reason + Revelation)—is, I believe, fundamentally flawed. Neither reason nor Revelation are fixed notions, and the truth of one may be simply incomparable with the truth of the other. At some level it may be that the university needs reason *and* Revelation, but not because Revelation delivers up some truths that reason just can't quite grasp. Rather, the truth of Revelation is *essentially* not available to reason. More important, the truth of Revelation is fundamentally distorted when formed upon the university's model of truth. When Pascal says that "the heart has its reasons that the reason knows not," the reasons of the heart are just not rational reasons. In the Pascalian use, "reason" like "truth" is operating in a wholly different context than that of "rational" knowledge. The context is so different that one could regard "reasons of the heart" as a mere rhetorical device, an expressive metaphor betokening conviction but no "reason." A strict scientific rationalist may well admit the Pascalian distinction, happily consigning "reasons of the heart" to subjective feeling. To be sure, people have certain emotional attachments but these do not add to the stock of human knowledge. The biographer who presents the facts of his subject's life adds nothing to our knowledge by a concluding paragraph making it clear that he really liked the person chronicled.

Relegating Christian belief to "*reasons* of the heart" has an initial attraction as a protection of faith, but if it is carried through to the conclusion that religion is after all subjective, there will be protest. In his most recent papal encyclical, *Fides et Ratio*, John Paul II singles out the denial of truth by philosophical relativism and pluralism as the besetting sins of the age. Roman Catholic Christianity has had a special concern for truth, revealed *and* rational. What concerns the pope is that claims for truth—including the *truth* of Christian faith—will be relativized and subjectified, so that religious belief becomes just one of a plurality of personal or cultural options all of which are equally legitimate—or illegitimate.

By allying faith with reason, the pope seeks to establish that the Christian religion, no less than rational science, lays claims upon the individual that go beyond subjective interests and position. The problem with calling on reason-as-universal as an ally with faith-as-universal is that faith may then be reconstructed at some deep and unconscious level on the model of rational truth, which, it is the contention of this book, is a fundamental mistake. In the quarrel between science and religion that has marked the modern world since the time of Copernican astronomy, the churches have often unwittingly presented their case for Christianity on so-called scientific grounds—a strategy of doom for faith. Thus the quest for the historical Jesus with the hope that verified "scientific" history would establish Christian claims. Thus biblical literalism's placing of the "facts" of Genesis against the theory of evolution. And thus the Roman

Catholic enthusiasm for a species of Thomism that point by point, reason by reason, gives the appearance of demonstrating the truth of faith.

While it is heartening to have the pope defend reason, reason has not always repaid the compliment. Because Christianity makes *universalist* claims for its truth, it appears to invade the territory of universalist reason. Strict rationalists hold that only reason holds the field of universality, and thus the Christian claims for universal Revelation are false and pernicious even on matters of theology. In the words of the great apostate emperor, Julian: "Reason enables us to attain a knowledge of the divine essence quite independently of any disclosures on the part of Moses, Jesus, or Paul. [The God of the Bible] is short sighted, resentful, capricious, sectional and particularist. . . ."[1] Modern rationalists use the same epithets—maybe absent "resentful." Believers do not stand in the universal posture of reason, they are "particularists"; belief is "capricious" and "sectional" (sectarian), the assertion of mere subjectivity against the common, universal truths that only reason can affirm.

The relation of *fides* and *ratio* is an ever-present issue for Catholic academics and their universities and colleges. When the American Association of University Professors (AAUP) promulgated its statement about academic freedom in 1940, it made a grudging exception for religious colleges, allowing that they might put some restrictions on inquiry because of prior faith commitments. If, in the recent reflection on academic freedom, the general secretary of the AAUP declared that the exception was no longer necessary for Catholic colleges since they had become so open, one is not sure whether to rejoice with the AAUP or fret with the pope. If the whole Truth is rational truth, and the university is the instrument of rational truth, then there is no place for *fides* in the academy. Faith becomes an extracurricular activity. So it has come to be regarded at mainline institutions; and so it seems to have become at many nominally Catholic colleges. The pope may have a proper concern.

John Paul II's defense of reason has been widely hailed by academics within and without Catholic higher education. It is not clear, however, that his defense of the truth of faith will win ready acceptance in the general academic community. In any defense of truth, whether of reason or Revelation, it is important to understand that this grand notion operates quite differently across a variety of contexts. As *Fides et Ratio* itself affirms, "a single term conceals a variety of meanings. Hence the need for a preliminary clarification."[2] And yet it is confusion about the context of "truth" that is the greatest problem with *Fides et Ratio*. As Richard Bernstein noted in his commentary on the encyclical:

> The word that is used with perhaps the greatest frequency . . . is
> *truth*. But it is used in a bewildering variety of ways: "ultimate
> Truth," "absolute truth," "universal truth," "the fullness of truth,"
> "the different faces of human truth," "the truth attained by philoso-
> phy," "the truth of Revelation," "Jesus Christ as the truth," "the
> unity of truth," "different modes of truth," an "ulterior truth that
> would explain the meaning of life," "the truth of the person" are
> phrases repeated throughout the letter. Although it is clearly as-
> serted that there are "different modes of truth," and that ultimately
> there is a harmony and *unity* of these truths, there is virtually no at-
> tempt to stand back and reflect upon the different *meanings* of
> "truth" and to show us precisely how they are compatible. Nor is any
> attempt made to show us how we are to reconcile conflicting claims
> to truth. But this is the issue which must be confronted if one is to
> *justify* the claim that the truths of reason and faith form a harmo-
> nious unity.[3]

Bernstein's commentary is on the mark. Only if one can disentangle different
meanings of the word "truth" and then discuss their relations can one hope to
bring any harmony to faith and reason. Clarifying the varying meanings of
truth is the fundamental ground for any discussion of the nature of a Catholic
institution of higher learning.

In this and the next two chapters I want to sketch out three important but
significantly different contexts in which the word "truth" functions: scientific,
artistic, and religious—specifically within the Jewish-Christian religious tradition. While there is legitimacy to the use of "truth" in these differing contexts,
confusing the contexts of usage leads to profound misunderstanding. Depending
on our understanding of the varied meanings of the word "truth," a *Catholic* university will either be a contradiction or a contrarian academic community.

Prior warning: there is no way to discriminate among the varying contexts—
at least one of which is "religious"—without indulging in some necessary theology. Of course, if one is convinced that there is no *theos* about which one can
offer some sort of *logos*, this may seem like warning the reader that it will be
necessary to indulge in the science of Santa Claus, at which point the rationalist reader will lay down the book. However, since our problem is the idea of a
Catholic university, there is no way to avoid theology. In the long run, one
may well reject the idea of a Catholic university, but before doing so, it is
worth attempting to see what such a notion entails. Further, for the sceptic
and nonbeliever, I think that the theological position of Judaism and Chris-

tianity is sufficiently peculiar that the usual rejections of religion relative to higher learning miss the mark. Walker Percy recognized the oddity of these religions and gave a fresh perspective on the familiar faith versus reason debate: Judaism and Christianity are "not members in good standing of the World's Great Religions."[4] They are not spiritual regimes for enlightenment but they are a life lived. Franz Rosenzweig, the great twentieth-century century Jewish theologian, was even more explicit in separating off the "belief" of the Jew from the kind of credal truths that seem to clash with the truths of scientific reason: "The belief [of a Jew] is not the content of a testimony, but rather the product of reproduction. The Jew, engendered by a Jew, attests his belief by continuing to procreate the Jewish people. His belief is not in something: he is himself the belief."[5]

UNIVERSITY TRUTH: REASON AND SCIENCE

Any useful analysis of Truth should start with a commonsense model: the truth of fact, the truth of propositions. The dominant model for verifying the truth of propositions is science, broadly conceived. It is certainly the modern university's model for truth. What is crucial to science is the methodological stance of the scientist, which is characterized by its commitment to reason. I am not using "reason" here in the sense of the modern philosophic quarrel between rationalists and empiricists. Whether knowledge is derived from sense experience or ideational construction, both sides would agree on the need for the researcher to be *neutral*. Rationalists appeal to common reason, empiricists to neutral, given sense data. The scientific mind is either a transcendent spectator or a blank slate. In either mode the scientific (rational) observer is neutral in the sense of bracketing out "particularist" characteristics: sex, nationality, religious belief, time, place. Max Weber called the modern academic method "ascetic" as a way of noting the strenuous denial of all those aspects of personal life that must be transcended to participate in the scientific life. Descartes's ascetic withdrawal to the purity of the *Cogito* is an initial model for the attitude of "pure" science. There is no female or Chinese or Buddhist physics and results are time and space neutral. If the observer is neutral, so are the data. A neutrino is the same wherever, whenever, and no matter what one's sexual orientation.[6]

The scientific model may seem to fail when one turns to other parts of the standard academic curriculum. The nineteenth-century historian Leopold von Ranke may have been naïve to claim that his histories described "how things really were." Historians write from their own times and interests, which inevitably color their accounts. Nevertheless, Ranke rightly stated a necessity for historical study: no matter how colored a history, it must not be fiction. The historian must refer to data that would be open to any other investigator regardless of her personal characteristics. Open data for open minds is a dictum even for "humanistic" studies. The literary critic who claims that Shakespeare was the Earl of Oxford, misogynous, misandrous, or that *Lear* is a flawed play, argues from data he expects others to accept as proof. It is not his *personal* opinion or feeling that counts as scholarship. (I have to tell my students who give me their personal opinions about Plato that I am not interested in their autobiographies.)

In the ideal of science, *any* observer should have access to *available* data—thus the insistence of natural science that experimental results be duplicable by other experimenters. Such stringent conditions cannot, however, be applied in all circumstances. The contemporary historian cannot observe the past about which he writes. Even in natural science, we must sometimes rely on nonrepeatable observation. If the first astronaut to land on Mars is also the last, then her observations will have special authority. The astronaut would be a *privileged witness*. Reliance on the privileged witness as an *authority* does not, however, fundamentally deviate from the scientific model. Perhaps only one astronaut made it to Mars, but the assumption is that any other astronaut could confirm or disconfirm the initial report. In the case of history, if we happened to have H. G. Wells's time machine, we could travel in time as the astronaut travels in space. The time machine would allow later observers to confirm past historical facts. The privileged witness assumption is a conditional: *if* one were to be in the same situation as the privileged witness, then one would be in a position to validate the report. Unhappily the conditions for reconfirmation are technically impossible (no time machine, no appropriations for further Mars exploration.)

I have explicated the authority-of-privileged-witness scenario because it is often taken to be the model for Revelation, for Christian truth. In his commentary on *Fides et Ratio*, Alvin Plantinga offers his interpretation of John Paul's view of faith and reason as derived from Thomistic thought:

> [T]he Thomistic reason for observing this distinction [between reason in philosophy and faith in religion and theology] is that to know or believe something by way of *faith* is to know or believe it on the basis of someone else's say-so, testimony; but what you learn by yourself, by way of reason, is something that you "know better," something that has a higher epistemic clout. . . . For example, if I

know the Fundamental Theorem of the Calculus on the authority of
my mathematician friend Paul, I don't know it as well as if I had
learned the appropriate bit of mathematics and come myself to see
how the proof goes.[7]

The pope defends reason and philosophy because it can know better, with
surety, certain great religious truths like the existence of God and the need for
an ultimate purpose in life. What it cannot know finally are the answers sup-
plied by faith as derived from the testimony of Jesus. Applying this sort of
analysis to the university, one would then regard Christian Revelation as a sort
of fortunate "add-on." Since most of us are not mystics or those to whom God
speaks in burning bushes, we have to accept the authority of privileged witnesses. Like the astronaut who has been to Mars, only Moses went up the
mountain. In the New Testament, "Only the Son knows the Father." Jesus is
the source of a truth about the will of the Father that he and he alone knows. Jesus is the authority, a privileged witness, and we come to believe the truth that
he reveals. The function of the church is to pass on the truths revealed by the
privileged witness. As for the university, it should no more exclude the biblical
privileged observer than the report of the Mars astronaut or an anthropologist's
account of a remote and vanishing tribe.

The problem with biblical Revelation-by-privileged-witness within the
university context is that the biblical witness so often seems either dead wrong
or wholly implausible. A responsible biologist will reject the literal version of
Creation as literal falsehood. The science of Creationism is no science at all.
That Joshua stopped the sun in its tracks is a miracle of astounding implausibil-
ity. Putting Revelation-by-privileged-witness into the methodological critique
of university rationality rapidly undermines the credibility of faith. So it has
been since the monumental conflicts between Darwinism and the denominational colleges of the late nineteenth century. But the real problem with truth-
by-privileged-witness as the model for Christian truth is not how shaky it is for
the university, it is that it undermines Christian faith.

Truth-by-privileged-witness denies the central tenet of Christianity: the
unique status of Jesus of Nazareth. Jesus does *not* say, "I am revealing a truth."
Rather he says, "I *am* the Truth." If Jesus were only a privileged witness he
would be a prophet, not a Savior. Islam is very clear that Mohammed is "the seal
of the prophets" who *reports* the word of God. The Prophet is privileged but is
in no way "divine." Muslims regard Christian claims about the divine nature of
Jesus as blasphemous, an offense to the One God. Blasphemy was also the ac-

cusation of the Sanhedrin in the trial of Jesus. Any privileged witness—even a prophet—is theoretically dispensable. As earlier noted, Mohammed is so "dispensable" that some pious Muslims believe that the Prophet was illiterate. He did not write the revelation but served only as a writing instrument of Allah.

If there is a problem for Christianity with the status of the witness, there is a parallel problem in terms of *what* is revealed. In the normal case of a privileged witness, that which the witness reveals is something that some other might well have known or come to know when brought face to face with what the original witness revealed. But in the Christian case, God is and remains an eternal mystery. Only the Son *does* know the Father.

For traditional Christian faith, Jesus is more than a privileged witness; Jesus is the "unsurpassable Word of God" (Karl Rahner's phrase.) As Savior, he is the indispensable Word: "*I* am the Truth." If Jesus *is* the Truth—and the Way and the Life—then his relation to God is more than witness; Christians say he is the Son of God and all the Trinitarian complexities begin to unfold. But the problems are not only with the metaphysics of divinity, they are also with the nature of the following of Jesus we call "the church." What is the revealed truth that is taught, the *teaching* passed on by the church, and how does it relate to the truths of the university and human reason?

To understand the oddity and subversiveness of Jesus' claim "I am the Truth," consider the normal expectations surrounding university teaching. The role of the teacher is to reveal and display the truths of the subject. The aim of the teacher is to create students of the subject, *not* disciples of the teacher. It is utterly subversive for the university teacher to say "I am the Truth" as if the only way to reveal the truths of the subject were through his personal powers. Contrast Jesus and the Buddha. The Buddha is a teacher, he preaches the Four Noble Truths; Buddhism stems from acceptance of those truths, not of Siddhartha Gautama. Buddhism is not the worship of Gautama; but Christianity is the worship of Jesus of Nazareth as the Christ of God. Christians are *disciples* of the Teacher. Recall Walker Percy's observation that the world's great religions, including Buddhism, are "spiritual regimes" for enlightenment. But that, Percy claimed, is not what Christianity is about at all. It is perhaps no mystery that Buddhism has been very attractive to a number of modern academics as an alternative to traditional Christianity. Buddhism is at least a *teaching*.

To put the problem most paradoxically, at a first approximation there is no Christian "truth" to be passed along, no "teaching" in the sense that a university professor would recognize. If there is a truth, it is not a teaching but rather the *Teacher:* Jesus is the Truth. What is handed down from generation to generation is Jesus as Risen Lord. For Protestants, it is through the living word of preaching that God is present to the faithful. For Catholics, one could say that the church is centered in the Eucharist, not in encyclicals. The Body and Blood of Christ—Christ's presence—is what is offered as the meaning of life, the ark of Salvation. Christians are disciples of the Teacher as he is present in the church. In the older Catholic ecclesiology the church is the Mystical Body of the Lord.

If there is no *teaching* that defines Christianity, then at one level there is a simple solution to the supposed conflict between faith and reason. The conflict is not between the truths of the university and the truths of faith, but between truths and Jesus as Truth. The "solution" is, however, a solution *per obscurans*. What can it possibly mean to say that Jesus is the Truth? In the interest of making their position more intelligible, Christian apologists may quickly sidle over from "Jesus is the Truth" to "Jesus tells the Truth." "Jesus is the Truth" is only a worshipful (flamboyant) way of stating the latter. For the reasons outlined above, this intelligible reduction of Jesus' strange claim cannot be made without a general reduction of his unique character (Son of God, the Christ, Savior) that has informed orthodox Christianity from the very beginning. So one way to resolve the relation of Christianity and the university would be to place faith in some misty region well beyond the capacities, interests, or cognizance of the university and the life of reason. It would leave faith unchallenged by reason, but would hardly be the basis for a claim by Christianity on the university as reason's institution and method. People who hold to nonsense—"This man is the Truth"—can hardly make claims on the rational mind.

A biblical literalist will reject this entire line of argument. When it is said that Jesus is the Truth, it means that the Bible is the truth as read. The supposed findings of science are to be judged by conformity to the biblical accounts. Are there fossil remains that suggest great antiquity well beyond the biblical past? Determined biblicists have suggested that they are artifacts of the devil intended to lead the faithful astray. Any God with his cosmic status could certainly stop the sun (or earth) in its course and also obviate all the normal astronomic sequelae. The foundational idea of biblical literalism is, paradoxically, the method of science. Thus one may talk about Creation *science* derived from the Bible as being on the same methodological footing as Darwinism. Biblical literalists are basic empiricists lining up biblical fact against the facts of scientific research. The catch is that they judge biblical fact to always win because it is "God's truth."

Biblical literalism is a losing strategy within the world of science. This has certainly been the verdict of the modern university that emerged after the quarrel with Darwinism and that sides wholly with science against Scripture. To play the game of science, one cannot regard some facts (biblical history) as unimpeachable. All factual claims are subject to further testing and review by experiment and theoretic placement. The test is not Scripture but the world as we find it in fact and theory.

The challenge for Christian faith in "Jesus is the Truth" is to show that this claim is not a simple "category mistake." This paradoxical statement presumably makes some deep spiritual sense—a sense which cannot be accessed by something more prosaic. In the next two chapters, I want to move toward the special character of "Jesus is the Truth" first by considering the nature of art and then the "failure" of art. I suggest that we must move beyond the "neutral" stance of reason in our understanding and valuation of art. Understanding art's meaning and value—the "truth" of art—offers an intelligible bridge toward the even more peculiar situation of "truth" in the Jewish and Christian religious traditions.

3

Art: Signatured Truth

I am convinced that Christianity is committed to the strange logic outlined in the previous chapter: what is "taught" is the Teacher; what is True is this Jesus; what is handed over is Christ's presence. The essence of Christianity is the presence of the Teacher, the presence of Jesus in the church. The notion that "truth" is somehow essentially bound up in a specific historical person ("I am the Truth") is fundamentally antithetic to the assumptions of universal reason and scientific truth. This was precisely the basis of Julian the Apostate's rejection of the need for Revelation attached to any historical person, whether it be Moses, Jesus, or Paul.

Given the biblical notion of Revelation coming to a chosen people and to specific individuals, and the even more uncanny notion that this Jesus *is* the Truth, one should surely expect rationalist rejection of the whole understanding of Revelation. The modern university with its deep commitment to universal reason should be anywhere from indifferent to hostile to special revelations. Julian the Apostate's complaints remain: faith is particularist, capricious, sectional (divisive), and has no place in the house of universal rationality.

So much for Christian faith. But what is startling is that just such "particularist, capricious, and sectional" claims are being advanced with grim determination within the university not by external religion, but by aggressive segments of the professoriat. A variety of movements—deconstructionism, neopragmatism, feminism, queer studies, to name a few—charge that the universal voice of reason is a sham and is written off as mere male patriarchy or heterosexual hegemony in disguise. Multiculturalism (to offer a generic characterization for the individual movements) demands that the *particularist* voices of women, blacks, and gays be heard in the icy mansions of academia. It is just these contemporary academic trends that have raised the issues of relativism and pluralism that so perturb John Paul II in *Fides et Ratio*. If it is every man, woman, black, white, gay, and bisexual for himself or herself, what hope is there for the truth of reason or faith?

The academic establishment has been as troubled by relativistic multiculturalism as has the pope and for precisely the same reason: the defeat of reason and universal truth in a welter of warring cultures and cults. As I tried to make clear in the preceding chapter, scientific truth is essentially *un*historical. For true scientific knowledge, all the characteristics that define an individual as an actual historical existent are bracketed out. The one who *knows* is neither male nor female, neither ancient nor modern. This is precisely what multiculturalists deny; they say it is sheer illusion to think that one can or ought to transcend one's particular history; there is no truth-as-*universal*, there is only my, his, and her truth.

This deconstructive urge certainly sounds as if it leads inexorably to the abyss of privatism, the sort of radical relativism that John Paul II rightly deplores. No doubt there are those who would revel in incommunicable individualism, but at least in the case of multi*cultural* claims what is demanded is the *true* voice of the group. Women are told to reject the *false* construction placed on them by a patriarchal society and assert their authentic voice. Searching for the authentic voice eventually undermines the simple relativism of multicultural enthusiasms.[1] It is the search for an *authentic* voice for women, blacks, gays—or the *human* voice—that is the concern of this chapter.

ART AS SIGNATURED

This demand for particular placement, for the historical voice, I will call a demand for *signatured truth:* John Doe's truth, Jane Roe's truth. From the perspective of universal (scientific-rational) knowledge, signatured truth seems to be subversive nonsense. Truth is common or it is nothing. If one turns to the arts, however, signatured truth is found to be fundamental. Whether "signatured truth" is a contradiction akin to "Catholic university" is the question to be addressed. On the surface it may seem radically idiosyncratic, but in a movement like feminism, Jane Roe's truth should reflect the *authentic* voice of woman, or, if not, Jane Roe should learn to speak with that authentic voice. The authentic voice is not, however, an abstract, nongendered voice, and it will carry the nuance of the individual. It will be Jane Roe's voice but as such reflect something larger than Jane Roe alone. How this mix of individual and authentic (larger, "universal") is possible can be illustrated best in the fine arts.

The notion of "signature" is fundamental to our understanding of art. The unique style of the composer, the unique vision of the painter, or the unique voice of the poet is integral to what is presented. Even when we do not know the names of the artists we give them unique descriptions—the Master of Three Angels, the Rhine Poet, and so on—because we believe that there is something essentially personal to the artist's work. Art works as signatured are *essentially historical* insofar as they are connected to and express particular visions with historical placement. The work is Rembrandt not Lievens, Beethoven not Rossini, twelfth century not fourteenth, Spanish not French. In contrast, Newton's theory is Newton's only *honoris causa*; there is nothing finally English, male, donnish, or seventeenth century about the inverse square law. When the artist dies or ceases his effort, the essential work stops. No one continues Keats. Again the contrast to science is striking. Because science is person neutral, one can continue the work of Newton by developing Newtonian mechanics.[2]

One may readily admit that there is something personal, or signatured, about works of art, and go on to hold that the variability of differing artistic visions precludes the very marks of objectivity and universality that are taken to be essential to any application of the notion of truth. In what sense then is there "truth" in the realm of the arts? Certainly not as propositional depiction of an *external* actuality. We may assess which portrait of George Washington is the most accurate, truest depiction of the man, which would be of interest to the science of history. But accuracy to historical fact cannot be the sense of truth in art.

"True" is used in art first of all in an *internal* fashion. We ask whether this is a *true* Rembrandt (or a forgery or the work of a pupil). Then we may ask whether some item is *truly* art. Neither of these uses of "truth" in the realm of art is mysterious insofar as there is an agreed upon method of assessing truth. There may be significant actual controversy about whether the item is genuine or whether it is art or junk, but the method of approaching the truth in both cases is agreed upon and, in the context of this discussion, *method* is all important. To the extent we are concerned with the authenticity of a work or its value *as art*, we operate in a manner radically different than when we ask whether a putative scientific theory is true. The morning paper carried photos of an hotel room in New York dripped with a thousand pounds of cheese. Is it art, or a practical joke on art, the public, or the hotel? How would we judge? We make the decision in a manner analogous to how we judge an authentic Rembrandt. We fit the present object into the already present history of what is clearly "authentic": the *already* attested works of Rembrandt, the *already* attested exemplars of art. The cheese room is ranged alongside something—Gaudí's Barcelona church?—and a decision is made to enter it into the history of *art*, rather than the history of jokes or psychopathology.

True art is what is valuable or valued *artistically*—not every drip of concrete or cheese may be valuable (real, true) *art*.[3] In the area of what is signatured, the criteria for value is an accepted *tradition*. The only standard for either authenticity or valuable art is the existence of actual valued exemplars. In the case of the genuine Rembrandt, there must be some canon of accepted exemplars against which a putative Rembrandt can be compared. Forgers are delighted when one of their forgeries slips into the canon because it makes it easier to accept the next forgery. "It doesn't look much like number 1 to 12, but a lot like 13 (the forgery), so it must be authentic." A similar pattern is followed in determining what is *truly* art. We rely on actual exemplars that are accepted as the real, that is, valuable, thing. Sometimes great exemplars can be stultifying to art. In the Paris Commune of 1848, the avant-garde artists of the day wanted to burn down the Louvre so that they would not be dominated by past exemplars.

Despite the dangers of evaluation-by-tradition, there is really no other modality available for assessment. The existence of and dependence upon tradition is not necessarily biased to the past. Comparison of present work to past exemplars affects past and present alike, and the past may not emerge the winner. It can happen that the newer work casts older work into the shadow, leading us to see that previous exemplars are less valuable than earlier believed because the newer work reveals with clarity what now seems awkward and muddled in the earlier vision. On the other hand, in a developed and deeply historical tradition such as the history of visual representation, we would be prepared to reject out of hand any new development that threatened to fatally undermine the value of Rembrandt.

The validation of art by placing works within a tradition clearly distinguishes art from the universal (nonsignatured) truth of science, a truth that is validated by common observation or experiment, not by exemplars. A sign of the difference between art and science is that in science one subsumes past theory into the present scientific structure. Newtonian mechanics is in a sense a local phenomenon within Einstein's more extensive cosmology of relativity. In art, however, as much as artists learn from and depend on previous artists, the past is not subsumed. Cezanne said his aim was to "redo Poussin in nature." Assuming that he accomplished that goal, Poussin nevertheless remains in no way "subsumed" or "refuted" by Cezanne or anyone else whom he may influence. Again, science continually swallows its history only to reformulate it in present theory; art is essentially historical, a tradition of exemplars.

The notion of true art and its validation within a *tradition* constitutes a fundamental rejection of the relativist assumptions of multiculturalism. In the peculiar way that opposites converge, the multicultural critique of scientific knowledge—unhistorical and universalist—turns out to be thoroughly *un*historical on its own grounds. If every reader has his or her own text, his or her own here-and-now interpretation, then historical placement is unnecessary or impossible and canonic works are only political artifacts. Thus the present-day canonic wars in American colleges. Denial of a canon is simply the denial of tradition, that is, the notion that works of art assess one another within a common history. But looking for a canon is not placing the dead hand of the past (dead, white, European males) onto the vital present, it is exercising the vitality of a tradition in which present works call into question the past and vice versa. Tradition is the available means for discovering the *authentic*. As noted previously, feminists are not advocating radical individualism. They are searching for the authentic voice of women as it has been suppressed in some texts, ecstatically exploded in others. This authentic voice is the "true" voice, it has "universality" but not the ascetic universality of natural science.

THE TRUTH OF ART

It is clear enough that works of art are uniquely signatured, and that we evaluate those works by assessing signatured exemplars within a common history or tradition. We talk about what is *truly* art and decide to consign cheese drippings to some other category of human effort, or to nonsense. If we value art, as we do, do we value it for its *truth?* Is there a sense in which works of art are true to something *external?* Is there something true about the world as seen by Rembrandt? To the extent that there is "external truth" in Rembrandt's vision, it necessarily moves beyond (or below) the scientific model of truth. The "self" of the rational, scientific mind is sexless, above culture, transcendent, without birth or death: a timeless, passionless observer. Actual human beings are *not*, however, timeless or passionless observers. The world that living human beings "know" is precisely the world of historical position, passion, and emotion that the transcendent observer ascetically abandons. Art as personally signed reveals the world as experienced by persons, historical humans embedded in sex and situation. One brings humanity to the arts, and the arts are, in turn, schools of humanity. In whatever sense the arts can be a school for humanity is a clue to the truth of art—and the place of the arts in the "school" of the university.

One might well admit that humanity only comes in signatured, historically particular works, an acknowledgment the multiculturalists then use to point up the difference between the universality of science and the variability of human sensibilities, moral, and aesthetic values. How can there be any external—that is to say, universal—truth revealed in art. The relativists whom John Paul II opposes hold that truth is unattainable because cultures differ too widely, there are no *human* universals, thus no universal art; art is only true locally. It may be that Shakespeare is authentic art to Western sensibilities but not to those grounded in other cultural traditions. For years, the artifacts of African tribes were placed in ethnographic museums because they were not regarded as art in the European *beaux arts* tradition.

The philosophical problems surrounding the universality of art's signatured visions requires extensive and deep considerations of a sort that is beyond the scope of this book. The key to a philosophical analysis requires distinguishing between what is psychologically "subjective" and the meaning of "personal" vision. The two are easily conflated since the personal is inherently "of the subject" in the sense that persons are identified by something "inside," the capacity of self-reflection. A player piano programmed to perform a Beethoven sonata might play with feeling but would feel nothing. There is then a confusion between the use of "personal" to indicate passing tastes and notions, as in "my personal opinion," and its use to indicate a complex, comprehensive, deep vision of life—what one would stake one's person upon. By putting myself—my person—on the line, I am clearly staking out more than my feelings. I am making an implicit claim: this is how the world is as a *person* (heart and soul) sees it. Rembrandt's vision is clearly *personal*—it is, after all, *Rembrandt's*. But what a vision! The difference between the passing and the deep sense of "personal" comes out when we note without contradiction that this art or that person is "good" even though we don't happen to "like" the art or that personality type. The mistake of subjectivists is to construct "personal" from the side of feeling. There is no contradiction in my saying Wagner was a great musician, even though I don't like his music. Of course, from the standpoint of transcendent science, Wagner is not a musician at all—one does not appropriate music good or bad as a matter of science. Only persons respond to music.

The philosophical issues involved here are complex. I confine myself to some obvious problems with the thesis of radical, incommunicable difference between cultures. The multiculturalist claim for a radical separation of cultures is, I believe, false in fact, a failure of nerve, and a simplistic method of affirming one's own views. That radical separation is false in fact seems clear enough from the existence of universal artists: the works of Shakespeare have had a rich history in Japan. Of course there is something different about them, starting with the obvious fact that the plays are translated into Japanese; but even the contemporary Royal Shakespeare Company does not perform in the manner of seventeenth-century England, or even in that of the nineteenth century or the 1920s. The very fact that African masks are now displayed in art museums rather than museums of natural history suggests that the art of varied cultures can be appropriated.

As to failure of nerve: erecting a multicultural sign post at the *beginning* of cross-cultural dialogue signals the basic futility of the enterprise. In proclaiming my broad tolerance of the other culture, I am also making sure that my own views are sealed from comparison and critique.

The paradox of great art is that it is on the one hand signatured, deeply historical, a unique personal voice and vision, while on the other it transcends its mere periodicity and personal quirks. Shakespeare is certainly a unique voice; he is also very much a writer of his age. We can dissolve him into a specimen of sensibilities, style, and vision that he shared with his contemporaries like Beaumont and Fletcher. Scholars do just that. But it is the mark of great art that while speaking from the person and of the age, it contains a core that can constantly be revived in radically different societies. If there is a *tradition* of art, it is not simply because there are historical precursors, it is because some of those historical precursors are more than historical curiosities. Tradition bears upon the present as the standard of value because great art of the past moves beyond its historical placement to comment on the present.[4] Great art is universal and true to the *human* condition. The feminist's search for the authentic voice of women would be futile if there were no female writings that were exemplars and touchstones of true female sensibility.

If one of the marks of truth is universality, one can plausibly argue that there are universal artists and universal works. If at least some art works did not transcend their historical particularity, there would be no ongoing tradition in the arts, no possibility of assessment other than local fashion. It seems plainly mistaken to claim that value in art relies on ephemeral taste. But if there is transcendence and universality in art, it is clearly *not* the transcendence and universality of science. If Shakespeare is a universal artist, a cynosure of the poetic tradition, it is not because he ceases to be a Renaissance artist writing his uniquely powerful verse. We are likely to attribute Shakespeare's universality to a breadth and depth of vision into so many aspects of the "true" human condition that a person of any age and culture could understand some—probably not all—of those aspects as present in his or her own life, times, and culture.

When we understand the mind of Shakespeare, are we neutralizing our own perceptions, becoming a blank slate analogous to the transcendent mind of the scientific investigator? We cannot be an epistemological blank slate for the arts because if we achieved such transcendent neutrality, we would be constitutionally disabled from appreciating what is presented. What is valuable is a signatured voice, a deep *personal* vision. Only signatured persons can read signatured persons. Descartes's sexless, bodiless, apolitical thinking *thing* is positioned precisely to avoid all the prejudices of particularity. But if we read as persons, we can be open to the voice of the other. I read Shakespeare, and Shakespeare *reads me*—that is the sense in which Harold Bloom can argue that Shakespeare teaches us what it is to be human. The interchange always takes place, however, between signatured persons. My reading of Shakespeare will carry my signature; if I have a "weak" signature, it may be only a trace element. (Persistence of the personal is the truth of the deconstructionist claims.) However weak or strong, *my* reading of Shakespeare is, one hopes, still a reading of *Shakespeare*. Wittgenstein's notion of "family resemblance" is helpful here. My reading of Shakespeare, Burbage's reading, Kean's, and Kurosawa's are not identical but they all have a "family resemblance."[5] In contrast, all physicists who read Newton share the *identical* idea. Members of a family are not identical but share a set of overlapping traits sufficient to place them in the same family. Wittgenstein remarks that "Stand over *there!*" is sufficiently clear without specifying longitudinal coordinates. Sufficient deviation and lack of shared traits places one in a different clan. "No, not there, over *there!*"

SIGNATURED ART AND UNIVERSAL
MORALITY: A DEFENSIVE DIGRESSION

If entry into the world of the arts is only via what is signatured (both the work and the reader/viewer/listener) it should be clear that this world is radically other than the world of science, which is deliberately and self-consciously unsignatured. What about the world of morals? Although the problem of morality is not my principal concern, a book treating the broad range of issues centering around the "Catholicity" of Catholic universities should say something about the subject, since the church claims sovereignty over "Faith and Morals." If the pope wants to assert the truth and universality of Christian faith, presumably he is also concerned with the universality of morality. Between the two—faith and morals—my basic interest in this book is in faith, since that is what seems to threaten and be threatened by the sort of "knowledge" thought to be the domain of the university. Thus I do not as such address the Catholic claim for infallibility on moral matters. My view on faith and morals in the context of Christianity is that whatever morals may be affirmed are derivative of faith and share its logic. This means that like faith, Christian morals lack the sort of universality characteristic of science. If such morals are universal, they are so more along the lines of universality in art.

One assumes that the pope has moral concerns in mind in his defense of Christian truth against the threat of relativism. There is a deep lesson of moral tolerance in the calls for *multi*culturalism, but one doesn't want to admit the Nazi culture or the cult of *thugees* into the list of the tolerated. We think that certain things are wrong with as much "certainty" as we know the world to be round. Our moral intuitions are correct here, but not because universal moral injunctions are to be understood as scientific statements. It is the value neutrality of scientific statements that gives them a universality; but universal moral truths are not value neutral. The universality of science and its neutrality stem from its descriptive character. The facts, just the facts. But moral truth cannot be a matter of *fact*. If that were the case, moral and legal decisions would be quite straightforward. In a murder trial we know that someone has been killed; we may know that X shot Y to death. But was it murder? To answer that we have to examine such "interior" mysteries as motive, psychological state, belief, whether the defendant is lying, and so on.

If we say that "Murder is wrong" is universally true, it is because we mean "Wrongful killing is wrong." That is an analytic truth, not a valued discovery or acclamation of fact! It is the apparent analytic character of moral truths that has led sceptics to argue that moral judgments are nothing but expressions of a culture. We learn the rules of the "language game" of morals for our society, but there is no more truth to such rules than there is to the rules of chess. An alternative denial of truth for morality is the claim that moral judgments are only expressions of feeling. "Murder is wrong" means nothing more than "This is a killing and a kind I don't like." On these views, moral truth is infallible either because it is an analytic statement (game rule for your group) or it is an irrefutable statement of feeling.

It is no defense of universal morality, however, to regard moral statements as analytic truths or as exclamations of feeling. Someone who merely reaffirms the analytic moral judgments of his society or wafts along on his feelings is not the paradigm of the moral man or woman. Rattling off analytic moral claims specific to my society will not *prove* to anyone not sharing that ethical geometry the right and wrongs of the conduct in question. Catechizing the youth in the analytic judgements of the culture will not produce a moral actor, only a moral reciter, a moral reactor. Reduction of moral claims to statements of feeling obviously reduces any universality since feelings are notoriously varied.

The problem for moral truth is how to break out of its infallibility as either analytic to the culture or subjective to the speaker. How does morality relate to "reality" beyond local custom or local (my) feelings? The clue to answering this puzzle lies in the method of learning to be moral, the root problem of which is avoiding mere rote or emotional whim. If *the* model of learning is "science," one can be certain that morality will never be learned. The value-neutral outlook demanded of the impersonal investigator constitutionally prohibits moral assessment. Unless one is prepared to simply give up on this issue in sheer moral skepticism, we need a different model for moral learning and appraisal. The method of the arts is helpful insofar as art can only be appraised from within the world of persons, what Dilthey called the *Lebenswelt*. We can learn morality to the extent we share in the world-as-seen-by-other-persons. It is vital to hold, then, to the notion of *person*, understood not as my ephemeral feeling tone, but as my internal vision of an acting, judging self. In the arts we see the world through the personal vision of the artist. Great artists offer great visions of the world, offering a meaningful world because it is a world *full* of meanings—in contrast to mere personal, that is, "subjective" opinion, which is a world of limited, idiosyncratic meaning.

We teach morality by revealing how it feels to be *inside* the experience of another. Learning about *human* value is learning about signatured individuals, real or imaginary, who have specific placement as men, women, children, princes, paupers, and so on through the unending human set of variations. In the process we learn about our own "inside" as we learn about that of each other, and come to see that the world in terms of weal and woe looks just so from the highly specific standpoint of the other. Certainly telling stories is *the* pedagogy for the moral instruction of children. Understanding the little engine that could or the prince that wouldn't is basic moral tutelage. Plato censures the stories of the gods in preliminary pedagogy for fear that future citizens will learn the wrong lessons about fear and pleasure. Telling stories over time develops a reciprocal relation between the stories told and the one receiving the story. Ideally, we "progress" from simple stories with a clear moral point, stories with blackhatted villains and whitehatted heros, to stories that reflect the complexity of feelings and emotions as they are worked out not in fairy tales but in the dense world of specific histories. We learn that one may "smile and smile and be a villain" and that terrible things have been done out of "good intentions."

Those who equate moral judgements with a type of feeling are not wholly wrong but what they fail to appreciate is the "social construction" of feeling—how feelings are learned, schooled, shaped, and enriched. The good *person* is the one who has the *right* feelings—or at least knows what the right feelings should be—when faced with a particular circumstance. The good person is not the product of ephemeral moods. Acknowledging the social construction of feeling is not by any means to open the door to moral relativism, unless one assumes in a spirit of empty tolerance that other societies' constructions of feeling are hopelessly opaque one to the other. This "artistic" model of moral tutelage insists that we can learn from different social constructions—as we do from different styles of art. What we do not learn is a final moral geometry.

In the pedagogy of morality, how do we know what are the "right," that is to say, the truly moral stories? It would be comforting to believe that there was a litmus test, a theory, or even a definitive code sanctioned by God, but none seems to be available to morality, just as there is no *theory* of art that can develop the scrupulous eye, ear, sense of the connoisseur. Finally, we judge conduct to be right or wrong in the context of how it fits into a life narrative lived with and among others. Moral development and stature is more likely to arise from living in the world of Dickens and his poor, Dostoevsky and his crazed fanatics, Walker Percy and and his anesthetized moderns than from reading Kant. Great stories become the exemplars of great feeling and great lives against which the most learned moral catechisms seem to falter.[6] The position suggested here is directly counter to the trend in Kantian ethics. For Kant, examples are the "child's go-cart" of moral philosophy; we give examples to illustrate the moral law but in the end we must rationally apprehend the *law* in itself. I prefer the Wittgensteinian notion that there are only examples.

ART IN THE CURRICULUM

If one assumes that the arts uniquely reveal the human world *because* they are signatured, one could raise the issue of whether they belong within the modern university with its commitment to the logic of reason and science. But it probably seems sheer nonsense to even suggest that the artists are somehow "out of place" in the modern university. There they are, all tenured-in like the physicists. If I raise the issue of the arts, however, it is because of the much livelier (or deadlier) question about religion in the curriculum. If there is current academic suspicion of religion, there has been past academic suspicion of the arts. After all, departments of the arts within the university are relatively recent developments. I attended the faculty meeting at Princeton at which the issue of a Ph.D. degree in musical composition was being proposed. One staunch opponent declared, "God forbid that Princeton would offer a Ph.D. degree for something *creative.*" The suspicion and disdain currently cast upon multiculturalism within the academy may be a late reflection of an earlier suspicion of the logic of the arts, a "logic" apparently rooted in personal visions and enthusiasms.

It is not difficult to construct an argument that the university should stick to strict science. There are distinguished institutions whose overall curricular trajectory is natural science, engineering, and technology—albeit with some residual "humanities" programs thrown in for whatever uplift or sheer relief may be provided by such "soft" subjects. Of course one can introduce art in the curriculum in the posture of strict science—at least of sheer fact. Much of nineteenth-century German art history concerned itself with the succession of styles or the influence of new methods and materials on artifacts produced. The value of art, its "success" as art, was not an issue, and certainly neither was the "aesthetic education of man." One might study religion in a similar fashion, scientifically, from an anthropological point of view, recording powerful and pervasive human practices and beliefs, while at the same time regarding the whole field of religion as superstition and psychic aberration. In short, one could introduce art or religion into the university curriculum as part of the *un*natural history of humankind. People involve themselves in such things for subjective pleasure or from psychic pressure, but to one who looks at the world rationally, the arts and religion do not look back.

It may be more than an historical accident that as religion has been ushered out of the educational curriculum during the twentieth century, the arts have been welcomed in. In many ways the arts are the functional replacement of the older religious commitment. The religious founders of the early American colleges simply assumed that one function, perhaps the principal function, of the university was education inculcating religion and morality. "For God, for country, and for Yale" was more than rhetoric. Nineteenth-century denominational colleges saw nothing out of order in suspending academic exercises for the annual religious revival. This earlier religious direction of higher education has been almost wholly erased by the advent of the modern scientific research ethos. However, while religion vanished as the bearer of value, the arts and humanities prospered as the secular descendent of the older ethical commitment: "For Man [and since coeducation circa 1970: Woman], for country, and for Yale."

Signatured truth in art attaches to morality insofar as it reveals the *Lebenswelt*, the *lived* world. Regardless of the elegance and persuasiveness of various attempts to dissolve human value, morality, and art into an illusion of the genes or a value-neutral dance of atoms, people go on *living* a world of moral choice and artistic value. Signatured truth also characterizes biblical religion but in a manner that goes beyond both science and art. The signatured character of Christianity is expressed in the claim I have already highlighted: Jesus' statement "*I* am the Truth." To understand that claim, and the general claims of Christianity, I want to explore the "failure of art." Although an explication of artistic signature introduces concepts and methods that recur within the religious dimension, in the long run the artistic model, like the scientific, fails to capture the peculiarity of biblical proclamations. The "failure" of art as a key to religion is the subject of the succeeding chapter.

4

Religion: Truth of Presence

In chapter 3 I sketched a "logic" of the arts in order to suggest that the value-neutral rationality of science does not command the entire territory of truth. There is signatured truth, truth attached essentially to the vision and insight of named individuals. As humans not angels, as living persons not transcendent observers, artists (broadly defined) reveal to us the truth of the human world of life and desire, passion and pride, good and evil. Art is always to and from the person and thus signatured, which means that it must also be appropriated by the viewer-as-person. A great *universal* artist is not universal because he obliterates history, sex, self, but because the sense of self expressed is so enriched that it can speak to other histories, other sexual identities, other selves. Art is appropriated as a dialogue of historical selves.

In this chapter I turn to the issue of biblical Revelation. The presumed problem for a Catholic university is the relation between reason and faith, reason and Revelation. One direct way of justifying the Catholic university is to demand that it take in *all* the truth there is. There are the rational truths of science and there are the revealed truths that we have through biblical Revelation. All well and good. But the danger in this approach is that the truths of Revelation will be construed on the model of the privileged witness, which is set within the forms of scientific, rational truth. It is an accident of history that we cannot appropriate something that was in fact seen by only one witness. Signatured truth, on the other hand, extends the field of truth and cannot be reduced to the truth of privileged witness, cannot be regarded as accidently restricted scientific exploration. I might be the next astronaut, but no matter what my genius, I will not be the next Mozart. Mozart is the truly unique conveyer of the Mozartian truth.

If one accepts the reality of signatured truth, then, in the university's broad quest for *all* truth, it should also find its place on campus. The arts do have a reasonably firm lodging in the contemporary curriculum, however vague the rationale may be for such inclusion. If biblical Revelation were to be regarded as an instance of signatured truth in the manner of the arts, then it might be legitimated for the modern university. In fact, the Bible is often taught in departments of religion as "literature," as one of the great exemplars of "spiritual" writing alongside the Lotus Sutra, the Vedas, or the novels of Dostoevsky. Coming to understand the Bible—and Christianity overall—within the modalities of art can be a valuable and instructive introduction to the "logic" of Revelation. In the final analysis, however, Christianity-as-art, the Bible-as-literature, fails to capture the power of religion either for historical believers or for the essential proclamation of biblical Revelation. In this chapter, I explore the positive points of comparison between art and Revelation, and then move on to suggest the ways in which Christianity-as-art is profoundly misleading.

REVELATION AND SIGNATURED TRUTH

By the proclamation "I am the Truth," Jesus is not, I have argued, taking on the role of privileged witness. However one may finally understand his claim, it would certainly seem to *signature* "Truth" to Jesus of Nazareth. At a first approximation, then, New Testament Revelation follows the pattern set forth for the signatured truth of the arts.

The creation and assessment of art for its truth, as I argued in chapter 3, depends on *exemplars*. It is not too much of a stretch to regard these exemplars as *revelations*. There is no inner natural necessity that leads to, say, landscape painting. Many cultures—even highly developed painting cultures—just don't do it. But if Poussin or Turner or Cezanne comes along and paints landscapes, these are novel revelations, exemplars for the "new" tradition of landscape painting. While it is true that artists basically learn from prior artists and that one can trace the precursors of a special genre like landscape painting, nevertheless the transition to landscape painting is a genuine novelty, invention, or inspiration. Literally, one moves what was in the background to the foreground and that is a radical and unpredictable turn in sensibility.

Without accepting the full-blown romantic view of "genius," there is a central truth to the notion that we depend on genius, the inspiration of the artist to create and initiate the reality, to begin or expand the tradition. Because the artist's work proceeds from no natural or rational necessity, it has been thought to be super-natural, coming from somewhere beyond reason or, negatively, below reason from the infinite chaos of the emotions. Positively regarded the artist is said to be inspired—in the spirit. The ancients literally thought the godlike muses were prompting the artist's work. Because the emergence of art is highly contingent (waiting on inspiration, a boost from the muses), art is deeply historical, dependent on what happens to be created.

The parallel to the role of Revelation in the biblical sense is striking. Contrary to the universal rationalism of Julian who held that reason alone could discover the divine essence, the Bible affirms that we can know God only through the historical Revelation of and to a *chosen* people—to Abraham, Moses, and latterly, Jesus—which initiated a tradition that became canonic and could be used to validate later instances of the ongoing history of Revelation. The Gospel writers did not refer to the Hebrew Bible for nothing! Biblical Revelation to patriarchs and prophets is held to be canonic for "true" religion as Rembrandt is for "true" art. That, at least, is the biblical and Christian claim.

Because art depends on actual individual exemplars, the descriptive, critical, and apologetic language that grows up around these initiating realities is relegated to paraphrase. Artistic criticism receives understanding and validation only in the presence of the art work. We have extensive descriptions of ancient Athenian wall paintings but none of them have survived. Lacking the actual examples, we really do not know what they were as art. I may tell you that van Gogh uses a thick brush and vivid colors, but until you actually see a van Gogh painting, you don't know van Gogh. Similar considerations obtain for religious revelation. Whatever is revealed in Jesus, theology and doctrinal statements are finally and only validated by the presence of that actuality. We don't start with theological doctrine and then instance the reality; we start with the given reality and then try to understand what there is about it that the theologian may be pointing to. The theological claim "Jesus is the Son of God" is interpretively read back into the life of Jesus by the New Testament writers and the church.[1] First there is participation in the life of faith (the life of the community/ church), out of which arises the secondary discourse of apologetics. Thus one must first be *within* the tradition of historical Revelation or artistic exemplars in order for theology or art commentary to make any sense. I believe it was Wittgenstein who commented: "You can't hear God speak to someone else, you can only hear him if you are being addressed—that is a grammatical re- mark." (If it wasn't Wittgenstein it should have been; it is his way of dealing with religious claims.) The "grammar" of understanding a work of art or God's word is that one must be addressed in the present by a presence.

While teaching a course some years ago on the philosophy of art, I asked the students to indicate with which of the arts they had some familiarity. One stu- dent said that he had no experience with any of the arts. Why was he taking the course? He wanted to get the theory of the thing so that if and when he ever did start listening to music or looking at painting he would be able to distinguish the good stuff from the junk. That certainly put Descartes before the course. My student had a perfect Cartesian mind: if one had the general theory, then one could fit the cases under the theory. But that is not at all how one comes to appreciate art. Only exposure, immersion, "living with" the art work will open that world and its values.

Pascal is often criticized for having said that one should practice religion, attend services, pray—even though one does not believe. His point was that only by practicing, by immersion in the religious life, can one access the value (beliefs) of the tradition. There seems to be a proper analogy in this advice for the arts. My student who did not "practice" any of the arts, would never be able from philosophic thought to come to appreciate the value of art. There is no guarantee that immersion will reveal value; individuals may finally decide that grand opera and cubism are opaque. There certainly are those who seem opaque to religious traditions.

The secondary role of doctrine is vital to understanding biblical religion. Jewish writers have been the clearest on this point when they insist that Judaism is not a religion of orthodoxy (right *belief*) but a religion of orthopraxis (right *action*). What *leads* the religious believer is not a statement of belief, a dogma, but some lived actuality. Thus Franz Rosenzweig's peculiar statement that the belief of the Jew is the "procreation" of the Jewish people. The living Jewish people are the belief. In the Christian tradition, liberation theologians have in- sisted that theology begins in and must grow from *praxis*, a term purposely cho- sen instead of the more conventional "practice," which is often regarded as the *application* of a prior theory or belief. The liberation theologian insists that there is no prior theory to be applied. One must first engage in a practice like the South American base communities in order to derive and properly understand Christian beliefs. Praxis in this sense is strictly analogous to how theories of art and critical descriptions grow only out of the actual experience of art and must be continually referred back to exemplars for interpretation. A less politically informed notion of theological discourse than that of the liberation theologians is Balthasar's statement that we must do theology "on our knees."[2] The Christian praxis of prayer leads theology, not the other way round. This is a point to which I will return later and at length.

So far the analogy of art and Revelation seems apposite. The problem for religion, however, is in the interpretation of *presence*. Even when immersed in the praxis of faith, to what are we present? I consider this issue of "presence" in the balance of this chapter. But before turning to it directly, I want to emphasize again the difference between the Jerusalem Tradition and a great spiritual wisdom like Buddhism. Buddhism is a teaching, a spiritual philosophy, that stands more or less on the same plane as, say, Stoicism. Because there are "doctrines" in the sense of *beliefs* about how the world of sense and desire are to be understood, one may assess and accept or reject these teachings. But in doing so, the presence (or re-presentation) of the Buddha or Marcus Aurelius is indifferent to the truth of the teachings. In Christianity, however, it is the presence and person of Jesus that is critical: "I am the Truth."

ART AND PRESENCE

It is useful to compare art and biblical Revelation because methods and practices that seem peculiar in the life of the church and synagogue have quite acceptable interpretations within the life of art. Further, comparing art and religion may seem to have great apologetic value for religion. Organized religion has been having a hard time of late, but the museums are crowded and drama festivals abound. If religion is in any way like an artistic "vision," one could soften or, perhaps, eliminate the controversies over dogma and doctrine (the scientific model of truth) that have marred its history and render it "unbelievable" to the modern rational mind.

I have argued against rooting religion in doctrine lest doctrine be construed as some sort of factual claim about the supernatural. But if the aim is to avoid confusing religious belief with scientific truth, we must be alert to the equivalent mistake of regarding religion as art. Art, as Freud properly noted, is an "illusion" that allows us to imagine and construct a more livable world. The artist reveals and shapes emotions with a clarity that the inattention and buzz of the everyday obscures. Because we recognize that art is an illusion, it is a benign illusion, and one that may even educate us toward refined feeling. Thus one might be led to follow the injunction to shape one's life as a "work of art"—to create a life full of human sensitivity and compassion. Religion, on the other hand, Freud judged to be an illusion that people take "for real" and thereby distort their lives. Robert Frost reflected this Freudian distinction when he said that poetry does not affect the real, it does not eliminate suffering, though (importantly) it "lifts suffering to a plane of higher regard."[3]

For what it is worth, reducing religion to art—or making art a new religion—hardly conforms to the actuality of religious history and practice. The Bible is really not a very satisfactory work of art for all the power of the psalms, the denunciations by the prophets, or Jesus' parables. Nor have religions offered themselves as artistic visions for contemplation; they claim to be disciplines, life commandments, and commitments. That is certainly how believers have understood religious teachings. To access the religious, one must in some sense move beyond art to life itself, what is "for real!" (I use "the real" throughout the book for this distinction, and enclose the term in quotation marks to differentiate "the real" from "reality" as that term is used in scientific verification. I have adopted "the real" in part because of its use by Lacan as something beyond the "Symbolic" and "Imaginary.")[4]

A perceptive differentiation between art and what I call "the real" can be found in Henry James's preface to *The Spoils of Poynton*. James relates how the novel came about. While attending a fashionable London affair, he happened to overhear someone telling of a messy inheritance and discerned in that story what he called a "germ," a set of complications that could serve as the narrative rudiments from which a novel might grow, though the actual events turned out quite differently than depicted in his novel. James reflected on the difference between life and art:

> Life being all inclusion and confusion, and art being all discrimination and selection, the latter in search of the hard latent *value* with which it is concerned . . . the artist finds in his tiny nugget washed clean of awkward accretions and hammered into sacred hardness the very stuff for a clear affirmation . . . for the indestructible. At the same time, it amuses him again and again to note how, beyond the

first step in the actual case . . . life persistently blunders and deviates, losing herself in the sand. The reason, of course, is that life has no direct sense of the subject and is capable, luckily for us, of nothing but splendid waste.[5]

Art is the luminous, clear, Platonic form: hard, golden, indestructible. Life, on the other hand, is all "inclusion and confusion," capable only of "splendid waste."

James points to what can be regarded as a failure of art. In the distinction he draws, art, powerful and important as it is, constitutes an "abstraction" from life as lived. Art is symbolic, something shaped into a "clear affirmation" that reflects the controlling sensibility of the signatured artist. From the standpoint of biblical religion, art must be transcended since it is *only* an illusion—thus reversing Freud's view of illusion and reality. A vivid example of the failure of art is expressed in Elie Wiesel's comment that only the art produced by children in the concentration camps is adequate to the experience of the Holocaust. Once the formative, cultivated sensibility of the adult artist starts to reshape the Holocaust events, as James extracted his "germ" from a messy history, the horror is placed at a distance and in a sense "falsified." The children's art, however, moves beyond symbol to what I call the "iconic."[6] A symbol becomes iconic when it *participates in the reality it depicts*. (Thus the various controversies about icons in the Eastern Church. Are the icons only *depictions* of the holy, or do they actually *participate in* the holy?) The art of children in the concentration camps is immediate, unfiltered by "Art," and thus it participates in the very event that is depicted.

The iconic artist hopes not merely to depict a reality but in some sense to make that reality *present* in the very work. The power of the icon is subtly different than that of even the greatest works of "normal" art. Great works of art are certainly *disclosive*. Heidegger discussed the disclosive power of van Gogh's depiction of peasant shoes. Somehow the being of the shoes and the life of the peasant is opened, unveiled. True enough. But that disclosure is still within van Gogh's powerful personal vision. Unlike the naïveté of the children's art, van Gogh's work remains a disclosive depiction, not an icon. We admire van Gogh's art and style; we do not—indeed, cannot—assess "style" in the children's work.

Great art is important; we need clarity from the artist because we lose the sense of things by submerging them in our practical needs. Artists reveal human truth in that sense. Yet, in James's view of art there remains the controlling, powerful sensibility of the artist. We confront the shoes, but only as mediated by van Gogh's strong personal vision. To confront van Gogh is a disclosive experience of art shaping reality. A Jamesian novel confronts us with an exquisite selective refinement of human intercourse. Insofar as we regard shoes (or society) for bare practical utility we ignore both Jamesian "waste" and the alarming clarity of vision offered by the artist.

The problem for the true artist is to find forms that are disclosive. On this quest there is no assurance that the viewer will understand or accept the artist's disclosive intent. Van Gogh's shoes may become a charming decoration, *The Spoils of Poynton* an elegant diversion. The "bourgeois" appropriation of art is an ever-present trap. Even if one is not stricken by bourgeois taste, one may from high aesthetic refinement appraise van Gogh in the powerful categories of art. Again, Wiesel's assertion is that the art of children in the camps does not "suffer" from the shaping sensibility of the "normal" artist, thus blocking aesthetic distancing so that the event can be apprehended as "present."

Contrast the naïveté of the children's art with a high art depiction of murderous reality, David's *Death of Marat*. The body of the assassinated leader lies in the bathtub, the wounds visible, blood dripping on the sheet. All is rendered with the scrupulous versimilitude that marks David's style. This must be "the real"! Not at all. David had viewed Marat's body in the room where he was assassinated. As painted he lies against a somber black emptiness that fills the upper half of the canvas. In fact, the wall behind Marat was white wallpaper elaborately decorated with everything from pistols to a large map of France. Wallpaper was part of the "confusion" of life that David left aside to make clear his assessment of the murder. The leader slain, blackness looms. We see the murder but also the artist's strong personal statement about it. But in the children's art produced in the camps, we get the horror of the Holocaust without any transcending commentary. The Nazi guard may be placed next to a primitive flower under a wooly scrawl of cloud. Reality escapes directed commentary and becomes more present in its terror.

Traditional Christian icons are not naïve. They are the products of a high art, but they obviously exist in a different space that cannot be related to the space from which the viewer apprehends them. This is "holy space," an "other" world is made present. One does not need to say, "This is a holy person"; the figuration *is* "holy." Iconic art as presence seeks to break down the aesthetic distance of "normal" art and even the moral input of the artist's shaping hand. At least that is what one would hope, but, of course, any viewer may fall into "aestheticism" so that even an artless depiction is read at a distance.

TOTALITY AND THE "HOLY"

One of the motives of iconic art is to present the world as a "totality," to go beyond the "merely artistic" into the density of *life* that lies beyond art in James's distinction. Yeats said that we should not "make light of the troubles of children. They are worse than ours, because we can see the end of our troubles and they can never see any end."[7] Children live in the present, having little sense of a past lived through, of suffering survived. To the child who suffers, that suffering is the totality of existence. The overwhelming reality of the concentration camp, the special work of a totalitarian regime, is captured in the totalizing vision that children inhabit by nature. A sense of totality arises when the distance between the viewer and the thing viewed is bridged, so that one is not merely a spectator but in some sense a participant. Elie Wiesel wants the "viewer" of the Holocaust not just to view but to participate. The psychiatrist Bruno Bettelheim, while imprisoned at Dachau, sought to avoid going mad from the destructive irrationality of the camp by exercising his professional transcendence and acting as an observer of inmate behavior. Children cannot possibly adopt such a mode of (scientific) transcendence, thus their artistic account of "the real" about the camps presented the thing-in-itself, with all its unmediated unstructured destructiveness.

I had the opportunity several years ago to review an excellent analysis of war photography. The study started with the first American war for which photography was publically available, the Spanish-American War, and proceeded chronologically through the Vietnam War. The trajectory of styles ranged from the artful to the artless. Early photographs were sharply focused, highly formalized, and captured moments of wartime heroism. By the time of the Vietnam War, however, the grainy, half-focused, partial glimpses of action, often the work of nonprofessional photographers, emphasized the manner in which the "fog of war" eludes artistic capture. Yet even with these provocative images of Vietnam, for all their immediacy, one knew that the reality of war was at a distance. A World War II photographer commented on the "disappointing sameness of it all." The mere act of fixing time in a photo, however murky, lifts the viewer out of the sameness of it all. And there is the noise, the smell, the cold and heat of war that make up the totalized experience.

War photographs are not "the real thing," children's art remains a depiction, icons are not the actual saint—but something about the manner of their presentation opens to "the real," throwing the viewer back on himself or herself. It is not the moral judgement of the artist (this is heroism, this is suffering) at work here; it is "the real" that engulfs the spectator who is not allowed to be a mere spectator. In Catholic Christianity the central ceremony of remembrance of the Lord's passion is said to constitute *real presence*, it is not merely a symbolic presence. Clearly the Eucharist is not the literal body of the Nazarene who lived two thousand years ago, but Catholics are right to reject the notion that it is merely a symbol or remembrance. Sacramental presence is iconic: it is a symbol that participates in the reality it depicts, just as the children's art from the concentration camps is a symbol infused with the very *presence* of the terrible reality depicted.

In order to illuminate an approach to "the real" and the idea of iconic art, I want to consider how and why certain movements in modern art play upon "the real" and thus move from "normal" art toward the iconic. The root notion of the iconic is that the reality must be made present to the spectator and that the spectator be made present to the reality. The "grandada" of modern art, Marcel Duchamp, epitomizes this sensibility. His great work *The Bride and the Bachelors* or *The Large Glass* is in the Philadelphia Museum of Art. It consists of two very large panels of glass, one above the other, on which the complex figures of a chocolate mill are depicted. When viewing the piece, one is not merely a spectator but also a part of the work as seen through the glass by other viewers. The spectator becomes part of the visual presentation of "the large glass." In the same gallery is Duchamp's last important work, *The Waterfall*; it is an erotic diorama that must be viewed by bending over and peeking through the keyhole of an antique Spanish doorway. Again, the spectator is not the distanced appraiser. The viewer is also the one looked at and an erotic voyeur at that! Duchamp's intent was to break down the "bourgeois" or "aesthetic" attitude toward art, the attitude of good taste in which the art work was a beautiful object *out there*. In contrast, Duchamp puts the viewer "on the spot." One is "in the picture." Looking at Duchamp's most infamous work, *Fountain*, a urinal that he attempted to exhibit at the New York Independents show in 1917, one should ask, "Why am *I* standing here looking at a toilet fixture with the same rapture as I would view a Bruges Madonna?" Why indeed! Existentialism, whatever its various oddities and internal disputes, valuably exploited the German word *Dasein*, which, though often simply translated as "existence," means literally "to be *there* (Da)*. Duchampian art forces the viewer to be *there*.

Many of the wilder reaches of contemporary art are nothing but post-Duchamp. In installation art, for instance, the viewer enters a room filled with rocks or sandbags or paper flowers or glass tumblers or almost anything or nothing. The viewer does not stand "outside" the work of art, a voyeur of beauty. Rather one is *in* the work of art. The stance, meaning, attitude, emotion of the spectator is not a reaction "out there," but part of the meaning of the whole installation-as-event. The prevalence of the erotic in contemporary art is not merely social protest, it is deliberately provocative, involving the viewer not merely as spectator but as sexually present. The viewer, again, is a presence in the art, not absent in external contemplation of a vision given by the artist.

What is the point of the post-Duchamps sensibility? In one sense it is an attempt to transcend the conventional meaning of art in the direction of presence that Wiesel finds in children's art.[8] It follows the sensibility expressed in Hemingway's *Farewell to Arms:*

> I was always embarrassed by the words sacred, glorious, and sacrifice. . . . I had seen nothing sacred and the things that were glorious had no glory. . . . There are many words that you could not stand to hear and finally only the names of places had dignity. . . . Abstract words such as glory, honor, courage, or hallow were obscene besides the concrete names of villages, the numbers of roads, the names of rivers, the numbers of regiments and the dates.[9]

In the "fog of war," the only realities are place names and dates, places where one can be *present* in space or time, not caught up in the rattle of great ideas and ideals that war has utterly destroyed. In *Farewell to Arms* one bids farewell to the big ideas; for the post-Duchamp artist it is also "Farewell to Art" and the notion that art is a sort of moral repository of the true, the good, and the beautiful. Post-Duchamp "art" work is deliberately non-arty, deliberately crude, awkward, unfinished. When Duchamp's *Large Glass* was accidently cracked across its whole surface while being transported from an exhibition, the artist considered this happening to be a considerable improvement. It removed any suggestion of the artist's *finish*. A critic commenting on recent art trends—pop, minimalist, conceptualist, and so on (all of which are genuinely Duchampian)—summed up the intent of such efforts as the "drive to wrench art from its normal subject matter and materials so as to bring it closer to the chaotic vitality of everyday life . . . ."[10]

SCIENCE, ART, AND RELIGION

I have sketched three contexts in which truth may function. There is the propositional truth exemplified by the sciences; artistic truth; and truth of presence, which is the truth of "the real." Scientific truth despite its power and scope requires an ascetic transcendence of human all-too-human experience. Artistic truth engages with human life as lived, shaping and molding it, clarifying human passion, and giving to suffering Robert Frost's attitude of "higher regard." But finally art may fail before the enormity of suffering, the sheer "blunder" and "waste" of life, the horror of the concentration camp, the fog of war. One bids "Farewell to Art" for a postartistic sensibility that engages the very blunder (a cracked glass) and waste (display of a urinal) of life. The aim of this postartistic art is direct engagement with the confusion of life that Henry James wished to put aside in his search for the "germ," the hard nugget of ideality.

If life and reality are as James depicted them, confusion over against the shaping sensibility of the artist, the modern anti-art artist wants to bring "the real" in all its messy presence to the distanced viewer. Museum goers, accustomed to the controlled visions of traditional art, will ask why they are being presented with such an inchoate, unshaped, often erotic mess. Why indeed? Presumably there is a truth to be told that goes beyond even the most penetrating personal vision of the great artist. But that truth is beyond the clarifying abstraction of the scientific proposition or even, it seems, beyond the shaping sensibility of traditional art. The depiction of the truth of "the real" in all its "splendid waste" seems either impossible or undesirable—"too much reality."

It seems easier to characterize the revelation of presence in negative terms: the total madness of the concentration camp, the fog of war, the blunder of life. James did characterize life as "*splendid* waste," but there seems little that is splendid in the visions so far discussed. Even the critic's characterization of anti-art as expressing "*chaotic* vitality" may not be consoling. Nevertheless, if there is to be any place for religion, for the holy, I contend that it must be found in experiences of totalizing presence, in experiences of "the real." Rudolph Otto's well-known definition of the holy as *mysterium, tremendum, et fascinans* certainly links the sacred and what is mysteriously overwhelming. The anti-art "junk" on display is certainly mysterious (what is it?), fascinating (the erotic helps here), and "tremendous" in the sense of overwhelming: the viewer is *in* the work and cannot seem to escape to a safe aesthetic distance. One suspects that much of the anti-art is iconic not of the holy, but of the demonic; the modern artist's protest against the corrosive totalitarian ethos of commercialism or

sexism or whatever. Icons of the demonic and the holy both disclose life as totality, the utter presence of life to the utterly present self. The choice between
the demonic and the sacred may be the ultimate life choice.

UNIVERSITIES AND THE TRUTH
OF "THE REAL"

Undifferentiated usage of the notion of truth, as Richard Bernstein noted in his
critique of *Fides et Ratio* (see chapter 2), is likely to end in simple confusion.
Worse yet, from the standpoint of a religious apologist, one may conflate religious truth into something like ordinary (scientific) truth—only a tad more
mysterious. And the truth of art finally fails because it lacks the participatory
moment demanded of the iconic or the anti-art engagement with what is overwhelmingly "the real." We have then three types of truth: the propositional
truth of science, the signatured truth of art, and finally, a truth about "the real"
that escapes the categorization of science and the shaping power of art. "There
are more things in heaven and earth, Horatio/Than are dreamt of in your philosophy."

It is conventional for universities to proclaim on their official seal *Scientia et
Ars*—Science and Art. What if they were to add Hamlet's caution to the es-
cutcheon? My guess is that Hamlet speaks a *truth*. It is, however, a truth that
seems to proclaim the failure of the truths of universalizing science and also, in
its way, the failure of the truth of art, if art is directed solely at the "formal" order or is appropriated as refined aestheticism. Life is neither what we know nor
what we artistically craft; life ("the real") always eludes us or impinges upon us
beyond the best of those splendid efforts. Hamlet's caution placed in the university prospectus might be a proper caution to the eager student who expects
university study to answer the riddle of life. "Salvation? No, not here!"

If there is a truth in Henry James's notion that life goes beyond art and
therefore resists the clarity demanded by the artist and the scientist, what possible role can this impossibly dense, confused realm of existence have in the life
of the university? Can anything be said about the "splendid waste?" "Of those
things about which we cannot speak clearly, we ought not to speak at all" is
Wittgenstein's famous concluding line in the *Tractatus*. The only legitimate
propositions are the propositions of natural science verifiable by facts. And "the
world is the totality of facts." "Not *how* the world is, is the mystical, but *that* it
is. . . . The sense of the world must lie outside the world. *How* the world is, is
completely indifferent to what is higher. God does not reveal himself *in* the

world." Wittgenstein's well-documented disdain for conventional academic life might be explained by the contradiction between his deep interest in ethics, art, and religion on the one hand, and, on the other, his antiseptic restriction of academic legitimacy to the statements of natural science.[11]

Across the English channel, Jean-Paul Sartre's take on "existence" was also broadly dismissive of the entire university enterprise. Sartre saw a final absurdity in the too-muchness of reality. It is an absurdity that must be recognized over against the university's normal ideals of science and art. In his novel *Nausea*, the protagonist, Roquentin, is attempting the scholarly reconstruction of the life of the (fictional) Marquis de Rollebon. In the course of the novel, Roquentin has a great revelation of the density of existence, a density that everywhere escapes form and categories. Scholarly pursuit, he concludes, is absurd in the face of too much reality. Similarly with art, as Roquentin comments:

> I think they are fools who find consolation in the arts. Like my Aunt Bigeois: "Chopin's Preludes were such a help to me when your poor uncle died." And the concert halls are overflowing with the humiliated, the outraged, their eyes shut, seeking to transform their pale faces into receiving antennas. They imagine that their sufferings become music. . . . What jerks they are.[12]

Art does not lift suffering to a plane of higher regard. Sartre's anti-Platonic existentialism is the sour inversion of James's Platonic view of art. Art for James is "sacred hardness . . . the happiest chance of the indestructible." Where James looks happily at the "splendid waste" that is the confusion that eludes pure form, Sartre looks upon it mordantly: "soft, monstrous lumps, in disorder— naked with a frightful and obscene nakedness."[13]

If, then, there is truth to be disclosed to the effect that life, existence, "the real" runs beyond the neat orders of "normal" academic pursuit, it is not at all clear what stance, if any, university study might take to such truth. It is perfectly possible simply to ignore the too-muchness of existence. Science: "It goes without saying that what we *know* is only knowledge of the *type*, never of the actual existent *individual*." Wittgenstein: "Not *how* the world is, is the mystical, but *that* it is." The "how" of actual individual existence, that it is, goes without saying, so it is not said—either in the classroom, the lab, or the mission statement. Such a restriction leaves outside of university recognition all that has been "said"—or at least presented—about the ultimate absurdity, riddle, mystery of life and existence: Wittgenstein's mystical, Sartre's revelation of existence. Not the least among the evocations of ultimate mystery has been religion. If the experience of religion and its reflective commentary (theology) have any place in the university's claim on truth, it will have to be in whatever can and cannot be said about the density of existence.

Sartre was accused of being an antihumanist, a nihilist of value. Despite his protests to the contrary, there is something to that claim in the sense that the normal *values*—at least the normal values of the normal university—are undercut in the "obscenity" of existential revelation. The *value* of existential truth for Sartre is negative; it is a constant check on the pretensions of science and art—the "divinization" of art and science—which are primary university values. Wittgenstein was equally wary of the university's capacity to deal with the truly important values of ethics and religion but, unlike Sartre, he did not question the vital importance of "elucidating" those areas. In the language of anti-art, Sartre and Wittgenstein might be said to "put the university in its place" and that "place" is irrelevant to the confrontation with existence or the mystical. The word preached to the university is "humility."

From the standpoint of traditional Catholic thought, there is much value in preaching humility to the schools. What seems impossible to modern existential types from Wittgenstein to the anti-artist is the notion of a theology *within* the university and, worse yet, theology as queen of the sciences. Queens do, of course, tend to put folks "in their place"; the traditional hierarchy of studies culminating in theology would subordinate (humble) all the other arts and sciences. If God is simply another name for "the Overwhelming," however, a theology-of-the-overwhelming could not find a (legitimate) place for science and art. Too much God (Existence/the Overwhelming) in the university and there is no university left. That sort of Catholic university would be a contradiction. Whatever else might be said about traditional Catholic theology, it was at least *scholastic:* it provided a place for learning and art in the economy of life and Salvation. I later suggest how this more "positive" outcome for the university might be justified and even practiced in a Catholic university. I argue in particular that a Catholic sense of the "sacramental" is uniquely appropriate for the conjoining of church and university. For now, I want to emphasize that *all* universities would do well to ponder "the more in heaven and earth." Catholic universities are not absurd or contradictory in addressing the beyond, even though one may conclude that they derive the wrong message or—worse yet—that there is no message. But that is a truth claim.

In the life of the university, the final elusiveness of existence may be ignored for purposes of categorization, shaped as best one can to personal artistic vision, cheerily acknowledged as the "splendid waste" (of extracurricular life?), cursed for its absurdity, or accepted as overflowing gift (of God). Consideration of these options—and any others that might come to mind—would seem to be not wholly alien to university conversation if for no other reason than to heed Hamlet's warning to his school chum. Accepting Hamlet's caution does not settle the issue of discourse, if any, *beyond* standard academic pursuits. Perhaps Zen, with its practice of paradox and silence, is after all the appropriate discourse for the beyond.

5

"I Am the Truth"

The previous three chapters have dealt with truth in three distinct contexts: scientific verification, art, and what I call "the real." It is in the last category that the truth of religion—at least biblical religion—must be located and assessed. *That* there is the reality of presence, "the real," cannot, I believe, be denied; the issue is whether anything can be *said* about it. Wittgenstein consigned it to "the mystical"; in Sartre we are overwhelmed with its utter, unsettling, "nauseous" incomprehensibility. Catholic Christianity, in contrast, purports to say quite a good deal about the mystery of "the real"—the All in All that is God. There are dogmas to be affirmed that apparently characterize "ultimate reality." Karl Rahner, who was particularly fastidious in the face of ultimate mystery, at least characterized it as *Holy* Mystery, his preferred locution for "God." To say that the ultimate real is "holy" is to say *something*—and is a direct contradiction to claims that it is "obscene" (Sartre) or the scientist's ultimate reality: "dumb" matter. (Whatever else one might say in gratitude to atoms, quarks, and the like for shaping themselves up into human beings, even producing a Beethoven, I would not go so far as to proclaim them "holy.")

A claim to some "definitive" word about the mystery of the existent may seem to create an arena of potential contention between academic fact and Catholic faith. The exact location of that possible contention is not, however, easy to define and is the subject of the next chapter. If, however, one were content to leave religion in Wittgenstein's "mystical," there would be no potential clash of any university claims and Christianity. It has been suggested that the Zen *koan* is a "post-linguistic use of language." Once you have a language with definitive meanings you can assert profound contradictions for their emotional shock value. Playing with language—serious play for the mystic monk—is no threat to the sober statements of science.

This chapter is directly theological, specifically christological. If there is to be some understanding of the relation between Christian statement of dogma and the truths assessed by the academy, there should be some account and analysis of what it is that Christians believe. *What* Christians believe cannot, however, be separated from the strange "logic" of creedal statements. While this chapter discusses the content of belief, it also deals with the logical or "grammatical" issues of belief. Content and mode of statement cannot finally be separated. Given the central problem of this book, the relation of academic freedom and Catholic dogma, knowing what Christians claim and how those claims are presented is crucial. I do not pretend that I can "prove" the validity of Christian belief—indeed, I am inclined to think that "proving Christian belief" is its own species of contradiction. What I hope to do is to indicate at least some of what is meant when Christians say that they believe in Jesus as Lord.

I have chosen to center Christian belief around Jesus' statement "I am the Truth." Obviously there is much more in the developed liturgical, ethical, and theological character of Christian faith than what appears in that single statement. At the same time, I think that the very strangeness of the statement expresses the special, transcendent claims made by the Christian church about her Lord.

My argument has already rejected the possibility that dogmatic belief statements are like factual scientific claims. The problem with factual claims is that they are person neutral, *un*signatured. Whatever else Christian religious claims may be, they certainly seem to address us as persons, individual beings of fear and passion, good and evil. The transcendent observer does not enjoy or suffer such experiences. One enters Christian truth through the venue of signatured truth. In the previous chapter I discriminated between art as signatured and what goes "beyond art" into anti-art and "the real." While "normal" art describes the world-as-seen-by-persons, it remains the world as *depicted*, not the world the viewer is *in* as a participant. Both science and "normal" art retain a distance between the knower/viewer and the work at hand. Anti-art and religious presentation, on the other hand, place one *inside* the event. The viewer is "on the spot"—part of the action in an anti-art "happening"—in the religious context faced with a fundamental life decision.

Anti-art seeks to present the "existential" density, mystery, and confusion of "the real." Being open to that presentness can only occur for a *participant*, one who does not assume the distanced stance of the scientific spectator. "The real" is a "mystery," which Gabriel Marcel characterized as a "problem which encroaches on its own data."[1] The self, for example, is just such a mystery: I cannot stand outside myself as a neutral observer of myself. The "I" that knows escapes the "I" that is known. To my self I am a participant, not a spectator. That I am a participant may be masked, however. I am often "absent" from myself and may need to be propelled into the truth of presence, my own presence. The truth of presence arises when I am both present to myself and the world is sharply present to me. Dr. Johnson's famous remark that nothing concentrates the mind so well as a sentence of hanging points to the double aspect of presence. A present sentence of death (a worldly event) brings my *presence* to myself front and center—because *I* soon may be altogether *absent* (from the world).

Various philosophers and artists have emphasized the intransigence of sheer presence. None have done so more determinedly than the anti-artists. Christian theologians should acknowledge the crucial importance of any movement that so effectively directs our attention to presence. But where the Christian differs from the anti-artist is on the issue of whether (or how) there is a "word" for such existential revelation. Can *one* say anything about final presence? Is there any sense in which this final reality can be "comprehended"? What exactly is "revealed" in the opening to "the real"? Given that art is inherently signatured, can "the real" beyond art—Henry James's "splendid waste"—be signatured?

SIGNATURING "THE REAL"

I have made much of the fact that "normal" art is signatured. Oddly enough, this is also true even of anti-artists: the Duchamp collection at the Philadelphia

Museum of Art is the work of *Duchamp*. The strangeness of anti-art, however, is that the artist signatures what seems to be unsignaturable, and that which is signatured seems without detectable impress of the artist. Often Duchamp did not "create" objects so much as he "found" them (*objets trouvés*)—the urinal, for example, or a French bottle rack. I saw a piece in a gallery in Montreal that did Duchamp one better. It was a "found" version of *The Bride and the Bachelors* (also the title of the Montreal piece). The artist had constructed a guinea pig cage on a board, in the center of which he placed a female guinea pig in an enclosure. He then introduced a number of male guinea pigs into the cage. Eventually the animals were removed; the artist glued the animal droppings to the floor of the cage, turned the board on end, and hung it as a "work of art" in the gallery. Clearly, the work was only tangentially related to the artist presenter's craft and signature. The aim of such works it seems is to thrust upon the viewer the sheer messy waste of things.

But why force such a perception on the viewer? Charles Taylor suggests there is a motive of "transcendence" in such art. By compelling us to "face the facts," the artist hopes to propel us into courage or despair. Taylor traces the impulse for such works to a Nietzschean transcendence of the ordinary, domestic, bourgeois values.[2] (Anti-art is antibourgeois if it is anything!) Taylor distinguishes between domestic goods (food, shelter, sex) and the hypergoods of heroic life (the courage of the soldier, the celibacy of the monk). In pursuit of hypergoods, one may abandon domestic goods. The monk fasts and abstains from sex. The soldier risks life itself. In classical times, it was the pursuit of hypergoods that were considered the highest value. In the modern bourgeois age, domestic goods have come to eclipse noble pursuit. Anti-art, Taylor suggests, expresses the Nietzechean urge to transcend domestic (bourgeois) goods for the hypergoods of the old nobility. For Nietzsche, the aim of life is not utilitarian—a philosophy he said only appealed to Englishmen—it is life at the edge, in danger, the ethic of defiance. Anti-art either as repulsive or erotic transcends the polite categories of bourgeois appreciation and the world of domestic goods.

It might seem that the function of anti-art is simply to throw the participant back on himself or herself. The proper reaction would be to flee the gallery in disgust or enter into the fracas at hand. Yet anti-art is also art; it is not just a mess, it is signatured. Can one signature the chaotic real? In a sort of parody of conventional art in which the artist signatures by impressing his or her definite style onto the medium, the pop artist simply signatures what is at hand. Andy

Warhol signs a soup can and thereby lifts it into the eternal realm of Art. Take that gesture into the religious realm. Jesus signatures existence, his very life itself : "I am the Truth." Christians claim that this life is raised to "the eternal." Final reality with all its sheer contingency, pain, waste, and confusion is signatured by this Jesus who is the Truth of such reality.

In anti-art, the artist signatures to emphasize the mess of existence. It may be to compel a Nietzschean recoil into defiance, it may be simply a desire to shock bourgeois values, or it may be a true gesture of nihilism. In Christianity, Jesus moves into the confusion of life and encompasses it, signatures existence as a place of God's presence. In creedal terms: at the heart of existential density there is God, the Holy Spirit, Jesus as Lord, the light comprehending the darkness, the Name that signatures life itself. When one is fully present to oneself, when the world looms up in utter presence, the Christian believes Jesus encompasses that presence. Jesus has signatured "the real." Even in the heart of suffering and death, there is person, signature, and Salvation of the everyday from birth to death.

APOSTOLIC PRIVILEGED WITNESS

If the central Christian belief is that Jesus signatures "the real," then grounding Christianity on some set of doctrines, a "catalogue of truths," is inherently flawed. A catalogue of truths might be offered by the scientific privileged witness, but Jesus is not to be so regarded. The sole Mars explorer can present a compendium of facts about that planet. The failure of that quite satisfactory scientific model for Christianity is manifest: the truths presented are not signatured to the explorer; any old observer could have/should have reported the same truths. But Jesus is the indispensable and unsurpassable word of God. Jesus is God's signature ("word") on human history. Only thus is he "Son of God" and not the last of the prophets. He who says, "*I* am the Truth" transcends the privileged witness.

But, one could counter, Jesus is the source of the source: it is the Gospels and the Bible overall that are the "source" of Christian belief. Jesus may surpass the state of privileged witness, but his disciples, the apostles, the women at the tomb, are privileged witnesses. They were the unique observer witnesses to events, and we believe on the basis of their reliable testimony. The church of apostolic succession passes on the reports of privileged witnesses.

"Privileged witness" as so far discussed has been a term within the area of scientific description. The Mars explorer describes facts that only she has seen, but those facts are in principle available to any other observer. In that sense, it would be misleading to think of the apostles as privileged witnesses. What they report is seen through the eyes of faith, not the eyes of a neutral observer. In the tradition there is *apostolic* witness to *faith*, but that is quite different from the privileged witness of the fortuitously located scientific observer. The problems with the apostolic witness as "scientific" in any sense are manifold. In the first place, these witnesses are not notoriously reliable. The extended and continuing puzzle about the "historical Jesus" is indication enough that it is exceedingly difficult to reconcile the conflicting stories of the synoptic Gospels, John, the testimony of the Epistles, and third-party evidence. When it comes to the central matters of religious faith—the birth of the Messiah and the Resurrection—the accounts are vague, confused, and puzzling: the tomb was empty except for the shroud, no—there was an "angel"; the Resurrected warns against touching his body but seems quite able to eat fish with the apostles on the shores of Galilee.

The matter of historical accuracy from apostolic privileged witnesses is enough of a problem for the Bible, but the theological problem is fundamental. What would count as *sacred* scripture? Is it the factual versimilitude of the account? I think that would be the last thing that would be expected. In the first place, what is being "reported" are the "mighty acts of God" and one would properly (and piously) suppose that such actions escape human conceptual and descriptive capacity.

Let us suppose, for a moment, that the Gospels form a third-person memoir of Jesus. How does this compare with a first-person memoir, which seems to have become a literary fashion? In the latter, one gives an account of one's life, right? Yes and no. Yes insofar as we recall events; no in the sense that we cannot recall our birth and, obviously, our death. Spinoza, in cataloguing things about which we are certain, started with the existence of God because that could be deduced rationally. Of things about which we are uncertain, however, our birth must come near the top of the list. We don't remember it (an unreliable source of knowledge anyhow) and so we have to rely on someone else's testimony that it really happened—and we know how dicey depending on witnesses can be. Both our birth and death are not events upon which *we* can comment; we don't recall the first, and we won't be around to offer our thoughts about the second. This means that for humans, any *inner* meaning to birth and death escapes our capacities to recall, feel, understand—they are "mysteries" to our conscious life. Birth and death are always reported from the "outside."

To everyday human consciousness, birth and death are, one might say, blank spots, an arbitrary beginning and end. We just happen to be here and one day we will happen not to be here. "So it goes," in the words of Billy Pilgrim as he considers the thousands dead in Dresden. What is startling about the Gospels is that Jesus' birth and death are not taken as mere happenings. There is a "story" for both his birth and death, which are, one might say, part of God's "memoir." That is a large claim, but for the Christian it becomes the basis of the belief that the historical particularity of each and every individual—this, my birth and this, my death—are more than what just happens ("so it goes"). The story of Jesus that contains a birth story and a death story, both stories included in God's story, becomes the foundation for thinking that all persons are caught up in God's story. Jesus is the symbol, parable, icon, and reality of that quite incredible idea.

Again, modern anti-art is instructive. Much of it is a "happening"—a term that is used for certain avant-garde "theatrical" performances. The guinea pig *Bride and the Bachelors* is a happening. These happenings are ambiguous in their meaning. On the one hand they may be presented for the sole purpose of undermining conventional meaning. Hemingway, as we saw in chapter 4, dismissed the vocabulary for big ideas, preferring only place names: Palermo *happens* to be where I am, that at least has "truth," unlike "glory, honor, patriotism." On the other hand, signaturing a happening suggests that there is some sort of meaning lurking in mere happening. In Christianity, Jesus (or the Father) signatures the happening of this life and death. The mere happening is a happening that is then more than a mere happening. Andy Warhol published an autobiography of sorts titled *A*. "A" was the first word in the book, which was a strict minute-by-minute chronicle of twenty-four hours in his life.[3] It was an autobiography similar to his twenty-four-hour film *Empire State*, which was a filming of the Empire State building with a single fixed camera. What is presented in the autobiography and the film are meant to be the facts without Warhol's comment, shaping, imprint—whatever. But, of course, he signatures the works and they are then made more than mere happenings (presumably).

Given that in our personal lived experience we have no "story" of our birth or death (like *A*—these are what happen to us), it is not surprising that the Gospel writers have no available template for the basic idea that the life and death of Jesus are *not* mere happenings, but part of a larger meaning and story. The accounts offered are "myths," stories as full of mystery and confusion as one would expect to find in the attempt to convey what is simply not part of our common human experience. To say that they are "myths" is not, however, to say that they are fraud or fairy tale. In Jesus' death, something beyond the mere happening of death happened, some powerful insight occurred, something that is properly called "Resurrection." There is a conviction that Jesus is not finished by the happening of death. But how one might "describe" a life beyond life (before or after) is not something for which we have sober categories of experience.

Returning, then, to the apostles as privileged witnesses, they could not be such in the manner of our Mars explorer. Whatever Resurrection means, it cannot be a simple describable "fact." How would one distinguish Resurrection from resuscitation? Jesus is not Lazarus; he is not "raised" into more of the life we know, he is raised into God's life—which is a final mystery.

ICONIC WITNESS

If the Gospel accounts are not privileged in the scientific, descriptive mode, a Christian could claim that they are privileged as *iconic*. Consider again the children's art of the Holocaust first discussed in chapter 4. Descriptively it is hardly "literal"; the children were not prodigies who could draw like Ingres. Were the Nazi guards really giants in black on gray against the delicate stick-figured children and the one colored flower in the corner? No. But the nonliteralness of the depiction in its naïveté makes the reality present to us today in a manner that would be screened out by the filtering sensibility and moral overlay of a mature artist. In the iconic mode, the children for us are witnesses; using a term from the vocabulary of the church, they are *infallible* witnesses. The children's art makes present the horror of their experience—a horror that resists the most artful form and scientific description. It is the very incomprehensible terror of the event that is conveyed.

The apostolic witnesses were participants in the life of Jesus and the narrations offered—albeit not directly by apostles but by the later Gospel writers—have an iconic character, or at least should be read iconically. In that sense, the New Testament materials are unsurpassable witnesses to the reality because they *are* the reality. This is a difficult notion to explain because it may be interpreted to mean that the New Testament is a fiction about Jesus. An anecdote from Wittgenstein's life may help. He and his friend Drury attended evensong at a local church. Here is Drury's account:

> [T]he preacher chose as his text: "It is expedient for you that I go away: for if I do not go away, the Comforter will not come unto you."

> After a few minutes Wittgenstein leaned over and whispered to me, "I am not listening to a word he is saying. But think about the text, that is wonderful, that is really wonderful."[4]

For Wittgenstein, the text itself was revelatory, was "wonderful," while the explanation, exposition, whatever of the preacher was useless. Elsewhere Wittgenstein characterized religious statements thusly: "The whole weight is in the picture"—a statement that approximates my notion of the iconic. An example he offered was Michelangelo's *Creation of Adam*. If we try to move beyond the picture to some subject depicted we lose the meaning. Does God really have a white beard? In his discussion of so-called primitive religion, Wittgenstein was sharply critical of the notion in J. G. Frazer's *Golden Bough* that the rituals were scientific blunders by people who thought that these strange actions would influence the weather: "When Frazer . . . narrates the story of the King of the Woods at Nemi, he does this in a tone that shows that something strange and terrible is taking place. . . . If one puts together the account of the Prince King of Nemi with the phrase 'the majesty of death' one sees that the two are one."[5]

The New Testament writings as iconic present the reality and they suffer diminishment when interpreted in a preacher's sermon. The ritual of the Mass or the slaying of the King of the Woods carry their meaning on their face—"the whole weight is in the picture"—and are degraded when interpreted as expressions of "belief," for example, as the naïve scientific blunders of primitives or apostles. If there are beliefs (church dogmas)—the often weak or wrongheaded attempts to capture the inherent majesty of the "picture"—they are secondary.

Under what circumstances does iconic presentation seem appropriate? The reason that the children's art is appropriate to the Holocaust experience lies in the *totalizing* character of that experience. Recall Yeats's comment quoted in chapter 4 that we should not underestimate the suffering of children. Lacking a sense of living through pain and suffering, a sense of before and after, suffering for children is their whole world. The Holocaust experience was like that: a whole world of evil and pain and nothing but. The art of children in the camps captures this character of encompassing evil because children totalize their world. The Nazis must have understood this aspect of childhood, for psychological studies of concentration camp inmates showed that the Nazis deliberately sought to infantilize the prisoners because they would then be easier to control.

Religious claims characterize "the real" that is *total* reality. If religion exists in the realm of "the real," then the only way to reach "the real" as-totalized-experience will be through the iconic. The iconic sign envelopes and encloses us in the reality signified; we are not transcendent spectators of science or art, we are directly involved at the very core of our own existence. Birth and death are the markers of sheer existence, they are mysteries. The reason that miracle birth and Resurrection elude straight description is not just that we have no memory or experience of them, it is because when a sense of our own birth and death is evoked we engage in the mystery of our own existence. To understand my death is to understand that I will not be, that this unique center of consciousness will simply be no more. William Saroyan spoke for everyone when he said on his deathbed, "I knew that everyone had to die, but I thought there might be an exception in my case." We all know as a scientific fact that we must die, but we do not realize our death. Tolstoy's *The Death of Ivan Ilych* recounts how a self-assured official comes to realize his death—Ivan Ilych becomes his death, death is his world. Speaking of his earlier failure to realize death, Tolstoy begins his account, "Ivan Ilych's life had been most simple and most ordinary and therefore most terrible."[6]

Anti-art as a happening confronts us with the sheer contingency of things, not the least of which is our own contingency. We are a happening, born just then, dying whenever. In facing the unfinished assemblage of happenings in anti-art, we are compelled into the raveled borders of our own "accidental" status. Realizing our contingency by participating in the contingency of the anti-art happening violates our sense of meaning. We ask, "What is it?" "Why should I spend time looking at this junk?" "What possible meaning can be expressed by a room full of plastic spoons?" Often the motivation of the anti-artist may not only seem nihilistic, it may be nihilistic. Anti-art aims to deflate and destroy the big and little messages and slogans that mask the meaningless contingency of our existence. The purpose is to prove to another Ivan Ilych that a life that seems simple and ordinary is "most terrible."

Christian proclamation, the "message" of Christianity, can only be heard when the meaning (or meaninglessness) of sheer existence—this, my life—is evoked. I cannot receive such a message as a transcendent observer because the transcendent observer is above the mere contingency of birth and death. As knowing mind, I am eternal, without the accident of birth, body, sex, and condition. Thus the phrase that scientific knowledge is always *sub specie aeternitatis*. If the Christian message is delivered, it will have to be in the iconic mode where I am a participant in the reality evoked. To repeat the Wittgensteinian injunction: "You can't hear God speak to someone else, you can only hear him if you are being addressed—that is a grammatical remark." Unless called by name, my unique historical marker, the message is not heard.

Insofar as the Gospels are iconic, they are privileged openings to a realm that it seems eminently "rational" to recognize and recall, though abstract "reason" is debarred from characterizing "the real." "The real," if it is to be properly recognized, must be recognized in its overwhelming, "incomprehensible" character. The reason, *ratio*, in play demands a proper proportion of self to that which is perceived. Proper ratio, "reason" requires a proper sign or symbol as the thing "known." As iconic, the Scriptures are Holy Scriptures: they incorporate the reality of God in the same sense that Byzantine icons do not simply depict the holy, they are holy. The Gospels are indispensable rules of faith in the manner in which the art produced by the children in concentration camps is indispensable. The children's art, by making present the reality of the Holocaust, cannot be surpassed in their "truth" to that experience. Jesus says that we cannot enter into the Kingdom of Heaven unless we become like little children. We cannot receive the message of the Gospels unless like children we experience "the real" as a totality, as a whole, as overwhelmingly present. Conversely, the Gospels, like anti-art, make our fears and hopes present, demanding participation and decision in the face of death.

In the case of Christianity and the church—particularly the Catholic understanding of church—the primary iconic manifestation of the reality of Jesus as Christ is not, however, the Gospel accounts but the Eucharist event. Before there were Gospel narratives, it is clear that the Christian community evoked the presence of its Lord in the Eucharistic meal. The theology of the Eucharist follows the logic of signature that has been central to this analysis. Jesus signatures the bread and the wine: "This is my body . . . this is my blood." (Recall Warhol and the soup can.) The *words* of the Gospel can easily be put at a distance—that is the nature of words; eating bread and drinking wine are a more immediate and better vehicle of the iconic presence of the life, body, and blood of the Resurrected. The very strangeness of signaturing the bread and wine as Jesus breaches the distancing, appraisive stance of words—which are, after all, only symbols.

THE APOSTLES' BELIEF

I said at the beginning of this chapter that I would not try to prove the truths that Christianity posits about the meaning of existence. I also said that I am not certain that the attempt to prove religious beliefs is a sensible notion anyway. Because "proof" finds its best lodgement in the ascetic neutrality of science, I do not see how any proof of Christian claims would be possible. If one remains a spectator to the happenings of life (or of anti-art), the message—in the case of anti-art "There Is No Message!"—will never be received.

If, however, one abandons any notion of proof, it remains necessary to indicate what believers are up to in their strange behavior (venerating consecrated bread) and making outlandish statements (that the bread is the body of Jesus who was resurrected). Santayana called Christianity a "splendid error." He admired the ideals and, one might say, the daring of the whole thing. It just happened not to be true. Much of modern advanced thought is not nearly as generous. Christianity (religion in general) is not splendid error, but straight nonsense.

To understand Christian belief, let me start with Paul because he sets forth so insistently the core structure of the Gospel narratives, despite the fact that in the genuine Pauline Epistles there is no reference to Jesus' active ministry, no reference to the Sermon on the Mount, no account of the miracles, no suggestion of a virgin birth. Paul is totally focused on the crucified and resurrected Christ. "If Christ is not risen, then our faith is dead" is his summation. I believe this emphasis establishes the basic mode of interpretation for the narratives of Jesus. Without the mighty act of God encapsulated in the Resurrection, there would be the figure of a prophet, the teacher of wisdom, the moralist, maybe even the protorevolutionary. All these modes of interpretation have been used to construct narratives of Jesus. Any one such figure might command respect, but not the worship that has characterized the community's attitude toward its Risen Lord down the centuries. For traditional Christianity, the actual life of Jesus of Nazareth is, as it were, bracketed by "miraculous" birth and resurrected life. What is inside the brackets is interpreted from the standpoint of the overwhelming acts of God at that life's beginning and end. It is clear, in fact, that many of the stories about Jesus' ministry are retrojections of an Easter faith upon the actual events.

The Gospel story is, then, a "story of God," a holy story with a beginning and end that only a God could fashion. But for all that the Gospel tale is defined by its beginning and especially its end, like any tale it requires a middle. Years ago I taught a course on Kierkegaard, who suggested that the more difficult it is to believe in an Incarnate God, the more it is to be believed: *Credo quia absurdum*. A student seized on the importance of absurdity and concluded that God should have been incarnated as a clam: it would have been even more absurd and a greater feat of faith to believe. Shrewd student! (He went on to become a very distinguished theologian.) For all that one brackets the historical Jesus in the mighty acts of God, for all that one retrojects Resurrection onto that history, the actual preaching cannot become inconsequential.

Reconstructing the actual preaching of Jesus of Nazareth is complex and we depend on the exegetes. One cannot, however, perform a simple rejection of retrojection, bracketing out the worshipful faith of the Gospel accounts. Like any historical figure, Jesus of Nazareth is entitled to reflections back on his life from its ultimate outcome. When a lazy Sidney Carton gives up his life for another in Dickens's *Tale of Two Cities*, we are inclined to read more into his earlier life than if he had died drunk in bed. While Christianity is interpreted from the Resurrection, it is important for *humanity* that the one resurrected preached love and forgiveness. The mighty act of God-with-us would hardly be with *us*, with humanity, if it were only a show of divine birth and negation of death. Those are feats for a god and one would be mightily impressed. The Greek gods were always passing into human shape and then reverting to their immortal state. In the Homeric record, however, the Olympians had no basic care for humanity as such. Humans were pawns and client states in the quarrelsome relations of the immortals. But in the Christian view, the God-with-us is the God-for-us. That seems to be the message of the Beatitudes and the essence of Jesus' active ministry. In short, the Gospel story of Jesus is not an exercise in divine saber rattling. It is a message of hope and love.

THE PRESENCE OF THE LORD

Having "released" the historical preaching from the brackets of miraculous birth and Resurrection, I want to return to the theme of "existential presence" as an explication of the course of the Gospels and the eventual faith of the apostles. In the Gospels, Jesus is seen as a religious revelation. In terms of the previous argument, *religious* revelation involves totalizing existential presence. I am present to myself as the world is present to me. Jesus was such a presence to the apostles—at least in their better moments, certainly in the experience of the Resurrection. Being present to this Jesus must have been—must be—in some sense like the totalizing experience of children: there is no before and after; everything is present in the present, in the presence of the Master. Jesus was present to these men and women in a manner that did not permit them to withdraw into the usual sort of distanced appraisal we make all the time, every day, of even our best friends and lovers. When we speak of "charismatic" personalities, it is something like this overwhelming sense of presence that is meant. Just to be in the presence of the great one is sufficient. All sense of distance is lost in the force of the charismatic other. Jesus calls his disciples not through a teaching, but simply says "Follow me" and they do. Those stories in the Gospels where Jesus reads the thoughts of others are oblique testimony to the sense that in his presence one could not withdraw into the "private" self.

The experience of presence is a totalizing experience. In love, one says, "Marilyn was the world to me." Suppose, then, that what the disciples saw in and through Jesus was a totality of existence. He was *the world* to them. For a pious Jew, Jesus-as-world would have to be in some way blessed-of-God; anything less would be idolatry. To whom else could I give my whole self? Who else could I call "Lord"? Who else but God is the whole, the source of inner and outer, the one who knows our hidden thoughts and tends the lilies of the field? In our common experience we do fall for lovers and charismatic types, but usually we retain some distance or at least compartmentalize our fascination with presence. The rock star groupie who sells all that he has and follows the Grateful Dead is thought to be more than a little unhinged. The groupie forgoes her own life in idolization. After all, even Elvis was only mortal (really!).

If, however, one does sell all one has and gives over one's life to the charismatic other, that could be "rational" if the charismatic figure is regarded as someone in whom my life is not "lost" but enhanced, enlarged, regained. Again, I am using "rational" deliberately here in the sense of what would be a proper ratio, a commensurate response. One "rations" one's emotion to the reality attended to. To rage maniacally over a misplaced memo is "irrational," an improper ratio between emotion and occasion. Of course, in the ordinary groupie experience it is the sense of living a larger life in the celebrity that compels, and yet most of us regard such idolization as "irrational." One may, in fact, regard all idolization and devotion as irrational, an affront to sturdy individualism. No one would rationally give up one's life for another! Take that stance and love becomes a dubious idea and religion impossible.

Whatever else one might say about the complex story of the New Testament, it seems clear that the disciples (at least as depicted by the Gospel writers) did see in Jesus a life of *total presence*. He was their all-in-all. As such he lifted them, all those he touched and those to whom he preached, out of the isolation of their distancing, separate selves (out of sin), making them wholly present to themselves because they were in his presence. He was their Lord, the Way, the Life, the Truth. Now, of course, these good fishermen and the others gathered around him might have been bewitched and finally deceived in their enthusiasm. Jesus was, we may think, just as mortal as thee and me, hardly deserving the idolization shown him by his followers. A good man, a serious prophet, but still human, not after all—what shall we say?—a God!

The option of de-idolizing Jesus for good purposes is always available both for reasons of sensible science or measured morality, but that was not the apostolic turn. To the extent Jesus was the world for the disciples, he was Lord and blessed-of-God. Anything less would have been blasphemy against the Holy One. It is Jesus' charismatic authority—forgiving sins is God's prerogative, for only God fully knows the human heart—that led to his accusations before the Sanhedrin. Suppose, then, that one is caught up in this person of Jesus. How would one deal with his scandalous death on the cross? If you truly believed that Jesus was a revelation of wholeness, of "the real," then, whatever the fact of death, it could not be final. If Jesus was experienced as presence that removes me as a spectator on life and thrusts me into its very midst, then his definitive *absence*—Jesus' death as a finality—would be like my death, the death of my world, and the "death of God." It would mean that when the whole reveals itself, when I enter fully into the whole, am fully present as in the day before Dr. Johnson's sentence of hanging—life's meaning is drained away. In a Sartre short story, a man facing execution concludes that "death disenchants everything." Having experienced Jesus as Lord, the apostles did not regard death as "disenchanting." Many people lose "faith" at the death of a loved one. The disciples had an experience of reassurance that God continued to "watch over Israel," that the one in whom they had placed their life was not dead but held in God's life.

To proclaim the kerygma that the Lord is risen—that Jesus is the Way, the Life, and the Truth—is not something that one might be led to only after a trip back in a time machine to verify that the tomb was empty. The proclamation emerges from a complex, deep religious history of the Jewish people. I do not suggest here that "resurrection" was merely a logical deduction out of Jewish tradition and the apostles' view of Jesus during his active ministry. I am inclined to think that the Gospel accounts of the desertion and demoralization of the disciples after Jesus' death reflects actual history: something happened that was "resurrection" and that converted their disillusionment into proclamation of the risen Lord. It would be in keeping with the *event* character of biblical revelation to regard this something as an event.

To proclaim Jesus as Lord one has to start from what might be called a "high

Jesusology." Only if one begins with an exalted view of what is specifically and historically human—such that individuals in their unrepeatable historical existence are worthy of justice and Salvation—is it possible for that Salvation to be mediated through a named individual, Moses or Jesus. Otherwise Julian the Apostate would have been correct that human "salvation" comes through escaping the particularities of specific history, adopting the transcendent tranquility of the rational spectator. For the rational transcendent mind, death just doesn't count, and certainly the *body*, that mere existential happening, is not resurrected. The individual is wholly caught up into the mind, the world of imperishable truth. For Judaism and Christianity, it is because God is present in named patriarchs and prophets, not in the elevated mind, that we can take just any old Tom, Jane, or Jonah as having exalted value. In Jewish thought, it is "necessary" that God reveals himself in and to a variety of individuals in specific historical circumstances. In Jesus, so the Christians maintain, this history of revelation is maintained and fulfilled.

THE WORD OF LIFE

I approached the truth of Christianity via the notion of signatured truth. If Jesus claims "I am the Truth," that certainly seems to signature whatever is at stake to Jesus. Within the Jewish tradition, God reveals Himself only in and through an historically chosen people, through signatured individuals. There is, then, nothing unusual in that tradition about exalting this individual Jesus as presenting/representing God's word. But the Christian claim goes beyond the exaltation of the patriarchs and prophets. Jesus is claimed to be the fullness of God's word, the Truth that encompasses the mystery of existence. As science is the word for reality as abstract type and art the word for its personal shaping, Jesus is the "word" for "the real" beyond form, beyond science and art. Jesus is a "saving" word as *the measure of final reality*. What "utterance" could encompass, comprehend the density, confusion, "waste" of actual life? To measure the mystery of life, the "word" would itself have to be a *life*. "Word" is adopted in this case as "that which reflects a reality." If the reality to be reflected is Jamesian "life," it will not be the shapely form of a Jamesian novel. Anti-artists who seek to go beyond art into the "splendid waste" of life give us only a slice of that life and that waste. Only a "word" that is a life or a life that is a "word" could "depict" life. Jesus as the Word, Jesus as the Truth, is not a circumlocution for a scientific proposition or doctrine, not even a great tragic poem. It is very life to very life.

Several years ago the *New Yorker* extracted a quote from the preface of a newly published atlas, whose editors were explaining the characters and virtues of various types of maps. The flat Mercator projection had obvious distortions; better was the globe. But, concluded the editors, even a globe was a distortion because it wasn't "the right size." The *New Yorker* retorted, "Well, the hell with it!"

The point of a map or a globe is precisely that it is not the real thing repeated. Only in a weird sense does a penny, say, "map" another. Using this terminology, it would be incorrect, I think, to regard Jesus as a map for life in the manner of an ethical paradigm. For Jesus the image is *too small*. Jesus meets the fullness of our existence that resists the clarity of model, paradigm, and map. One penny does not map another penny; it stands alongside the other in fullness. Jesus does not map a human life; he stands beside each human life in its fullness. In that sense, Jesus is greater than the prophets. He does not deliver a moral message, a commandment or consolation for human life. In Jesus there is life to life, a presence as "companion." Jesus as life to my life is the heart of the Resurrection, the continuing *real* presence of Jesus to each and every person who calls him Lord.

A literary example may give some sense of what is at work in this Christian belief. At the conclusion of a short story by John L'Heureux, *An Expert on God*, a disbelieving priest chances on a deadly auto crash on a lonely road. Managing to pry open the car door, he reverts to his official role and anoints the teenage driver:

> He began to pray, aloud, which struck him as foolish: to be holding a dying boy in his arms and reciting rote prayers about our father in heaven. . . . What could he do? What could he say at such a moment? What would God do at such a moment, if there was a God? . . .
>
> His doubts became a certainty and he said, "It doesn't matter," but it did matter and he knew it. What could anyone say to this crushed, dying thing, he wondered. What would God say if he cared as much as I?
>
> [A]t once the priest, faithless, unrepentant, gave up his prayers and bent to him and whispered, fierce and burning, "I love you," and continued until there was no breath, "I love you, I love you, I love you."[7]

Life's final truth is chanciness, the blundering accident, the awesome density of existence, and suffering. If there is any Salvation, any "Word," it is to be held, to have the presence of the Other who says, "I love you."

Note the irony of the title L'Heureux chooses for his story: An Expert on God. This expert, it seems is "faithless, unrepentant." He cannot state a doctrine because he does not believe. Nevertheless, he asks whether it matters to hold a "crushed, dying thing" and say "I love you" until no breath remains? Being present to another, present to one unconscious and dying, saying "I love you"—all this may be nonsense, none of it may matter. Yet somehow the priest knows that it does matter. Jesus is *the* "expert on God"—not because he announces some hidden fact or message like a privileged witness, but because he is present to humans in all the blunder and chanciness of life. If we are held once and for all by the "expert" who says "I love you," there is Salvation. Jesus promises to send the Holy Spirit to the apostles. The word in Greek is *parakletos* and it has been variously translated as "advocate," "consoler," and "comforter." It means literally "the one who stands by" as in the German translation: *der Beistand.*

Christian belief in Jesus' Resurrection is essential for this salvational faith. We can easily understand that when a great master or teacher dies his "message" remains. Plato's philosophical message is as alive today as it ever was—just take a look at the scholarly journals in philosophy. The question for Christians is whether life in all its density can be saved by such a message. A Platonist would say that it could, but only at the price of discarding existential density to live in the realm of Ideas, beyond what is dense, historical, particular, mortal. Anti-Platonists like Sartre or the avant-garde anti-artists insist on the intransigence of existence, life in all its chaotic reality, in the face of which their message is that there is no "message" that can save this mess, there is no salvation. If, then, in confronting the totality of the existential—the chaotic wholeness of "the real"—there is no message that can be applied to life that is adequate for salvation, our salvation can only be possible by "applying" a life to a life. It would be like the L'Hereux story: having a life wholly present to my life. Not dying alone, but in the arms of one who says "I love you," one who knows suffering and death, one for whom the density and chance of life is as real as it is to every human.

Because they believe that only life "saves" life, Christians *must* say that Jesus *lives.* Platonists may be "saved" by a message that lives after the philosopher, but Christians are not saved by Jesus' message, they are saved by his presence—a life that holds my life in birth, suffering, and death. The Christian hope for personal resurrection is grounded on the belief that, as Jesus lives and holds us, so we share in his life beyond death.

Wittgenstein summed up this argument:

If he did not rise from the dead, then he decomposed in the grave like any other man. *He is dead and decomposed.* In that case he is a teacher like any other and can no longer *help*. . . . So we have to content ourselves with wisdom and speculation. . . . But if I am to be REALLY saved—what I need is certainty—not wisdom, dreams, or speculation—and this certainty is faith. And faith is what is needed by my *heart*, my *soul*, not by my speculative intelligence. For it is my soul, with its passions, as it were with its flesh and blood, that has to be saved, not my abstract mind. Perhaps we can say: Only *love* can believe the Resurrection.[8]

The Christology offered above is clearly influenced by a variety of contemporary philosophical and theological tendencies. Just as clearly it is not likely that this was the cast of the apostolic witnesses. The most plausible interpretation of the New Testament writings as they were conceived by their various authors is eschatological. History was coming to an end; Jesus would return within the life of those living. One could say, then, that the faith of the Gospel writers was false, misplaced. Jesus did not return as expected. I would argue, however, that the eschatological cast of the New Testament writings rests on a deep foundation for which imminent apocalypse is only a powerful metaphor. What is crucial is the nexus of ideas built into the Bible around the concepts of Creation, Covenant, and Salvation/Resurrection. As is repeatedly said, the biblical God is a God of history. The cosmos has a history, it is created. God covenants—striking an agreement with a people in the freedom of their history. God is at one with history, and Christians see God-with-us in the historical figure of Jesus. New Testament eschatology at its core claims that history—including that of the world as created and of individuals—stand before God who judges that history; judges as he also loves and saves that history.

RESURRECTION: FACT, ART, ICON

In the previous chapters I suggested three types of truth and modes of expression characteristic of each. There is the factual claim for truth of science that is open to any witness indifferently. There is the signatured truth of art in which correspondence to fact is irrelevant because we are interested in the personal insight, emotion, evaluation of the artist. Finally there is the truth of presence that is present in iconic art, which goes beyond the shaping hand of the artist toward the very presence of the thing depicted. "Christ is risen" can be regarded as science, art, or icon. As science the claim is implausible, and even if it were verified, a resuscitated body does not serve the theological claims of Christianity. No matter what manner of Resurrection experience the apostles may have had (ghost, "body," apparition, dream), they could not on the basis of empirical evidence have concluded that Jesus was "with God," a risen "Savior." These latter are confessions of faith about who Jesus is as Christ, and are beyond any demonstrable facts of experience.

In contrast, as a statement of art, "Christ is risen" may have powerful currency. The artist may use the story of Jesus to express a personal shaping of the world. "Death be not proud, for thou art not so" proclaims the human spirit. Great paintings of the Resurrection are testimony to spiritual heroism. In that sense, "resurrection" is true of what it means to be nobly, defiantly human. There is something correct in approaching the Christian doctrine of Resurrection through the human signature of art. It has the great advantage of removing Christian claims from the arena of scientific fact. Resurrection is not a scientific claim but a sort of moral demand or spiritual protest. We know, in fact, that the emergence of something akin to a doctrine of resurrection in later Judaism was a demand for cosmic justice. The innocent suffering of the past could not be left unresolved. Resurrection seemed a plausible cosmic correction. Imagining resurrection is a proper moral move.

There is something grand in the artistic projection of resurrection as a form of moral demand on final reality, but it may be only noble protest. Here Christianity may be what Santayana saw as a "splendid error." "Splendid" in its hopes and ideals; "error" in thinking that there was anything real in these hopes. Not Jesus, but Don Quixote is the Lord of Life. If, then, there is anything more to Christianity than noble metaphor and splendid error, one has to move beyond the truths of science and art to the truth of presence and the assertion of Christian truth as iconic.

The iconic "statement," in contrast to the simply artistic, seeks to make the reality depicted emerge directly, beyond the shaping hand of the one who formulates the statement. The "artless art" of the children in concentration camps makes present to the viewer the reality of the death camps. In the case of the modern anti-art artist, the aim is to block the viewer as aesthete, to insert each viewer directly into the total event. The boundaries separating the subjective viewer and the objectivity of the work are broken down. In Artaud or the Living Theater, the boundaries between the play, the actors, and the audience is breached. I am "caught" in the act of viewing when I peer through the keyhole at Duchamp's erotic diorama. Being caught as voyeur reveals me to myself as here now in this body, thus overcoming abstract spectatorship.

In the event of presence one has the experience that is characteristic of the religious, the revelation of the whole (me) to and in the whole (the external situation). It is an experience of *presence:* I am wholly present (in the sense that I am neither the scientific nor artistic spectator), and because I am wholly present external reality is now present in a manner that escapes factual assessment or artistic form.

Given the "logic" of presence, Christian belief statements—for example, "The Lord is risen"—are not strange scientific facts, nor are they noble and splendid artistic or moral illusions. Belief statements must somehow "contain" the reality of Resurrection present to me and for me. The iconic statement is not the actual event itself—to sense presence in the children's art is not to actually live in the shadow of the gas chamber. Still, the direction of the icon is toward participation in the very reality depicted. The children's art is not only a depiction of the Holocaust, it participates in the Holocaust reality; blunting the artistic moment makes the Holocaust present.

If Resurrection stories do not just "depict" Resurrection, but are directed to make present a Resurrection reality, how is that possible? What are the conditions for iconic signification and apprehension? The children were witnesses of the Holocaust and because of their naïveté the best representers of its inescapable terror. The apostles were witnesses, one presumes, to an overwhelming experience in the saving life, death, and Resurrection of Jesus. If apostolic witness is comparable to the sort of witnessing that confronts us in the children's work, there must be a sense the experience they "depict" is made present.

TO DIE WITH CHRIST

Reading a depiction iconically is not something that occurs automatically. One may find the children's art simply naïve and awkward. One can always retreat to an aesthetic distance. Presumably someone who knew nothing about the Holocaust would not sense any actual reality iconically depicted by the children; at worst their drawings would be thought to depict nightmares, not historical horror. The conditions under which one should—indeed, must—view the children's art are crucial. So with the Eucharist and Gospels as iconic. A necessary condition is that one must come to the "depiction" *as a possible participant in the history made present.* A contemporary viewer is not likely to be a Holocaust survivor, but there must be some realization of a still "present" reality and possibility that I might be a victim (or perpetrator) of such events. In the Christian case, we are not "contemporary disciples" yet we must be participants in the Gospel history.

A Jewish acquaintance was visiting the memorial to the children who died in the Holocaust at Yad Vashem in Israel. The memorial consists of a darkened chamber illuminated by five candles. The walls, ceiling, floors are half-silvered mirrors so that the chamber seems to be an infinite field of flickering points of light. (Note how the memorial is iconic: the visitor is in the work; one walks through it as in an anti-art installation.) As one moves through the chamber, a voice reads the names of the 1.5 million victims. My acquaintance had brought his teenage daughters. While they were passing through the darkness, one of the daughters heard her name being read. She was undone. Of course, it was not her name only but also belonged to another young woman, one who had perished in the camps. Yet hearing her name placed her in the reality of the experience memorialized. As a Jew, the young woman was specially vulnerable, then, to the threat presented in the Holocaust; the reading of "her" name made that fact all too palpable. The memorial at Yad Vashem made the Holocaust present to her as a participant in Jewish history. The Jewish community of which she is a present member has taken upon itself the essential task of remembering the 6 million dead. The motto of that effort has been "Lest we forget!" Preserving this memory has been, in turn, not just an exercise in historical truth and completeness, it has been a sign for the present; a complex sign that demands grief and vigilance, an attitude toward oneself as a Jew with such a heritage of agony, and an attitude toward the world that in time of terror largely turned its back.

Let me analogize this vivid and recent Holocaust story to the Jesus story. First there must be a recognition of an actual history, minimally that Jesus existed and "suffered under Pontius Pilate." More important, the one who hears this story must in some sense be a "participant hearer" in Jesus' history. The young woman as a Jew is inextricably caught up in the Holocaust; it is her own Jewish history of past tragedy, present threat, and continuing concern. The one who would read the Gospel as icon must also be a participant in some way in the Jesus story.

One is born into Jewish history. Jews by birth who believed that they had abandoned Jewishness as enlightened thinkers or just "good Germans" were starkly reminded of being Jewish by their Nazi oppressors. One is not born into Christianity, but the Christian claim is that all people are born into the existen-

tial dilemmas and religious responses of humankind: the various creeds, litur-
gies, and meditations with which humans have repeatedly tried to transcend,
face up to, or evade the "splendid waste" of life. Like the "good German" who
did not regard himself as part of Jewish history, one may think it possible to opt
out of the religious concerns of the race, but that is a delusion. One only masks
the "splendid waste" of life.

When humanity faces "the real" there seems to be a very limited repertoire
of choices: ignoring, defiance, denial, and whatever it is that Jews and Christians do and believe. One can evade the messiness of sheer existence in the valued and precise mode of science or the "laziness" of the mundane. One can,
when faced with intransigencies like death and suffering, defy them: "Death be
not proud!" There is "denial" in the special sense of Buddhism, which finds the
root of suffering in earthly desire. Deny desire and one achieves a peace beyond
pain. Judaism and Christianity do not ignore or defy, nor are these religions
spiritual wisdoms that reduce pain and suffering to the illusions of desire. The
Jerusalem Tradition is deeply earthly—Franz Rosenzweig's procreation of
the Jewish people. Desire, suffering, and death are all too real and defiance in
the face of them a blasphemy toward the Creator. Salvation requires that suffering be taken on, lived through. For Christians, the suffering of Jesus is real
and suffering is a human reality not to be evaded. In the dark chamber of human
history, lit with flickering memory, the Cross calls the name of everyone.

It is a paradox that the Jewish and Christian religious sensibility emerges
around the problem of suffering—a paradox because it is the problem of suffering that for many seems to bar belief in God. If there is a loving God, why is
the world so full of suffering, suffering of the innocent like the children of the
Holocaust, the child with incurable cancer? But the denial of God because of
the problem of suffering is itself paradoxical. If there is no God, the reality of
suffering is no longer a problem. If the denial of God means that final reality is
purely naturalistic, the working out of physical laws, then suffering is "just one
of those things." Does anyone blame evolution for strains of defective DNA? If,
then, one is truly troubled by the reality of suffering, simple atheism won't help.

Elie Wiesel was debating the Holocaust with a famous rabbi. Wiesel asked,
"How can you believe in God after the Holocaust?" The rabbi replied, "How
can you *not* believe in God after the Holocaust?" Wiesel offered a grand Jewish
reply, "If that is an answer, I do not accept it. If it is a question, I accept it." That
seems to sum up the paradoxicality of suffering in the biblical tradition.

The children's art of the Holocaust thrusts us into the overwhelming, incomprehensible mystery of their suffering. The "mystery of evil" is made present. Hannah Arendt's "banality of evil" is itself a claim for mystery. How could a mere clerk like Adolph Eichmann be the instrument of such terror? The Christian also focuses on incomprehensible suffering: the figure on the cross. As there is a mystery of evil in the Holocaust, there is a mystery of evil in the Crucifixion. There is no lightening of the problem of suffering by lesser numbers, the suffering of many and the suffering of a single one. In the standard critique of unsophisticated utilitarianism, if one aims for the greatest good for the greatest number, would it be moral to improve the general happiness significantly at the cost of prolonged and terrible torture of one innocent child? No, the suffering of anyone, any *one*, is enough; it reveals the essence of suffering as that which cannot be tolerated. If one lived in the utilitarian society so founded, clearly all the "happy" majority would participate (in guilt) in the suffering of the single innocent.

Christianity could have developed in the manner of Holocaust remembrance. The church message would be "Lest we forget,"—forget the suffering of the innocent as exemplified in the cruel death of the one who preached love and forgiveness. The message could be completely secular: do whatever we can to make certain that this never happens again. This is a valid lesson and is well taken up by Christian liberation theologians. What is startling is that the Christian community went beyond this powerful lesson and proclaimed that the one crucified, in that very suffering, became one with God, taken beyond suffering into God's life and blessing. Wiesel again. He tells of the brutal execution of a young boy in the concentration camp. The youngster was hanged but, being small, he was not heavy enough to cause the noose to snap his neck. His death would be a long and painful strangulation. The prisoners were marched by the suffering child. One prisoner was heard to ask as they passed, "Where is God?" To which another replied, "Hanging there!" This was the exclamation of the centurion at the foot of the cross, "Truly, this was the Son of God." It has been the Christian proclamation down the ages. In an utterly implausible reversal of the notion that it is in the face of human suffering that God seems to be absent, unconcerned, null, void, the Christian claim is that it is especially in our suffering that God is uniquely present to humanity.

If, then, the creedal statements are iconic, these are the conditions. There must be some actuality: the Holocaust in modern Jewish history, the life and death of Jesus of Nazareth for Christians. One must recognize oneself as especially a participant in that history. In the case of the Jewish people and the

Holocaust, the connection is obvious. In the case of humanity in general, the Christian will insist (along with all those who hold other religious views) that we are all faced with the "mystery of existence." One can, of course, "ignore" the general "holocaust of history" (if I may be permitted to appropriate that term), but to the religious of any persuasion that is tantamount to the "good German" illusion. If one faces directly the mystery of existence, one can still question whether the Gospel or Eucharist is iconic of that mystery. Maybe the mess of anti-art is the true icon, proclaiming futility, nihilism, and despair.

I will not argue about the "proper" interpretation of "the real" that is opened and made available by iconic presentation. The chronicles of religion suggest that no one is brought to a sense of "the real" by argument. Something happens to open "the real" and its meaning. There are necessary conditions for an iconic presentation: some totalizing actuality, a sense of participation in that actuality. But how one comes to judge that the Christian icons of Salvation best capture the sense of our total life experience is beyond argument. One may turn to an experience of totalizing presence like the Holocaust and end with the ambiguity of Elie Wiesel's dialogue with the rabbi. How can you believe in God; how can you not believe in God? If there is any resolution to that dilemma, it will be because one *lives out a certain life* with God, without God. Liberation theologians are correct in noting the primacy of *praxis*. As one lives out the experience of a "base community," one comes to see how Biblical language takes on meaning. In a later chapter I suggest that it is only in a life of prayer that one might come to the truth of Resurrection.

One must live a life and judge from the inside; one participates in a history with or without God. Of course just saying that one lives a life with or without God is not to say that one is actually so doing. There are enough religious hypocrites in every age to prove that. (We have not spent as much time pondering "hypocritical" atheists, but there are bound to be some.) Protestantism, Catholicism, and Orthodoxy in their various ways insist that one cannot come to believe, one does not believe, except within some life, some life moment and experience. In Protestantism, it is the Word preached, the live word addressed to the congregation that carries a sense of iconic participation. The serious majesty of the Word preached carries conviction. I have discussed at length the Catholic sacramental life of presence. Orthodoxy is the historical home of icons; the rich ritualism of Orthodox service can have a compelling effect in establishing belief in a deeper, higher order of reality.

The biblical scholar Luke Timothy Johnson has pointed out how the "academic" study of the Bible essentially distorts the meaning of the text. The Bible exists within a worshiping, sacramental, liturgical community as an instrument of its sense of life meaning. In this respect, one may say that the King James version is better because of its worshipful dimension than the flat "historical" translations presently offered. The fact that Christians often chant the biblical text would suggest that there is something else going on than gathering facts. Academic readings of the Bible may assume that the text directs the practice of faith rather in the manner that an instruction manual directs how to assemble a new lawn mower. No one chants instruction manuals. Such "external" reading is often put forth in "fundamentalist" attitudes toward the Bible. In various ways, Catholic, Protestant, and Orthodox (and Rabbinic Judaism as well) would insist that the Bible can only mean something within a living community. First one is a Jew immersed in Jewish history including the Holocaust, then the children's art speaks to that history.

There is no guidebook for assessing the truth of the iconic. Should I finally accept icons of futility or faith? This book is not about to decide that issue—and I doubt that any book could. The questions I am interested in here are more modest. Assuming that one accepts the iconic presentations of the New Testament, or of the Catholic faith (hoping that the one does not exclude the other), how would that acceptance affect in any way the life of the university? How does Jesus' "I am the Truth" relate to the *veritas* proclaimed on the university's shield?

6

Academic Dogma and Catholic Freedom

The previous chapter was decidedly theological. It seemed only fair to give readers at least a sketch of what might be involved in the central truth claim of Christianity, the definitely strange proclamation that Jesus is the Truth. I will return in the later chapters to how this specific Christian theological claim may impinge on the university. Before moving to that issue, however, it is necessary to make explicit central assumptions that govern the life of the university. In addition I want to discuss theology in general—not just Christian theology—as it relates to university study. Later I discuss some leading types of Christian theology as they may or may not be supportive of the academy.

The university assumption most immediately at issue for a Catholic university is academic freedom. Indeed, it is assumed to be so central to the life and ethos of the modern university that it can properly be called an academic *dogma*. In this chapter I want to reverse the normal assumption that it is the university which is "free" and theology which is "dogmatic" by examining three crucial academic dogmas, relating to competence, morals, and the existential life of the university. There is, I would contend, dogmatism good and bad. A defining truth for an institution, because it defines the institution's very enterprise, may fairly be understood as an institutional dogma, the violation of which is properly labeled "heresy." This is no less true of the university than of any organized communal activity. It does not mean that the dogmas are beyond some sort of dispute. But the disputes lead to institutional definition and are not easily admitted to the parry and thrust of argument within the everyday life of the academy.

Not only is there a proper use of academic dogma, there is a useful sense in which one can speak of a kind of freedom accessible only through theology. In the light of a certain sort of theological freedom, it is the university that appears dogmatic in a bad way. Presenting such a paradoxical reversal of the normal rhetoric may shed light on the complexities of the issues involved in conjoining "Catholic" and "university."

FREE SPEECH VERSUS ACADEMIC FREEDOM

It is crucial to any sensible discussion of academic freedom to distinguish it from the civil right of free speech. Because of state interests in preserving domestic tranquility, modern pluralistic democracies grant very broad license to speech. One may preach capitalism or communism, Anglicanism or atheism, advocate or condemn the use of marijuana. The sole limitation for free speech is provocative speech, speech that moves others to immediate and destructive *action*. Thus the classic example of Oliver Wendell Holmes: one cannot shout "Fire" in a crowded theater. The state, the entity that permits free speech, is in the long run concerned primarily with *actions* not opinions. It is only when speech is directly and immediately linked to action or where speech *is* the action (conspiracy, fraud) that there is "state interest." When the state attempts to legislate opinion, it shows itself foolish or totalitarian. No vote of a legislature could settle the truth of Darwinian evolution.

In contrast to the civil right of free speech extended to any citizen for any belief, however bizarre, academic freedom is a limited privilege extended to a restricted set of individuals who must offer special warrants in order to exercise that right. Academic freedom as a "term of art" in American universities was the creation of the American Association of University Professors (AAUP). When academic freedom was first defined in 1915, it was intended as a right reserved to those faculty who were engaged in advanced research. Hence the title of the organization: the American Association of *University* Professors. Academic freedom was a function of advanced, attested, specialized *competence*. Just as a neurosurgeon must demonstrate advanced competence in order to be free (licensed) to perform complex surgical procedures, so only those with demonstrated high levels of competence were assumed to have the freedom of research and publication.

The difference between freedom of investigation based on competence and freedom to speak your mind in the public square is profound. What if politicians had to be licensed as competent students of politics, culture, American history, and ethics before being permitted to campaign? In the world of the university, academic freedom has been significantly broadened since the restrictive meaning it had in the 1915 declaration of the AAUP. College faculty and even secondary school faculty may and often do claim academic freedom to justify their choice of curriculum or pedagogy. Nevertheless, if one considers the usual course to tenure and its guarantee of academic freedom, it is *competence* that is being assessed as the basis for granting a special privilege.

It is not at all puzzling that the notions of academic freedom and free speech should be so frequently fused and fuzzed in a democratic society, but complete failure to distinguish the two is disastrous both practically and theoretically to the university. The exclusionary authority of the university expressed through the learned disciplines is crucial in distinguishing the university from the nonexclusionary openness of the public square. It is no accident, I believe, that academic freedom arose as an articulated principle for American universities as late as 1915. There were precursors of the notion at least as far back as the *licentia docendi* of the Middle Ages and the *Lehrfreiheit* of Humboldt's nineteenth-century University of Berlin. If, however, one looks more deeply at these earlier claims for "freedom," the philosophic bases are subtly and vitally different. Humboldt's *Lehrfreiheit*, for example, envisioned a sort of spiritual freedom of grand thought, something similar to the freedom from the mundane advocated by the ancient Stoics. In its context it was a sort of cultural resurrection of the Prussian spirit after the political disasters suffered by the nation at the hands of Napoleon. Modern advocacy of academic freedom largely rests on the Cartesian assumptions embedded in the Enlightenment, assumptions that have seen their most powerful and persuasive results in the modern natural sciences. The rise of science and the rise of academic freedom in universities are intimately linked.

A powerful and pervasive rationale for academic freedom in the sciences rests on the neutrality of the observer and the observed. Once one accepts Cartesian asceticism of the mind—the transcendent observer without political, ethical, ethnic biases—one may trust that what is observed is not colored by existing prejudice. Add to that the notion that what is observed is itself value free—mathematical forms, atomic particles, simple ideas (Hume)—and one may conclude that the risks of accepting falsehood have been drastically reduced. A neutral observer viewing the value-free facts is a fully adequate check on the observations of all other observers. Science eliminates historically embedded prejudice.

The connection between natural science and academic freedom in the university is sufficiently close that it has caused one observer to comment that the university needs science more than science needs the university. That science can exist quite well without the university is substantiated by the fact noted in an earlier chapter that, well into the nineteenth century, science was practiced outside of and often in opposition to the universities. More telling, in countries with strong ideological pressures, advanced natural science is not practiced in the universities but in separate research institutes. The former Soviet Union was a case in point. The Soviets needed advanced physics for their weapons programs if nothing else. They could not stifle research but they could not allow the politically neutral freedom of physics to "infect" the universities.

The connection between academic freedom and the natural sciences, between academic freedom and the Enlightenment, with its assumption of a transcendent "Cartesian" mind, may be *the* crucial issue in understanding the problem of a Catholic university. Catholic universities seem to many critics to resemble Soviet universities, that is, to be institutions with ideological blinders, lacking academic freedom. If there is a defense against this damning charge—at least for Catholic universities—it will rest upon how one assesses the adequacy of academic freedom based on the Enlightenment model of natural science. Or, more broadly, the model of a university based solely on the model of the "neutral" observer.

THE DOGMA OF COMPETENCE

Academic freedom based on disciplinary competence is a meta-truth of the current university world, an infallible dogma about university life that cannot be violated under pain of fundamental heresy. Academic freedom seems fully revealed and appropriately justified in the natural sciences. Quantum physics, for example, has such deeply funded results and broadly accepted procedures that problems with its exclusionary authority among university competencies hardly ever arises.

Academic freedom is not an "anything-goes license" for opinion. When a pair of chemists claimed to have achieved cold fusion, the results were quickly rejected by a panel of expert physicists because the experiments failed to meet the canons of acceptable physics. It was a clear example of the exclusionary power granted to an attested discipline. (A colleague of mine who was on the investigating panel referred to the cold fusion claim as the "three miracle theory." If one could have three successive miracles, cold fusion would be possible.) No one in the public square would forbid the scientists from continuing to claim the truth of cold fusion—certainly a harmless proclamation to the teeming masses—but cold fusionists are excluded from "true physics" with the same rigor with which Galileo was sanctioned by the true church.[1] (We do not, happily, burn cold fusionists at the stake or even confine them to house arrest.)

It is not clear in the cold fusion case whether academic heresy was at issue. The cold fusionists were up to a point playing by the rules, the standards of competence in physics. The problem was that they seem to have fudged results, misunderstood observations, and generally fell into various blunders of procedure. One is allowed to be decidedly wrong, but within the rules.

Academic heresy goes beyond just getting it wrong or being an incompetent experimentalist. In the social sciences and the humanities, competence in discipline and methodology may themselves be highly contested. Academic conservatives regard feminism, gay studies, and the like as political advocacy with a thin patina of scholarship—the intrusion of the public square into the stricter confines of scholarship. Certain aspects of feminism, ethnic studies, and deconstructionism are regarded as *academic heresy*, denial of the fundamental academic dogma. Those "studies" fail the meta-truth of competence; they are not disciplined methods toward universal truth but idiosyncratic, individualistic, subjective opinion decked in the gaudy pseudo-scientific turgidities of postmodernism. (Such is the polemic of the *odium scholasticum*.) Theology, a special concern of this book, may be utterly banished as mere idiosyncratic belief, trotted off campus entirely or carefully isolated in the historical appendage of a divinity school.

The dogma of competence is not a truth *in* the academy, it is a defining truth *for* the academy. Rejection of *any* sort of demonstrable competence may qualify one only for the public square and the irrationalities of politics. Violation of the preferred definition of competence is academic *heresy*. Heresy hunting is, to be sure, a dangerous enterprise whether in church or academy. Ecclesiastical history amply and sadly demonstrates it is all too easy to dismiss an opponent as a heretic. One uses the ultimate weapon rather than the complex task of straightforward argument toward refutation. Nevertheless, whether academic conservatives are right about deconstructionists, or the statutes of the University of Paris from 1215 about David of Dinant (see chapter 1, text at note 4), it is clear that there are modes of thought and action that utterly subvert accepted methods and competencies.

If competence is *the* essential dogma for the university, it is obvious from the above that its meaning is not beyond dispute. Defining competence is subject to significant reflection and debate—debate that may well occur within the university. The difference between such debates and normal arguments about the the size of the universe, cold fusion, the causes of crime, and whether Shakespeare's plays were written by the Earl of Oxford is that as one defines the competence dogma, one defines the boundaries of the university itself. If *Hamlet* turns out to be the earl's work or that of a wayward space alien, it will make no difference to the ongoing work of the university. But if one decides that casting runes is a way to settle academic disputations, the sense of the academy is fundamentally altered.

Because the competence dogma defines university boundaries, it is easily ignored as one is caught up in the daily business of teaching and learning. Universities and their denizens are notoriously oblivious to their defining dogmas—thus the utter confusion of curriculum committees trying to specify what is essential to higher education. Universities that claim to know about everything from galaxies to governments spend almost no serious time understanding themselves. Basic university dogmas are assumed and used, not reviewed and examined. This blissful unconcern is not by any means fatal. Assuming the good of some at-hand discipline leads to lots of interesting results. Dogmas are recognized usually when they are under attack. The challenge of feminism to the Cartesian "dogma" of transcendent mind is a current instance in which the university community has had to consider its basic defining character.

Since academic freedom based on competence is *the* fundamental dogma of higher education, and since the character of competence is not self-evident, as one specifies "competence" so one will decide which "studies" are compatible with the university. In regard to the central concern of this book, the "competence" of theology may be systematically excluded as the nature and range of *academic* competence is defined. Some basic university dogma about disciplinary method may become dogmatic (bad) if it is demanded that only that preferred methodology be the sole measure of competence. (At least that is how those excluded will regard such academic high-handedness.) One could offer the experimental method of the hardest of hard natural sciences as the *only* acceptable methodology for truth, asserting a powerful hegemony over all other alleged competencies. Poets would be ushered from the Ideal Institute of Physics with the same polite determination with which Plato sent Homer into exile in the *Republic*. If my earlier characterization of the arts as *signatured* truth is accurate, artistic truth is no truth at all for physics, so art would be quite banished from the quad. I have argued that if the poets go, so will the faithful since Christianity also rests on signatured truth. One can restate the problem of academic freedom and Catholic dogma as a quarrel about the nature of competency. Does some academic dogma about competence—for example, that competence pertains only to universal scientific truth—exclude the Catholic (and artistic) "dogma" of signatured truth? That was the claim as long ago as the Emperor Julian, who saw no need for the revelation through named persons.

MORAL DOGMA OF THE ACADEMY

Because academic freedom makes a "dogmatic" demand for some definition of disciplinary competence, it is possible that the competence dogma be restricted to the methods of natural science. There are technical institutions that at least approximate that model. In fact, however, almost all universities in the United States include a broader range of competencies than the strict scientific model would permit. Competence is currently interpreted broadly to include astrophysicists and artists despite the quite divergent warrants offered for "competence." In a large sense both astrophysicists and artists can, it seems, make reasonable claims to ways of sorting the true and the false, the genuine and the sham. One is not, presumably, left in the arts with mere subjective opinion. As previously discussed, the methodology for transcending mere opinion in the arts—the "method of authority" (reliance on authoritative tradition)—is crucial for their place in the academy, and that methodology has analogous application for religious faith.

If one were to confine competence to strict science—*especially* if one were to do so—one would have to deal with additional dogmas that go beyond direct competence in any of its modes or guises. And the absence or violation of these criteria would/should/could cause one to be to be excluded from the company of scholars. This is to say, therefore, that even if the first and necessary dogma of the academy is competence-toward-truth, there is also an ethical dogma to be asserted. Again, this dogma is not a truth *in* the university, but a truth *of* and *for* the university, a fundamental defining characteristic. The ethical dogma is most clearly revealed if one were to confine the university justification to strict science. Because human beings are not transcendent minds (on the side of the investigator) or mere specimens (on the side of the investigated), there are certain restraints on the sheer pursuit of knowledge that must (moral "must") be attended to by the academy. The ethical treatment of biological subjects (animals, humans) is not merely an external imposition and interference on the pursuit of science, but an inherent obligation that scientists must recognize.

One of the values of placing the arts *within* the university is that they offer a powerful statement about the personal, the fact that human beings have an "inside" that is a center of freedom and value. If one brackets out entirely any consideration of the truth of inner, personal life, then the most an experimenter could record is a typology of external behaviors. This attitude and approach is the scenario of the fictional "mad scientist" or the actual Nazi medical experimenters. The mad scientist is "mad" precisely because he considers himself only as a transcendent observer distanced from historical humanity. But there is a double distancing: on the one hand the scientist transcends feeling to assume an impersonal, "godlike" stance presumed to be the position of the ideal (neutral) observer. ("Aren't you playing God, Dr. Frankenstein?") On the other hand, the subject of scientific observation is distanced by being treated as a mere *specimen*. The physician sees his patient only as a case of cancer, not as a suffering, individual human being deserving moral concern.

There may also be "mad" artists, apart form the stereotypical image of the artist as bizarre and eccentric. The species of mad artist I have in mind is akin to the mad scientist: the conductor who regards the orchestra members as machines in the service of Music, the painter who abuses his models and cruelly portrays them on his canvas for the sake of Art. As in the case of the mad scientist, there is a denial of the person for the sake of the discipline. The mad artist seems paradoxical—and for that reason is often given more tolerance—because she is abusing the person at hand for the sake of revealing something personal, her artistic perception of human life.

Insofar as the university is an institution created by, sustained by, licensed by individual human beings and the human community, a necessary condition of its existence is humane concern and behavior. The university is not a creature of the gods for the sake of pure science or glorious art. It is not Jonathan Swift's floating island of Laputa. The mad scientist is excluded from the guild because he violates a necessary condition for research. Pleading academic freedom in the pursuit of sheer truth (or Art) will not prevail. The ethical dogma of the university denies to the university final transcendent value whether it is the transcendence of science or the transcendence of art. Humanity is not to be sacrificed even on the high altar of knowledge or beauty.

There would be a necessary contradiction between an academic competence dogma interpreted as transcendent science and Catholic dogma interpreted as the reality of the historical, individual and personal. Because Catholic dogma asserts the irreducible truth of the individual, it would be excluded from an institution dogmatically commited to transcending the personal in the interests of scientific truth alone. When, however, one includes an ethical dogma as a defining characteristic of the university, the claim of the individual and personal are legitimated and Catholicism may find some lodging in the larger reality of the academy. Catholicism may support the ethical concern essential to the university, but in the long run religious claims extend beyond the merely ethical. To illuminate what *more* is involved, one must raise not just moral issues, but issues of "salvation." Even for the university.

EXISTENTIAL DOGMAS FOR THE ACADEMY

A third dogma or meta-truth for the university relates to what in earlier chapters I have discussed as the truth of "the real"—the area of truth within which religion functions. I label this the "existential" dogma of the university. In discussing the signatured truth of the arts, I indicated the radical difference between legitimate scientific interest in the universal, the species or type, and the artist's interest in and expression of the unique and personal. Within the university, the artist serves to remind us of the power of the personal and its vision. I also discussed the arts as the necessary pedagogy of the ethical life. Despite the value of the personal and ethical vision in art, I went on to discuss the "failure" of art. Much as we admire and need the artist's mastery, one may, as in the example of the art of the Holocaust, come to reject such mastery as failing the chaotic reality that confronts us. In a collection of essays pointedly titled *Admitting the Holocaust*, Lawrence Langer is at great pains to show that art does not "admit" or reach "the real" that is is the Holocaust. In several essays he cites Jean Améry, an Auschwitz survivor, who expresses the issue of art and the Holocaust in a memorable phrase: "No bridge led from death in Auschwitz to *Death in Venice*."[2] Recall, then, the earlier quotation explaining underground anti-art: "The drive to wrench art away from its normal subject matter and materials so as to bring it closer to the chaotic vitality of everyday life . . . ." If one hopes to point to "chaos" either as terror or "vitality," one may need to go "beyond" Art.

In the most general sense, one might say that the university's task is to *order* experience for the sake of knowledge or, in the case of the traditional arts, for the truth of human experience as revealed in the ordering sensibility of the artist. But contemporary anti-art movements regard this urge toward order as fraudulent to the sheer chaos, painful or exuberant, of "the real." The children's art of the Holocaust in its failure as art reveals the chaotic obscenity of the camps. It demonstrates the failure of the bridge from Holocaust to Art. To the extent that the university is committed to order, what stance can formal study or traditional art take toward the chaos, splendid or obscene, that is proclaimed as the final truth by "the real" of human existence?

Explicitly or implicitly the university will manifest an existential dogma in how it understands and relates its inner methods and achievements to "the real." The pejorative "ivory tower" is but one expression of how the university's supposed distance from life, reality, experience can be regarded. As old-fashioned as it may sound, the existential dogma for the academy relates to "the meaning of life"—specifically in this case *the meaning of academic life.* Where exactly do the exquisite intricacies of scientific knowledge and the deep personal insights of the arts and humanities fit in the final meaning of life, ultimate reality, the "really real." Or, if life is chaos or "waste," can there be any meaning? Perhaps the ivory tower is humanity's best shelter against meaningless chaos.

The difference between an existential dogma for the university and the competence and ethical dogmas is that there apparently exists a range of choices for this dogma. The university will have an existential dogma, but not all universities will have the same one. Whether there is a connection between some proper definition of "higher learning" and the choice of existential dogma is a complex matter. I argue eventually that a special Catholic understanding—not necessarily that of the official church—is particularly apposite for the university. Before reaching that point, however, it is helpful to elaborate more fully the general problems of "the real" and its relation to the university world.

Assuming the *fact* of radical existential presence, how does recognition of this truth impinge on the life of the university? Direct attention to "the real" may seem too elusive for the crisp standards of academic thought. If so, the university for the sake of modesty might acknowledge "that there *are* more things in heaven and earth . . . than are dreamt of in your [academic] philosophy." Academic spokesmen may mutter, "Well, of course. We never pretended that the university could address such 'profound' questions as 'the meaning of life.'"

However, happily or unhappily, the contemporary university currently looms so large as the proscriptive guardian of Truth that such demurrals may not be quite believed—even (or especially) by those who utter them. Given university prominence as *the* authority for Truth, and the diminution of the traditional "meaning-of-life" institutions (the churches), the public may well conclude that the university from its tidy tower has *de facto* pronounced on all issues, to wit: "meaning-of-life" concerns are unscientific, irrational, idiosyncratic, so far beyond sense as to be nonsense. *Contra* Hamlet, there really isn't anything *not* contained in our academic philosophy. Well, anything worth talking about!

To recognize that the university in its mainline studies of science and art is finally embedded in an existential reality that resists enclosure does not, of course, lead necessarily to a *Catholic* university. It could lead to the denial of the university altogether. An atheistic Jean-Paul Sartre asserted that existential reality eludes all categories, manifesting itself in the sort of bloated "too much-ness" that confronts the protagonist of *Nausea*. Immersed in Sartrean existential reality one would look back on science and art, the "rational" activities of the university, and see them as "absurd." A Sartrean university is as much a contradiction as a Catholic university could ever be.

IGNORANCE, TRANSCENDENCE, AND GRACE

While I have noted that there are various ways in which the university might address "the real," they all seem to be variations on a limited set of themes. The simplest stance of the university and the most practical is simply to *ignore* the problem. Essentially this is the position of the scientific experimenter who, for all practical purposes, ignores the sheer individuality of the specimen under the microscope. It is not Ichabod Toad but any frog that is the subject of biological truth. One may, however, go beyond practical ignorance of existential density and consciously seek a "spiritual" transcendence beyond the chaos of the everyday, of life's unhappy happenings.

Platonism offers one paradigm of such a position. In his death scene, Socrates simply denies the reality of death as anything of real import. Death is not "the real." Insofar as he has pursued his philosophic inquiries, he has a lived the only life worth living. Socrates is a genuine academic hero: the only thing that counts is the pursuit of " knowledge." There is a profound difference, however, between Socrates' pursuit of *ethical* knowledge and the modern pursuit of natural knowledge, natural science. Socrates was burlesqued by Aristophanes as a distracted cosmologist, but that is not how Plato presents him. For Plato,

Socrates is not Aristophanes' "mad scientist" disdaining family ties for cosmic truth. He is the precise opposite of the Sartrean protagonist swamped by the nausea of existential density. For Socrates, sheer existence and its marker, death, are nothing, they disenchant not at all. For Plato, what is real are the Ideas and Forms—Henry James's "nugget washed clean of awkward accretions and hammered into sacred hardness." The confusion of existence is to be transcended, shaped and molded into a philosophical work of art, a thing of order and beauty. Existence is "denied," left behind in the way that Socrates says his body will be left behind with death, but he, Socrates, will either be elsewhere or not at all. The "really real" of Plato is not James's vision of life and its "splendid waste"; it is the Ideal.

The worst that could be said about the modern secular university might be that it *is* the Platonic academy (more or less): a grove removed from "the real," living in a world of Forms and Ideas, denying by transcendence the import of existential reality. That "worst" is not so bad! What is lacking in the pure Platonic academy and its search for ethical knowledge? The poets. It is in this respect that the modern university most clearly deviates from the pure model. For Plato, the arts have the essential fault of depending on historical individuality, what I have called "signatured truth." Signatured truths have two linked defects from the standpoint of the Platonic academy. In the first place they are *signatured*, which means that they are truths attached to some named person—for example, Homer's vision. For Plato, truth is always of the Form, not the particular. Socrates is forever noting that it is not he, Socrates, who is refuted or triumphant in argument. Socrates is easily refuted, Truth is not. The notion of signatured truth would be a contradiction in the Platonic academy: a particular universal. Worse yet, though some particular poet might trip upon *the* truth, poetry lacks method. Plato regards poetry as dependent on inspiration—a method that was notoriously unreliable and difficult to validate. It is not an accident, then, that in the *Republic*, the poets are censored. To the extent that the arts relate to individuality and "what happens" (inspiration), they must be suspect in any philosophy that holds that the "really real" consists in transcendent Forms and Ideas accessed only by some ordered methodology.

Socrates is concerned with ethics as ethical *knowledge:* the good life is conformity to an ethical ideal in which sheer individuality is left behind. What remains is the philosophic mind. This aspect of Platonism is forcefully carried forward in the neo-Platonic development of Stoicism. The two great Stoic philosophers are Epictetus, a slave, and Marcus Aurelius, the emperor. Historical *position* (slave or emperor) is of no interest or importance to the tranquil rational mind in tune with eternal Forms.

It is not wholly accurate to accuse Plato of disdain for the arts; rather he wishes to refashion the arts as didactic of the good life. The *Republic* is the supreme *philosophic* poem, which replaces Homer. Since the topic of this chapter is academic freedom, it is worth noting that the founder of the Platonic academy was hardly a champion of "freedom" as it is championed on the contemporary campus. On need only point to the censure of the poets to raise the ire of modern advocates of academic freedom. Thus Karl Popper saw Plato as a protofascist who would countenance academic freedom only for a universalizing method, censoring any claim for individualized, nonuniversal truth.

In the modern context one might regard natural science as *the* method for discovering the universal Forms, and it is the universality of truth and method that is the key to academic freedom. Natural science would not be Plato's method, but the lack of a universalizing method—in his case "dialectic"—would be a fatal and exclusionary flaw for admission to the academy. Poets fail such a fundamental test of university/academic competence because they depend on inspiration, not a possessed skill. What skill they have with language or poetic form is irrelevant to the poet's inability to demonstrate that what she says with such eloquence and charm is ethically and universally true. It is the very ability of eloquence and charm to distract us from the universal truth that makes the poet a dangerous person in the state.

The modern university should not overlook the historical quarrel between philosophy and poetry that we find in Plato. For better or worse, the modern university has accepted the value of individuality as manifested in the arts. The poets have been welcomed back from Platonic exile. But the faculty member who complained at Princeton about introducing a Ph.D. program in musical composition because the university should not be granting a doctorate for "creativity" shows that Platonism is not dead. *Artistic* freedom might still be regarded by some as the determined enemy of *academic* freedom: the freedom granted to methodological competence and universal truth. Checking the value of art as genuinely creative, the voice of the muse, seems much too vaporous. Artistic freedom may license nothing more than personal passions assessed by ephemeral fashions of the mob. There was a recent furor at a noted art school where the student's "artistic" presentation involved live sadomasochistic sex. Given that sort of goings on, Platonism may seem attractive.

I have expanded on the Platonic academy because in so many ways it re-

sembles the modern university in its attitude toward "the real." Clearly in the
natural sciences, it is the search for some universal Form that counts while the
individual is cheerfully discounted. That is very Platonic. When the arts are
allowed to enter the modern grove of academe, they are granted "artistic license," aka academic freedom. But are the arts even then really taken *seriously?*
Plato took them most seriously because they might depict and encourage an
ethically bad life. It is simply not clear whether we tolerate the variety of the
arts because they do, after all, only reflect fashion and are a form of "entertain-
ment." Where the modern academy as either science or art differs profoundly
from the Platonic academy is that Plato saw philosophy not as a learned discipline—and certainly not as "fashion"—but as a life strategy. As Pierre Hadot
has amply shown, ancient philosophy was a "spiritual exercise," a "way of life."[3]
If poetry lifts suffering to a level of higher regard, fine, but that is not "salvation." For Plato and then more clearly for the Stoic neo-Platonists, "higher regard" was reality itself and suffering was thus overcome. To the philosopher of
tranquil mind, knowing that reality is transcendent of mere existence makes
suffering an "illusion." Thus the Stoic claim that the wise man is always happy,
even on the rack.

In investigating the relationship between Catholic faith and academic life,
the Platonic heritage is enormously important. The modern academy instantiates many of the modalities of its ancient predecessor: methodical inquiry, transcendence of mind toward the universal. What the modern academy does *not*
claim—at least explicitly—is that this modern "academic" way is a "way of
life." In an ironic inversion of the spiritual exercises of the founder of the academy, modern study is "merely academic," that is, not finally intended to solve or
save life's inevitable confusion. At least that is what most academicians would
say if offered the Platonic challenge.

Rejecting the Platonic way of life would seem to leave the modern university with two options. One is simply to ignore the whole issue of the way of
life, of "salvation." The university is simply agnostic on that subject: "Not my
department!" More aggressively, having surveyed the power and prestige of
university studies, it can declare there is no "salvation"—worse, pick your own
way of life. Plato was mistaken to think that "knowledge" removes us to the "really real" beyond the travail of this world, the academy today declares. Knowledge is a good to be pursued for its own sake, but it does not pretend to
encompass "the real" or to transcend it except as artifice. Poetry has its place in
the modern academic array, but it is not salvation either. The poet says: "time

held me green and dying / though I sang in my chains like the sea." Poetry is the song that lifts suffering to a higher regard and that is valuable, but it does not lead even to Stoic transcendence.

It is obvious where a *Catholic* university enters into these options about salvation. It will clearly reject the Platonic model of salvation through dialectic and transcendent knowledge. Where the modern university explicitly or implicitly falls into a Platonic spiritual mode, Catholic belief is fundamentally alien to such a venture. A Catholic–Platonic university is a real contradiction; the concept contains contradictory ways of salvation. On the other hand, Christianity rejects the notion that there is no salvation. If the university were to declare implicitly by its presumed hegemony over truth that life, existence, "the real" is unsalvageable (too dense, too messy, splendid waste, chaos), Christians would insist that Salvation *is* possible. A Catholic–Sartrean university is also a contradiction. I will not here try to justify the Christian choice, I only wish to indicate how it might enter into the inevitable dialogue between knowledge and "the real," form and the density of life, intellectual contemplation and Salvation.

THEOLOGY AS QUEEN OF THE SCIENCES

I have suggested various ways in which the notion of a Catholic university would be, as Shaw maintained, a contradiction. A university dogma that restricted legitimate thought to natural science with all that implies about the universal neutrality of the investigator and the investigated would banish Catholicism because of Christianity's allegiance to signatured truth. Catholicism would have a place (at least a niche) if the methodology of the university encompasses the signatured truth of the arts. And Catholic belief in the signatured truth of the one who says "I am the Truth" would support interest in the individual voice throughout history. It would be a guard against the "mad" scientist.

But Catholicism goes beyond and "contradicts" the notion that signatured *art* is the "last word," even though that word lifts suffering to a higher regard. Christianity is not a literary gesture into the darkness of life; that is what separates believers from those who regard the Bible as great literature. Humankind may do more than "sing in [its] chains like the sea." Catholicism claims that there is more to reality than knowledge and even artistic form. We must come to terms with that "splendid waste" that is life itself. We are not saved from life by science or art; rather are we saved from life in life by a Life (Jesus) into Life. There is a way of *life* and that way is neither science nor art; one must plunge into life in the manner of the anti-art artist who wishes to confront us with "chaotic vitality." Duchamp said, "Art as religion? Why it's not even as good as God!"

The word "Catholic" in "Catholic university" makes two generic claims: there is a way of *life* that is salvational; and that way of life is radically signatured. Both claims are interpreted and justified in relation to the Hebrew Scriptures and the life of Jesus of Nazareth who is "the Way, the Life, and the Truth." How do these central Christian beliefs relate to the university way? Does the university think that there is a way of life that is salvational? One answer by academe is no, there is no salvation. Another is yes, it is the Platonic way through knowledge and artistic form. Catholicism rejects both answers. There is Salvation and it is in the realm of the signatured—but a signatured that goes beyond artistic form into the very density of life and death.

The crucial question posed by the university at this point is whether any claims about "the real" and counterclaims are discussable. As suggested earlier, for many academics religion is "below discussion." To even raise the question about whether accepted university models of thought are "salvational" would, I believe, baffle and annoy many, maybe most, faculty. "Salvation" is not the academic task—and the very idea of it may be thought to be mere nonsense and whistling in the dark. Nevertheless, the university cannot entirely escape the existential question. It will, as said, explicitly or implicitly position itself relative to life, a way of life (there is none), and "salvation" (don't even think of it!). Some academic existential *dogma* will constitute a fundamental defining characteristic of the university task itself: a dogma about the university's life and meaning.

That there are assumptions—meta-truths, dogmas—for any university does not mean that those assumptions are not subject to discussion and debate, even if the form and method of those discussions deviate from the standard methods used within the everyday life of the university. Obviously there is significant and heated debate about what is real *academic* competence. Because such debates are about basic assumptions, the very definition of the academic enterprise, they are "meta-discussions" not usually or properly part of the "normal" work of the university. Wherever and however this debate is carried forward, that arena would claim to exercise defining sovereignty over the university as such. If physics were *the* model of the university sole and entire, then it is clear that other subjects would be ordered, valued or disvalued, according to that *university* model.

In addressing the existential position of the university, formulating its existential dogma, the discipline properly called upon is theology or a "reasonable facsimile thereof." "Theology" seems a not inappropriate designation for whatever investigation might be undertaken that purports to assemble considerations for "a way of life" as it relates to the ultimate, to "the real." Insofar as "theology," its facsimile, or its utter rejection determines the status of the university as way-of-life, theology would be queen of the sciences. To say that the existential dogma is theological is not in itself to settle any religious claims as such. Sartre, for instance, is a dedicated "theologian"—dedicated to spelling out the radical consequences that follow from the nonexistence of God. As noted, Sartrean atheism stands in sharp opposition to the ways of the academy. No salvation even at *L'École Normale Superieure!*

One need not pretend that "theological" disputation on the existential status of the university is as simple, straightforward, and crisp as a chemical equation. Presumably the issues at stake are the most profound, murky, and complex of all. The issue, however, is whether the existential issue can be ignored. In one sense it certainly can be put aside: chemistry and economics have their own autonomy and produce valuable knowledge under anybody's theology or lack thereof. But if the university claims to encompass *all* that is legitimate for human consideration within the array of its usual academic subjects, from what authority does that claim over legitimation arise? It must be a view above and beyond the disciplines themselves. It is the philosophy or theology *of* the university that is at issue. When one moves to the meta-level of considering the range and legitimacy of the academic pursuits, the existence issue regarding the meaning of the academy to life itself will emerge. The academy's great skills will be placed within and among the life tasks of humankind for good or for ill. Plato will invite us into the grove of academe as a spiritual exercise, a way of life unto the eternal. Catholics will point to another way of life and seek to understand the relation of knowledge to their way of Salvation.

Whether Catholicism acts as a prophetic check on covert academic pretension to salvation, or whether the biblical materials offer vital insights into the ultimate place of knowledge and art in the road to salvation, it cannot avoid intersection with the university nor can the university simply dismiss Christianity's existential dogma without violating its own claims, positive or negative, about the university and "life." A minimal defense of a Catholic university is that it embodies a certain existential dogma, and since all universities explicitly or implicitly have some existential dogma, it would be as high-handed to simply exclude the Catholic choice as it would be the Platonic way of existential transcendence.

CATHOLIC FREEDOM AND ACADEMIC DOGMA

So far in this argument, I have only tried to indicate that the "theological" issue of the university cannot be ignored. Catholic theology and Sartrean atheism may both make claims (or assaults) on the basic character of certain academic self-understandings. One might fancy that in an ideal university with full academic freedom and open debate, there would be a Department of the University staffed with Platonists, Sartreans, Thomists, and those who thought the whole argument over the nature of the university "nonsense." Presumably there would be interesting and complex debates in this odd department about the academic enterprise. The model would not offend the sensibilities of the Committee on Academic Freedom of the American Association of University Professors (AAUP) because everyone would be given full opportunity to put forward arguments.

There are two crucial differences between this meta–Department of the University and, say, the physics department. First, is it at all capable of advancing wisdom in the field of its investigations? Second, if it does actually possess some way of assessing the value of arguments about the nature of the university, would/should its conclusions have any effect on the actual university of which it is a part?

As to the first matter, it would seem quite out of keeping with the basic competence dogma of the university to have a Department of the University that failed in competence. Presumably there is something more to the discussion of the nature of the university than trading personal opinions and anecdotes of practice. If there is some disciplinary competence—or an array of competencies—about the type of knowledge, ethical obligations, and existential stance of this sort of institution, then there would be some conclusions or directions toward conclusion.

I will simply assume that in my fictional department, while it is indeed possible that there would be disagreement, there would be a clear sense of what is good and what is bad *university philosophy*. If there is or can be no ordered wisdom about the university, its competencies, its ethical responsibilities, and its meaning, then there should certainly be no such study. Broad-scale failure in a philosophy of the university would lead one to wonder what, if anything, are the foundational elements of "university." What constitutes a "discipline"? Should there be a Ph.D. in musical composition? What experiments are ethically allowed? Will academic life be a *full* life? These questions, if they can be answered or even pursued with some degree of discipline, lead to the second matter distinguished above, about whether the Department of the University should have some practical, institutional consequence. Without an ordered meta-discussion about "the university," the academy becomes a geographical expression, a mart where whatever might pass as study can find a lodging. This is not wholly objectionable. It avoids false or early closure; it may elevate the less worthy to established standards; it certainly keeps peace within the quad.

When universities were founded in the Middle Ages they were crowned with a school of theology. Whatever else the theologians might have brought to the intellectual table, they would at least have offered an ordered locus for discussion of the relation of learning and life. That would seem to be a discussion worth continuing. A Catholic university should have a considered view in depth about the nature and role of the arts and sciences as they relate to the passions and needs of humankind. The Catholic university holds that Salvation is a deep human quest, that the very best of university thought and art is not salvational whatever its genuine value and importance. Despite the failure of any academic (Platonic) dream of salvation, one need not abandon Salvation as illusion. A theology grounded in historical Revelation legitimates ways of thought and action that go beyond the capacities of science and art.

The first consideration for a *Catholic* university does not, then, bear upon the competencies of varied disciplines within the academy. Physics is physics is physics and so on. Existential dogma, Catholic or atheistic, only(!) positions the range of learned competencies and artistic achievements relative to "the real" and the issue of "salvation." It is not stretching a point or terminology to place any such consideration in the realm of "theology." Theology is that study which assesses "the real" and sketches out strategies for Salvation (if any) in the light of "the real." The question about the salvational range and capacity of normal academic studies does not in any direct way encroach on the academic freedom of the various disciplines. Darwinian evolution is a scientific theory as well established and as open to justification or critique by competent biologists as one might wish. However, when Richard Dawkins declares that Darwinianism proves the truth of atheism, one has the sense that he has strayed from biological argument.[4] Even if one thought Dawkins's arguments sound, a Christian might well conclude that at most "some god" was discarded. There is, however, something useful in Dawkins's efforts to prove the nonexistence of God insofar as they at least make a claim upon the theological. As frequently noted, many academics consider the issue of "god," yes or no, undiscussable and uninteresting. Dawkins at least finds it capable of being decided and interesting enough to polemicize extensively on the subject.

The issue in regard to some considered and self-conscious existential dogma for the university is directly implicated in the legitimacy of theology. Since the university demands "competence," is there any ordered discipline, any competence, involved in assessing existential issues? One can, as noted, simply ignore the matter. Individuals who find the university salvational are like all believers exercising their options. There are those who just find university study fun and distracting from the mundane messiness of domestic life. And so on. Whatever else one might say about a *Catholic* university, it takes the task of the university with utmost seriousness, worthy of and capable of assessment within the largest considerations of life and its meaning.

The title of this chapter reverses the normal juxtaposition of academic freedom and Catholic dogma. If academic dogma precludes salvation because "the real" is beyond its ken, then Catholic belief might *free* one from the limitations of such a dogma and the oppressive chaos of life, the meaningless mess compulsively thrust upon us by aggressive anti-art. (It is interesting to note that many of the most aggressive and "outrageous" artists are or were Catholics— for example, Warhol, Andre Serrano, Robert Mapplethorpe. It takes a disappointed believer to proclaim "No Salvation!") Instead of "the real" as the ultimate threat of meaningless, an assault on and mockery of university pretense, the Catholic holds that "the real" is "with us," is not finally utterly alien to humanity and its ways—even university ways. Salvation in "the real" frees the university to pursue its well-disciplined ways.

In the next chapter, I want to reprise some of this same territory in terms of the issue of infallibility. The Catholic Church's claim for extensive infallibility in the area of faith and morals seems distinctly alien to the university's urge for everlasting inquiry and methodological skepticism. There may be university meta-dogmas, but these may exist only to justify doubt and discovery in the daily tasks. What then for church infallibility?

7

Fallible Church and Infallible Academy *or* Infallible Church and Fallible Academy

In the previous chapter, I argued that a Catholic university would first and fundamentally be a comment upon and a commitment to a certain *existential* dogma for the academy. In this chapter I want to reprise that argument in the terminology of fallible/infallible. It is one thing to argue that there must be some existential dogma at the back or front of the academic mind, it is quite another to argue that the Catholic Church grasps that dogma infallibly. To understand the complexity of the issue one has to look at the sense of fallible/infallible in *both* academy and church.

FALLIBLE ACADEMY

The conflict between church and academy is often stated today as a conflict between a Catholic claim for infallibility in matters of faith and morals and the commitment to fallibilism in the university. University study is eternally investigative, ready to throw over even the most cherished doctrine on the basis of better evidence or more powerful theory. Without a doubt this is the preferred rhetoric of the day regarding the work of the university. Despite its fixity in academic apologetics—dare one say its "dogmatic" position—the fact is that this philosophy for the university is relatively recent, dating more or less from the end of the nineteenth century. Progressive thinkers of that period, Charles Sanders Peirce (who invented the term "fallibilism"), John Dewey, and William James among others, posited the continually correcting vision of true science in opposition to the "tenacity, authority, and a priori reasoning"[1] that infected theological discourse. Thorstein Veblen summed up in 1908 what has become the standard posture of the modern academy: "[M]odern scientific inquiry comes to rest only provisionally; because its prime postulate is that of consecutive change, and consecutive change cannot, of course, come to rest except provisionally."[2]

It is obvious that a philosophy of "provisionalism" will recoil at the thought of "infallible" dogma despite, as we may say, the dogma of provisionalism. What is most interesting is to consider the radical change wrought by fallibilism on the understanding of science. Fallibilism replaced a philosophy of science derived from Francis Bacon, which dominated school science in the earlier period of American higher education until its destruction by the progressivists. Bacon, in revolt against the tradition-ridden "dogmatism" of his time, demanded empirical proof as the only standard for true science. Only induction from observation and hypotheses fully confirmed by observation would be admitted as "scientific." The direction of Baconianism was toward certainty. Until one had the empirical evidence at hand, there was no certainty, and science was only interested in certainty. As Julie Reuben amply chronicles in *The Making of the Modern University*, it was Darwinism that destroyed the Baconian model—destroyed it not only in its postulated theory but in the implications it had for scientific method.

In a famous nineteenth-century debate over Darwinism between the German biologists Rudolph Virchow and Ernst Haeckel, Virchow rejected Darwin's views on Baconian principles. Evolution lacked empirical evidence—there was, for example, no fossil evidence of intermediate species. What is most interesting for the present discussion is Virchow's statement that it is only on the basis of *certainty* that science can "demand that full measure of liberty which may be called the liberty of science, or more correctly still, perhaps, *liberty of scientific teaching* . . . ."[3] In what seems to have been the complete opposite of modern assumptions, Virchow argued that freedom of scientific teaching can only be based on *certainty*, while Peirce et al. argued that freedom is demanded by the *un*certainty of scientific results. Virchow held that one can demand freedom only to teach the verified truth; anything else is personal speculation that one has no right to purvey. Fallibilists, on the other hand, allow one to guess, conjecture, and speculate in the belief that the continual checks and revisions of ongoing science will eliminate what is spurious. *Contra* Virchow, John Dewey wrote a whole book called *The Quest for Certainty*, the burden of which was that such a quest was futile; there was no certainty, only inquiry.

As Reuben notes in passing, there is a curious paradox in fallibilist views: it is supposed that conflict (among investigators) will produce consensus. Peirce, who was the deepest thinker of the group, saw the problem and posited what he called "agapistic evolution," the notion that there was a benevolent "metaphysical" trend toward truth in science, that scientific truth was not just a lucky political agreement among the practitioners. The problem that Pierce solved in such a grand metaphysical way should give us some respect for Virchow. Despite all the courageous rhetoric of fallibilism and the continual change in science, we do regard change in science as *progressive*. Science is more than a consensus of fashion in physics. Finally, if we grant authority to science—and we grant it great authority—it is because there is a base of truth and certainty. Thomas Kuhn's seminal contribution, *The Structure of Scientific Revolutions*, has been read as if scientific revolutions were like aesthetic changes, variations in taste and fashion. It is an interpretation he was at some pains to reject. Einsteinian cosmology is a radical break from Newton; but, for all that, the truth of Newton—for example, gravitational calculations in local conditions—remain substantially accurate. Einstein's cosmology is broader and more comprehensive and can account for Newtonian mechanics. Einstein's theory constitutes *progress* in physics; there is no progress in fashion.

Baconianism is certainly wrong in its confinement of science to descriptive taxonomy. Science involves theory construction as well—indeed, theory construction is the more important aspect of science. But Baconians were correct in holding that somehow science must be grounded in verified truth. It is the power of verified results that gives authority to science, and in that sense Virchow also was correct that it is the basis of the freedom of science. One could, of course, base the freedom of science on the freedom we grant to taste. One is free to dress to fashion or not, adore or despise the current art scene. But we really do think that science is up to something more authoritative.

INFALLIBLE UNIVERSITY

If one circumvents the prevailing academic rhetoric either by historical perspective or a tad of analysis, one can discover if not an actually *infallible* university—that would be going too far—at least a university finally grounded on "certain" knowledge and a methodology of verification. At least this would be the case for the paradigm study of the modern university, natural science. I mentioned in the last chapter the controversy over cold fusion. In that instance, the physics community excluded the claims for cold fusion since such a process would have violated well-established physical law. However one might cast some shadow of tentativeness over physics, I am convinced that the investigation of cold fusion had more definitive weight than settling a squabble over the merits of the controversial "Sensation" show at the Brooklyn Museum, which featured Chris Offili's *Dung Madonnna*. Fallibilism about grand theory rests, I think, on two poles of "certainty." There is the certainty of observation at the beginning, and the postulated certainty to be attained by a consensus guided by agapistic evolution or some vague facsimile thereof. Empirical observation is given meaning by theory, but if the observation fails, the theory is in question. Einstein's predictions about the bending of light in strong gravitational fields awaited observation during a solar eclipse. The observation would have been idle were it not for the theory, but given the theory the observation had strong confirmatory powers.

I do not wish the trend of this argument to suggest in any way that the university is actually infallible; all the cautions about scientific progress are well taken. However, it is equally misleading to see the university fading into fashion. I am with the academic conservatives on this point—surely in the arena of the sciences at least. Science has *results* that seem to be as "true as true can be": the earth is round, the cosmos is vast, mosquitoes transmit malaria. If the claim about mosquitoes is not said to be infallible, that may be more a matter of intellectual taste rather than sober philosophy.

A further instance of the "infallibility" of science is the actual historical clash between science and religion. The classic conflicts (Galileo, Darwin) pitted the authoritative truth of science against the supposed truth of Scripture. It simply is true that the earth moves about the sun, not the other way round. It simply is true that species have evolved, that they were not created as is by God. One could say quite accurately that the quarrel was about what was infallible: scientific theory backed by observation or the Bible. The Bible loses.

Santayana said that historical writing was "myth corrected by further myth." One could on the basis of fallibilist rhetoric or its contemporary deconstructionist descendant think of the discourse of the university as a sort of ongoing myth making. In which case, I suppose, religious concerns could be just part of the mythological mix. But Santayana was being ironic when he said that myth "corrects" myth. Hardheaded scientists do not regard the Darwinian correction of Genesis as better "myth." One must admit that truth is the issue.

INFALLIBLE CHURCH

Having, I hope, resuscitated "Truth" (the motto of Harvard University), one must then give John Paul II credit for his concerns in the encyclical *Fides et Ratio*. The pope is duly and properly troubled about a universal slide toward mere fashion and away from a concern with truth. He is, of course, particularly concerned for the truth of faith and morals. But the university has its own established stake in the workings of *ratio:* it is not everyone to his or her own ethics and physics. In contrast to simple fallibilism, both physicists and popes seem to be back in the truth game.

The overall structure of my argument in this book is to differentiate the modes of truth cited in *Fides et Ratio*. As noted in chapter 2, Richard Bernstein criticized the confusion of "truths"referred to in the encyclical. If one turns to the question of "infallible" truth, one can only discuss fallibility/infallibility relative to the mode of "truth" being discussed. When it comes to matters of scientific "fact," it seems clear that science in either its Baconian or Peircian mode commands the field. No attestation from the Bible will carry any weight at all in the practice or development of science. Science has what one may call a "relative" infallibility over biblical truths.

If there is any sense at all to the notion of church infallibility, it must be in some area not covered by science lest it clash with the latter's achieved results or its ongoing methodology. Barring imperial science or imperious church, there should be no clash of "infallibilities."[4] The issue for the infallible church *vis-à-vis* the academy is whether the university circumscribes the total area of truth in either Baconian certitude or Peircian fallibilism. If one says that only scientifically observed empirical fact can be admitted into the legitimate academic discussion (Bacon), then church (along with art and morals) would be excluded, banished to a matter of political power, fashion, subjective emotion, or whatever. Baconianism places one "infallibility" in ascendency and denies alternate claimants. In contrast, Percianism denies infallibility on its face. It is not only the church that has it wrong about infallibility, science also has it wrong if it pursues a "quest for certainty." On either ground, church infallibility is rejected.

In the previous chapters I have attempted to discriminate the area in which Christianity properly asserts its truth: the realm of existential presence, "the real." This area falls outside the realm of science not because it is nonempirical but because, as observed, it escapes formulation. Science depends on conceptual formulation but, as Kant and half the philosophical tradition holds, "existence" is not a concept. To say that one hundred dollars *exists* adds nothing to the concept of a hundred dollars, though it can make a significant difference to one's bank account. That there is the sheer existent seems to be as empirical a truth as one could wish despite the inability to have a "concept" of existence. This innocent logical-seeming comment has been turned to lurid ends by twentieth-century existentialists and the anti-artists cited frequently above. In my discussion, existence has been equated with the sheer chaotic density of life, Henry James's "splendid waste," the mystic's overwhelming sense of grace. The essence of existence is to have no "essence," which is, however, more than palpable as a *totalizing* experience. One is not a conceptual spectator on existence. Rather one participates in existence, one is thrust into existence or has existential sense thrust upon one. Just as with the conceptual dollar and the existent dollar, I recognize the vastly important difference between my literary autobiography and my actual existence. The autobiography may go through fifteen editions; my life will not.

If it is the case that the Catholic claim for truth operates within the realm of "the real," there is a first-level "infallibility" to be noted that asserts *the truth of an existent presence beyond form and concept.* This is the existential *dogma.* The existent/"the real" is not something that admits of scientific verification or falsification. That "existent density exists" or "'the real' is real" is not a well-formed scientific claim like "the abominable snowman exists." "Verification" of the realm of the existent comes as a "revelation," as in Roquentin's sudden recognition of the density of life in the black roots of the chestnut tree (Sartre's *Nausea*). It is whatever "revelation" or "intuition" Ivan Ilych has when he becomes a participant in his own death. Revelation of the existent is not discovering a new fact; it is seeing what was already there before one's eyes in a new way. It is what we often mean when we say that we now *realize* something for the first time, like Ivan *realizing* the death he earlier had only abstractly known was his.

EVENT DISCLOSURE OF TRUTH

Revelation of "the real" seems to yield an infallible truth about life: "the real" is beyond science and art. What would one say to someone who seriously denied something like James's realm of "splendid waste"? The problem for infallibility in the Christian doctine of Revelation, the infallibility specifically claimed by the Catholic Church, is what can one *say* about the "how" of "the real." Christians and Jews—all the religious traditions—say something about the Ultimate, "effing the ineffable" as it were. They are not peculiar in this respect. If there is a first-level affirmation of the existentially dense, there seems to be an unavoidable propensity to "characterize" this realm despite the constitutional bar against conceptual or artistic formulation. After all, Sartre devotes pages to describing Roquentin's existential revelation in all its nauseous character. Mystics are no less prolific in writing about the ineffable.

The realm of existence may be just the seething chaos into which all human ideas and ideals dissolve—which is to say something "negative" about "the real." Christianity counterclaims that Revelation of the ultimate existent goes beyond nihilism. On the one hand, as a revelation of God, what is apprehended may be characterized as something like Meister Eckhart's "wilderness beyond Being," a realm in which all human aspirations and categories are radically questioned and relativized. Aquinas can properly say that his great philosophy is, in the light of such a revelation, "only straw." (Lacan characterizes this moment for Aquinas as the collapse of the symbolic before "the real." Aquinas might well have accepted that description.) But for all that the totalizing experience of God overwhelms human categories, for the Catholic believer the whole story from Creation to Covenant to the Christ reveals the Ultimate as in some sense *for us*, for something that is deep in the nature of being human. We do not recoil from existence into the clarity of science, the defiance or defense of art. We are urged to seize life, to accept suffering, minister to the lepers, care for the dying, and hold that Mercy outweighs our manifest limitations.

How can one assess and validate the varied claims about the character of ultimate existence? Is it rotting chaos, splendid waste, or redeeming grace? Do we ignore, curse, or thank when we are present to presence? Strictly speaking—that is, from the suppositions of scientific proof—there is no *method* for validating various characterizations of the existent. Sartre finds it horrible; mystics are transported with joy; Oliver Sacks, that most humane of therapists, says that there are times when he feels that there should be someone to thank for existence. One could, presumably, regard grumbling or gratitude as subjective traits, part of the delightful diversity of human emotions. The lapse into subjectivism is the only possible move if validation depends on the "objective" method of science. If there is to be a disciplined characterization of "the real," therefore, we must move to a different method. In religions the method is "revelation," whether it comes in a single moment of enlightenment like that of Prince Gautama or within a history as depicted in the Bible. Like the arts, revelation relies on historical moments, events, and authorities as the avenue for ordered assessment of the true and the sham.

The Cartesian/Enlightenment turn in the area of science and truth rejects any appeal to an historically given authority in favor of rational intuition, empirical observation, and the deductive process of mathematics. David Tracy spelled out the effect of Descartes's and the Enlightenment's "mathematical" method on the arts:

> This [Enlightenment] prejudice against pre-judgment disallows any experience of disclosure of truth by a work of art. In effect, Enlightenment prejudices have destroyed the truth disclosure of the work of art by removing its event character as a disclosure of truth. The work of art then becomes merely another object over and against an autonomous subject. . . . Eventually all judgments become matters of "taste."[5]

The "event character" of a work of art points to the fact that in art we depend on specific exemplars that happen to have been created as the standard for judgment of value. Instead of the "autonomous subject" exercising his or her idiosyncratic, immediate "taste" for the object at hand, one must, in appraising any work of art, assess it within the extant tradition of art: the authority of the already-valued exemplars. I reiterate what I said earlier: the fact that we depend upon extant exemplars in art does not necessarily make any particular exemplar indefeasible. That has been the mistake of the "beaux arts" tradition that sought to imitate, often literally, the "old masters." The method of authority rests on Tracy's "event character" of truth. There are exemplars and one comes to assess present against the extant, though it may well be that it is the past that is found to be defective in the light of the present. The method of authority creates and demands a dialogue of exemplars.

Art and religion both depend on the event disclosure of truth, although in art it falls short of providing what we take to be religious *conviction*. If one seeks to validate the *dogmatic*, the *infallible* sense of religions of which Catholicism is only one modality, the model of art is ultimately inappropriate. The splendid diversity of great artistic commentary on life from high comedy to bleak tragedy suggests that there is no resting point in our reactions to life. Religious believers' notorious intolerance suggests that there is something more fundamental (and more dangerous) at work than the multiple variations in artistic expression.

In the case of Christianity, Jesus is *the* event, *the* Revelation. Christians say that his life and death and resurrection are the fullness of God's Revelation. It is like saying that Shakespeare is *the* definitive poet. All poetry before and after is assessed relative to Shakespeare as the indispensable standard. There are certain titans of the arts whom one hardly believes can be degraded, but in recent avant-garde circles Rembrandt has been regarded as "hammy." *Sic transit gloria mundi*. No matter how lofty some extant "authority"/exemplar in art, his or her work may be diminished in the dialogue of exemplars that is inherent in the arts. Christians are not prepared to place their Lord in a dialogue of second thoughts.

DIGNITY AND THE DEFINITIVE

There is an obvious difference between the restlessness of art and the believer's "dogmatic" adherence to some definitive revelation. To grasp how Christians can regard the Revelation in Jesus as *definitive*, one must recall the basic Christian claim about "the real." Biblical religion holds that the *ultimate* category is the unique, the individual: an individual unique world of an individual God of Creation and the individual human being at hand. There is a *single* unique Creation; and the *single* unique person, Jesus, is claimed to be the measure, *the* Word of and for that Creation. Within a view of reality that validates radical uniqueness, my existent life becomes indispensable, unduplicable. My single life cannot be dissolved into the generic pool of genes or molecules. *Contra* the great myths of "eternal return" in other religious traditions, biblical reality is radically nonrepeatable. Finally, my *life* cannot be devalued in any dialogue or relationship with others. My art work is subject to such a dialogue of diminishment, not my self. My moral life is subject to appraisal for good or ill, yet I do not lose a fundamental dignity in that process. When we say that human beings have "God-given" rights it is not a mere rhetorical flourish, but is intended to place individual human dignity beyond the necessary and important appraisals of scientific acumen, artistic prowess, or moral character. There may be greater scientists than Newton, even Shakespeare may be surpassed; but no human as such can be surpassed in dignity. The claim that Jesus is unsurpassable and indispensable is an echo of—and for the believer the ground of—the unique dignity of each human being and the uniqueness of all of Creation. In short, I relate to my life in its unique, incomparable dignity; it is "the real" that I live within.

In contrast to my utter involvement with my *life*, the scientific mind may and should approach matters with a tentative air. Fallibilism about grand theory is in order. My best scientific hypothesis is open to testing and potential refutation. No matter how attached I am to my pet theory, *qua* scientist I can only rejoice in its refutation in the interest of scientific truth. The artistic mind is no less "open." In expressing my own powerful artistic vision, I do not "refute" other worthy works nor do I claim that my *oeuvre* is the end and fulfillment of art. My enthusiasm for Mondrian and minimalism does not mean that Botticelli should be sent to the basement. There is a rich and generous eclecticism in art that contrasts with the vituperative and destructive quarrels of religion. Attractive as the scientific and artistic mindsets may be in their tentativeness and open character, they are nevertheless problematic as *life* positions. Both science and art maintain a spectator's view of life; it is their glory and their limitation. It is immensely valuable to stand back from the sheer buzz of things to assess and appraise, but the question is whether in the long run we can (or ought to be) mere spectators on our own lives.

The most direct way of noting a limitation of the science or art as a *life* stance would be to see what happens to something like loving commitment under such conditions. Assuming I am a determined scientist, courageously willing to test any and all hypotheses, I turn to my marriage. Each morning I spend at least one hour scrupulously reviewing the pros and cons of the relationship. I even call in my associate, Professor Iago, to check and verify my love. So far each of these experimental sessions has confirmed my initial conjecture. But at bottom there really is no loving commitment here; regarding marriage as a continuously reviewed and tested hypothesis is precisely to deny the reality of the commitment. One could conjure a similar scenario of an artist who arises each morning to see whether her marriage conforms to some shapely expressive mode. The artist awakes like Madame Bovary into fiction, not into life. What does one do with the toothbrush in the sink, the proverbial burnt toast of life? (If you are an underground artist, you paste the toast to the canvas to note the difference between life and art!)

Noting the limitation of science and art when it comes to something like loving commitment is not to say that love and marriage are not subject to appraisal. The difference is that when such a commitment is rejected or broken, it is a life catastrophe. Wittgenstein says "the world of the happy and the unhappy are two entirely different worlds." The angry man lives in an angry world. Nothing works. The world of the happy man is different, though there are no special "facts" that make it happy. It is a matter of seeing the world *as* angry, *as* happy, *as* reflecting love. To lose love, to have love betrayed, does not change some fact *in* the world, it changes the whole world, the "boundaries" of the world. And the world is *my* world, my radical and unique grasp upon existence.

One does not regard the loss of love as a failed hypothesis or like a change of artistic interest from surrealism to abstract expressionism. In love one is a full participant in life, mine and thine. Love is not a spectator sport. Loss of love means that one is a different participant in the whole, in the world. There is a *definitiveness*, an *infallibility* about life as a participant event. The beliefs that I hold about myself as lover and my beloved are not everlastingly up in the theoretical air. I am unprepared to even consider proof of her infidelity. The "infallibility" of the beliefs entailed in deep commitment is revealed by the shattering of self that occurs when such commitments are betrayed and fail. Science and art dwell in their respective and appropriate tentativeness, but it is clear that one cannot and should not be tentative about one's own life and loves. Otherwise one would be an everlasting J. Alfred Prufrock, unable or unwilling to ask any "overwhelming question" because, presumably, in life there is "no great matter."

It is characteristic of religion to claim definitive commitment rather than to postpone a view of life pending scientific certainty or because of the need to be open to the newest turn in art. The philosopher John Smith rightly remarked that when the angels appeared over the stable in Bethlehem they did not say, "Behold I have brought you a topic for discussion." In the long run and deep down, I do not look on my life as a topic for discussion. Life-as-a-participant demands something more than tentative hypotheses. A dedicated scientist is not tentatively dedicated to tentativeness. When someone asked the great Kekulé what was his religion, he said "chemist."

I can see no way around the issue of infallibility. As a direction toward ultimate life commitment, Christianity as a religion does not offer a "topic for discussion." Infallibility of some sort comes with the religious territory; it is not a quirk of Catholicism. But if the religious turn transcends tentativeness, claims definitive, infallible certainty, and evokes commitment, one could certainly ask *which* religion? Should I be a Catholic or a Chemist? Religions and deep philosophies confront the problem of "the real"—the density of existence—and inevitably characterize that "experience." Even if "the real" is said to be waste or wilderness, it is characterized. Given the "incomprehensible" character of existence, the anti-artist's *chaotic* vitality, one connects to "the real" only by "revelation." The various religious, artistic, and philosophic "accounts" of the existent are in one sense like the exemplars of art. We must enter into these exemplars, consider them as revelations, and assess whether what they reveal conforms to our experience of life-as-lived.

The weighing of religious exemplars differs from the appraisal of art in that it is a fully participant appraisal. I can be an art connoisseur, but it is not clear that I ought to be a connoisseur of religion (or my life). When I enter into the great religious exemplars, I am compelled toward fundamental life choice. The characterization of the existent offered by those who have confronted and entered into "the real" is inherently valuable and one should cherish the "masterpieces" of religion with as much respect as one gives the great works of art. Religious masterpieces like the anti-art works make present "the real" when for matters of decorum we would just as soon not. Having been faced with "existence" we are not allowed the luxury of taste. More important and more controversial is the fact that we cannot be open to revelation without some already-present sense of need and commitment; religious masterpieces can be apprehended only from a stance of life vulnerability. We do not start or stand as connoisseurs, we stand "in fear of the Lord." "The real" then compels a life choice even if that choice is to flee in horror and disgust. When it comes to the clear choices among the great religious masterpieces, we are, perhaps disastrously, compelled to have our Yeas be Yea and our Nos, No.

A minimal condition of appropriation of a religious disclosure is the recognition by the viewer that he is in a particpatory event or experience. In chapter 6, I described how a young Jewish girl was undone at Yad Vashem through a sense of direct participation in the depiction of the Holocaust. She was called *by name*, and as a Jew was a participant in the very history depicted. The shock of pop art is that we already "participate" as consumers with Campbell's soup and Brillo boxes. In the case of the Gospel stories, a believer should sense his name being called as surely as the young girl at the Holocaust memorial. For the Gospel call, one must be in some sense a participant in a life under judgment for good and evil, a life of love and loss, abandonment, betrayal, death, and hope. To be sure, one may not be paying attention. There are idle tourists at Yad Vashem just as there are tourists through life and the Gospel. The Gospel stories, like holy icons, may just seem slightly weird and quite outside any present experience I might have. All those miracle stories and doves descending—fascinating stuff, perhaps, but not part of *my* life.

Having noted the necessity for *participatory* reading, I suspect that my argument already has a definite Christian cast. At least one could decide between being a Catholic or a Chemist. To a Christian the answer would be clear enough. The problem with the religion of Chemistry is that it adopts as a stance toward life the position of the transcendent observer. It is Platonism or Stoicism. The Stoics were not into life *participation*. For the Stoic, the position of the spectator (philosophic, scientific, artistic) was just the life stance that should be chosen. Their characterization of the existent was that it was a place of pain and confusion to be transcended by taking a more universal and cosmopolitan view. As for loving commitment, the Stoics, while not as bizarre as my marriage hypothecator, did suggest staying "loose" to such relations. Thus Epictetus:

> [I]f you kiss your child, or brother, or friend, never allow your imagination to range at large, nor allow your exultation to go as far as it will, but pluck it back, keep it in check. . . . [R]emind yourself that you love a mortal, and that nothing you love is your very own; it is given you for the moment, not forever or inseparably, but like a fig or a bunch of grapes at the appointed season of the year, and if you long for it in winter you are a fool. . . . What harm is there in whispering to yourself as you kiss your child, "Tomorrow you will die."[6]

The *rhetoric* of my argument about the need to participate in life is already on the other side of the Stoic option and into at least some shadow of Christian thought. The central Christian story of "the real" (God) immersed in the travail of flesh and body and death runs directly counter to the Stoic sense that "the real" is utterly transcendent to flesh and body and death. For the Stoic, participating in *life* is participating in *death*, and that is a threat to the tranquil mind. The Christian revelation of "the real" in the figure of a crucified Jesus presents a different life option than the revelation of "the ideal" presented in Stoicism.

How would one decide between the two—not to mention a host of other deep life choices? It is impossible in a sense to answer that question from some transcendent height because we are *vole nole* always, already involved in some life stance even if that stance is one of flight or distraction. (Malebranche said that "attention is the natural prayer of the soul." Lots of people are not paying much attention, *ergo* not much praying.) Appraising and choosing how one should participate in one's life cannot pretend to the neutral stance of the scientific critic or the artistic judge; we are already *in* life in some fashion that precludes such studied neutrality. Or, if we are in the mode of studied neutrality, we may see no reason to give up the freedom of appraisal for the chanciness and choice of life lived. People change or adopt religious life choices because they get knocked off a horse on the way to some other life destiny. Some God fails and another is born—or God dies once and for all. That at least is the dramatic course of conversions, and it is certainly true that people have either come to faith or despair by catastrophic life events.

I believe I have properly characterized Christianity and all the great religions by noting that they do not bring us a "topic for discussion." Put that way, one can see why the academy today has problems with religion, for much of the life of the university, at least in its modern configuration, centers around the discussion of this or that topic. In the days of the nineteenth-century denominational academies, classes were canceled every year for a week of religious revival; a *decision* for Christ was considered essential to the educational mission. The only modern equivalent that I have experienced was the week that classes were canceled after the shootings at Kent State so that students could make a decision for war or peace. When the academy in its commitment to fallibilism and everlasting discussion comes to the problem of religion (or of war and peace), it faces a deep paradox. Assuming that the matter of *religious* decision— that is, positing oneself relative to the existent—is genuine enough, how does one avoid distorting this arena of life and experience into a "topic for discussion?" The decision to avoid, deny, or flee from "the real" is itself a profound life position. The question raised by "the real" seems to be of such fundamental importance and seriousness that relegating it to taste, to the subjective, or to emotional temper seems as wrong headed as leaving physics to fashion. The issue seems grave enough to require "truth." Perish the thought that I should follow a "false" God!

A first problem for the university, then, might be legitimating the very *idea* of life commitment. One clear virtue of Catholic universities past was the presence within the life of the institution of life commitment. In former days this reality of commitment was conveyed by the presence of the sponsoring religious order. Michael Harrington mentions in an autobiographical writing how he was affected by the presence of the Jesuits at the College of the Holy Cross. They represented commitment to a way of life. Whether they individually or collectively met the demands of that way was not the issue as much as their visible commitment as priests and religious. The carrying out of the academy's ongoing discussion as part of the visible presence of life decision suggests a weight to the enterprise that might otherwise be invisible. The people who sponsored the place had, it seemed, faced "the real" and chosen a way. The university's "owners" did not *live* in the ivory tower.

If Jesuits in soutane were a visible proof of the "legitimacy" of life commitment in Catholic universities, it is not clear just how the secular university regards "vocation." Insofar as the university describes and assesses the range of human experience, one of the more peculiar quirks of humankind does lie in a taste for a series of interlocking notions: vocation, total commitment, infallible truth, absolute trust. From the standpoint of fallibilism one could regard this human trait as a methodological mistake. A strict academic might offer psychological and sociological explanations for fanaticism and bigotry. Such analyses are paradoxical if the analyst is as heroically dedicated as Freud to science, but they may well be criticized simply because they reduce by pathologization what many people consider the most profound human experiences. If, on the other hand, the university chooses not to exclude this range of human experience either by constricting its scope to pure science as in a technical institute, by some methodological exclusion like fallibilism, or by pathologization of "absolute commitments," just what treatment can the university in its methods and practices give to "the infallible"?

FALLIBLE CHURCH

In defending the *infallible* in its "proper" place, two crucial qualifications are necessary. The first concerns the fallibility of infallibility. Life commitment, unquestioning loyalty, and belief are high-risk undertakings. The risk is high because it is precarious. We are not to rush to commitment just to avoid being a distant spectator on life's passing show. We do not want to devote our life to a false cause, a false lover, a false god. Given the frailty of causes and lovers and the plethora of false gods, one is properly alert, wary, concerned. Kierkegaard was correct to say that faith is always "over ten thousand fathoms." Faith is never *grounded* in the sort of demonstrative surety that we can demand from science or even the careful assessments of art. Faith with its "infallible" commitment is thus highly paradoxical. On the one hand it is absolute, firm, the center of my very life; on the other hand it exists on the border of utter failure and collapse—"drowning" if one follows Kierkegaard's metaphor. Given the precariousness of infallible faith, it is clear that in a university setting one could hardly go about demanding simple conformity of "doctrine."

The second problem with infallible faith is how it is expressed in the Catholic Church, for example, in "official" doctrines and decrees, the rulings of Roman authorities, the infallibility of the pope. There are profound problems with such official pronouncements. Baron von Hugel commented after the Vatican I declaration of papal infallibility: "The council may have made the

Pope infallible, but they did not make him intelligible." Church statements are about "the real," the All-in-All, and thus in the strictest sense "beyond sense," beyond conceptual form and thus not "intelligible." The conflict between infallible church and fallible university is really a conflict between conceptual clarity and mystery. In what sense can an "unintelligible" dogma—for example, the "myth"/ mystery of Resurrection—conflict with the quite intelligible facts of science and history? How can the proclamation of a mystery intersect with a declaration of fact?

My argument has been that the "dogmas" of the Christian church are *iconic* presentations. Icons, if they work at all, are in some sense "infallible." There is no way that the art produced by the children in the concentration camps, as iconic, can lie about the horror that was experienced. Indeed, it is the very failure of art as depiction that conveys the full reality of the situation. In making present the reality of the event, the icon is primary and privileged, beyond contradiction and failure. But iconic infallibility is clearly *not* descriptive literalness. When the church presents its iconic reality, it necessarily presents "mystery." This mystery is not mumbo-jumbo, however; it is presentation of a reality that eludes fixed comprehension because of the participation of the viewer/believer.

It is difficult to construct a contradiction between the iconic infallibility of church dogmas like Resurrection and the "scientific" fallibility enshrined in university research and scholarship. A partial explanation of the conflicts between church teaching and ordinary teaching—scientific and historical fact— occurs as the *other* side of the iconic. Icons are, after all, *depictions* of a sort. An icon is not the reality itself, but a depiction that *participates* in the reality. As a depiction the subject matter of the icon may take on a life of its own and lose its iconic status. If the Eucharist is an iconic presence of Jesus, that is, a *real* participation in the Lord and holiness, one should not then dissect the host to discover its DNA or analyze the wine for a proper blood type. Sentimental piety and sceptical critics thrive on extrapolating from depiction toward ever more destructive literalism. Recall Wittgenstein's injunction: "The whole weight is in the picture." If we take Michelangelo's Sistine ceiling as a picture of God's creation, the weight is in the *relation:* a drowsy "Adam" and a force full "God."

More important in explaining the presumed clash of faith and fact is that, in affirming the central realities of Christian faith, one implies or strongly suggests numerous secondary claims. One may move outward to a host of derivative claims that are attached with greater and lesser immediacy to the central

reality of God-with-us. There is no need to block or discourage these derivative truths. If the Revelation in Jesus is Salvation itself, then it obviously reaches
into every aspect of life lived. The issue is the infallibility of those derivative
truths. The claims and postulates that fill the more than four hundred pages of
the new *Catechism of the Catholic Church* certainly do have a connection to the
fact of Jesus as present, the iconic infallibility of church and sacrament. But the
connection is not geometrical and deductive; a catechism of such length is an
interpretation not unlike that made of a literary work. Interpretations are not exercises in theological casuistry ending with Q.E.D. They range from the sensitive to the academic, the deep to the shallow, the central to the curious: Jesus is
"God"; God knows everything; Jesus is the greatest scientist of all times. The
theologians of Salamanca held that Jeus was the "greatest dialectician, philosopher, mathematician, doctor, politician, musician, orator, painter, farmer,
sailor, soldier, etc."[7] Well, no! Absoluteness of interpretation is a dangerous
enterprise. At the opening of Vatican II, the curial officials announced that the
assembled bishops were expected to take the Oath against Modernism, which
clearly was an *interpretation* of Christianity relative to certain notions like
higher biblical criticism, political liberalism, and the like. The bishops refused,
saying that the Apostle's Creed would be quite sufficient. Sometimes the Holy
Spirit arrives at just the right moment.

The central Revelation is an *essential mystery* and thus it is difficult to see
how the church's iconic presentation of the mystery—principally in the sacrament—or the *magisterium*'s derivative interpretations of that mystery can be
brought into definitive conflict with the truths that are the ordinary business of
the university. Indeed, in a paradoxical reversal of the normal rhetoric, it is the
scientific truths in the university that are thought to be definitive while many
church beliefs are considered, for better or worse, "interpretations," with all
the open texture that interpretation always implies. In terms of academic freedom for a Catholic university, it would seem that the space is relatively open for
varied statements on Christian doctrine with whatever checks on interpretation ordinarily prevail. This means that there will be sober interpretations and
ones that are far fetched. Someone claims that Jesus had a love affair with the
Magdalene, or that he was gay. No evidence, of course. Is the claim false? It is
certainly far fetched. One might put it into the "undecidable" category and let
ideological speculation spin out. If, however, the intent of the claim is to deny
the centrality of the Father in Jesus's life and the universality of Jesus' concern
for all in and through centering his life on God, then the claim is not *de fide*, of
the Faith, and would properly be rejected.

These reflections return to the problem of the church as teacher, the *magisterium* of the visible institution. Up to now, I have insisted on the radical difference between Christ as the Truth, Christ as the Teaching, and the iconic, sacramental way this is worked out in the liturgical and worshipful life of the church. The first and fundamental act of the church is to manifest the real presence of the Lord. Basically and finally, Christianity is an Easter faith or it is nothing. Paul was right. But, of course, this risen Lord was also the Jesus of history who delivered specific teachings and lived a life of compassion and sacrifice. It would seem only natural and appropriate to underpin these teachings with the proclamation of Resurrection. It is argued by some that one so favored of God as is this Jesus in Resurrection must have delivered God's definitive teaching in his active life. So if he said no divorce, then God must intend that there be no divorce. Jesus' words in the Gospel thus receive an absolute stamp of approval and constitute the message to be taught. Such a position seems a fair characterization of Gospel fundamentalism, and often sounds like the voice of the Roman *magisterium*—despite the fact that Catholicism is clearly not scripturally fundamentalist.

This claim for authority in the message of Jesus' ministry is not all wrong. It is important that the Resurrected One preached a message *for us.* However, the degree of surety that can be applied to specific commandments and injunctions from the "message" inevitably falls short of the infallible—what I would be willing to stake my life on.

There are various reasons for caution. Higher criticism raises serious questions about the authenticity of various texts. Such doubts are scientific in the same manner as one may doubt the authenticity of any ancient text, for example, Plato's letters. While it is certainly understandable that the Resurrection would be retrojected over the life and message of Jesus, there is the obvious danger that such retrospective insight distorts as much as it reveals. Did the historical Jesus ever declare himself Messiah? Did he actually foresee his fate at the hands of the authorities? It is one thing to evaluate a preaching of love and a sacrificial death as God-with-us, it is another thing entirely to say that Jesus himself regarded his actions through the lens of Resurrection. Such an interpretation is not only scientifically and historically dubious—people just don't have such foresight—but such views teeter on the brink if they do not actually fall into the pit of docetism, the theological heresy that denies the true humanity of Jesus. Docetism holds that the "historical" Jesus was only an "appearance" of God—God in disguise—and as such of course knew exactly what would happen just as the actor in a play knows how the final act will play out.

Docetism trivializes the historical Jesus and his status as one who shares our life. It is not God-with-us; it seems he was only paying a visit.

The fundamental problem, however, with pervasive infallibility of the Gospel preaching is the logic of *an event disclosure of truth*. The Christian "message" is a *signatured* truth: "I, Jesus, am the Truth." (Even if this is a retrojected statement in the mouth of the historical Jesus, it would be in the light of Resurrection a proper evaluation of that historical career. This was not, it turns out, just another prophet, this was God-with-us.) An event disclosure of truth is essentially historical; for all that it reveals truth, it is offered within the structures and assumptions of the historical time. Mozart could not have composed for a Steinway; Rembrandt could not clothe his Gospel figures in shirt and tie. In assessing and appraising any event disclosure of truth, there is always a tension between the materials or forms available to the artist and the message expressed through them. Utterly ignoring the conventions of Shakespeare's stage is foolish, but mere historical reconstruction of the Globe and its performance practices may obfuscate the essential. Is Christianity improved by returning to the practice of the first-century church, or is the continuing power of the message stifled by historical literalism?

In an event disclosure of truth, separating the embedded forms of the time from the continuing message is no easy task and conforms to no mechanical rules. Thus, in the controversial issue of women priests, how does one sort out the obvious historical fact of first-century Palestine—that no one in the Jewish community would have understood the notion of woman-priest (it would have been like a woman-father)—from the permanent theological reflection that all humans (women included) share the *imago dei?* To acknowledge that the problem of translating the truth embedded in an event disclosure is difficult, however, is not to lapse into subjectivism and caprice. We return again to the method of authority. Just as a history of assessment and appraisal creates a canonic body of exemplars against which we judge the value of present offerings of art, so the history of Christian commentary, theology, liturgy, and so on takes on an authoritative weight in assessing the essential Gospel message. The existence of a *magisterium* as the locus of historically funded authorities is in some sense a necessity. Without an ongoing, recognized history of canonic discussion, there would be no event disclosure of *truth*, that is, there would be nothing that would have weight in accepting or rejecting any single event as genuinely disclosive. One could not argue for women priests at all were it not for the tradition of *imago dei* or St. Paul's injunction that in Christ there is neither male or female.

Insofar as the Roman *magisterium* operates from such funded commentary, it's pronouncements have solemn weight. But this method of authority is fundamentally—if not fatally—cast within the event disclosure of truth, which means it can never come to the definitive closure available to scientific proof. It is science that can be infallible—the earth *is* round—while church pronouncements from authority are essentially revisable if not utterly fallible. But what is also "infallible," as I suggested at the beginning of the chapter, is the iconic presence of Christ in and as the church. Iconic presence is, however, a very different sort of truth from either scientific description, direct moral injunction, or the interpretive language we adopt for the central mysteries—for example, Aristotelian *transubstantiation* as *the* formula for the Eucharistic presence. To put the point most paradoxically, in the matter of the Christian message, what is *infallible* escapes the definitive (description, von Hugel's "intelligibility"), what is definitive (describable, intelligible) escapes infallibility.

What does this argument about the authority of the *magisterium* suggest for the actual reality of a Catholic university? The general principles should be clear enough. In the proper arena of infallibility there is a disconnect between the iconic truth presented by the church and the sort of scientific and scholarly truth conveyed in the ordinary life of the university. The point of juncture between church and university is focused on the existential "dogma" stated or implied for university truth. This is by no means a trivial consideration, since it underlies the importance and meaning of "the life of the mind" as it relates to the given historical existence of humanity—including the humans who are students and professors. Meditation on the proper existential dogma may have far-reaching effects on the manners, morals, pride, and pretension of the university. It will certainly affect the role of theology or, more neutrally, the study of first and last things as part and parcel of the educational task most broadly conceived. An institute of technology may have no truck with theology and its course on thermodynamics will diminish not a degree thereby. However, a Catholic university will hold that the event disclosure of truth is vastly important and that the Bible sets forth a powerful claim on first and last things. To neglect this deep human issue would be inappropriate. Further, the claim upon us of first and last things is hopelessly emptied if framed simply in the normal academic mode of ongoing inquiry. I may postpone writing the conclusion to my latest book until I get enough data and have reviewed various interpretations of other experts. What I cannot postpone is my life; it demands an existential dogma—even if at some later date the dogma fragments.

In the following two chapters, I want to make the arguments so far presented as concrete and specific as possible. Thus in the next chapter I offer a "thought experiment" that imagines a "Holocaust University." By imagining what might be involved in a university that remembers the Holocaust, my hope is to clarify what might be involved in specifically Christian "remembrance." In the following chapter I take a direct look at the most recent controversy surrounding the relation between the Catholic Church and the university as it has developed from the papal proclamation *Ex Corde Ecclesiae*.

8

A Thought Experiment: A Holocaust University

In order to advance the discussion of what Catholicism (Christianity) may add to the "normal"—at least prevailing—assumptions about universities, I want to offer what Einstein called a "thought experiment." Instead of a Catholic university, I intend to sketch a fictional "Holocaust university." If one understands and accepts what might be involved in such an imaginary enterprise, it may be possible to discover the conceptual tools and explicit structures that would be appropriate for a Catholic university.

Suppose that the Jewish community comes to regard the Holocaust as a marker for its history. Clearly this is not hard to imagine. Indeed, the diligent effort to preserve the memory of the Holocaust in memorials, museums, and ceremonies of remembrance suggests that, at least for the present, the Holocaust actually is such a central marker for the Jewish people. But push this supposition one step further; not only is the Holocaust *a* marker, it is regarded as *the* marker of Jewish experience. One sums up a universal sense of Jewish history from the Holocaust experience: history is a dangerous place;

one must be vigilant to ensure that the ever-present threat of destruction does not materialize. The lesson of traditional Judaism is only slightly different. History is a dangerous place from which one is rescued only by the almighty hand of God who chooses this people for his own. For traditional Judaism it is the historical event of the Exodus that is the paradigm for Jewish experience.

One could be universalist in regarding Jewish history. In the interpretation of many rabbis, Exodus is not the special marker only for the Jewish people. Because it is *God's* great action in history, it is *the* marker for all humanity. Even without a theological dimension, one could come to regard the Holocaust as a universal marker for human history. The Holocaust is only the most recent and visible manifestation of the nightmare of history from which James Joyce's Stephen Dedalus hoped to awake. Holocaust Jews are prophets and witness to pervasive "sin" in human history.

Is there any warrant for claiming some particular historical occurrence (Holocaust, Exodus) as *the* paradigm for history? One might counter that there are lots of historical occurrences and that settling on some single event or set of events as the central truth of history is overly restrictive and mistaken. Whether it is the Holocaust or the Exodus, the flowering of the arts in Florence, or the French Revolution, history is full of striking events. Why should one regard a memory of destruction as *the* paradigm rather than, say, the presumed triumph of democracy signified by the fall of the Berlin Wall? There is no easy answer to that question. It is, of course, characteristic of religions to offer an overriding paradigm or story as *the* key to existence: Exodus, the Buddha's recognition of suffering and death, the Crucifixion.

One could grant special indulgence to contemporary Jews for regarding the Holocaust as *the* paradigm event from which they understand their present position in the world. It could be the ground of everything from the Israeli defense policy to preaching in the local synagogue. But must everyone have a synoptic view of history? There may be a logical problem in answering "no." To deny synoptic history one looks on human existence as a great jumble of ups and downs, tragedy and farce. But that itself seems to be a synoptic claim. John Hick created a parable of two men traversing a countryside together. On the road they meet various adventures—some painful, others pleasant. One of the travelers holds that the country is under the control of a great prince and that the adventures they experienced are all tests that will be explained when they arrive at the city ahead. The other traveler believes no such thing. There is just the road and the succession of events good and bad. There is no great prince and the road does not end in the city of his rule. The second traveler takes no single experience as a marker of the journey—and yet the view that life is an ever-changing tumult of days constitutes a synoptic claim by which the journey is to be understood—or is not understandable, as the case may be.[1]

In Hick's working out of the parable there seems to be no way from the daily evidence that one could decide the issue between the two. The meaning or meaninglessness of this history will be determined only in the future. Both travelers have a "philosophy of history" that fits the facts at hand. (Hick argues that the first traveler will be proved correct when they arrive at the great city— "heaven" in the Christian tale. It is not clear what would disprove the Christian supposition since there would be no future state from which to judge.) But Hick may not have considered all the possible travelers. If there was a traveler who was a Holocaust survivor, he might well claim that there had already been an experience "on the road" that was so cataclysmic that it defined, colored, and qualified the entire journey. One need not wait for some proof at the *end* of the journey; already there has been a "revelation" on the road that defined the everyday.

I think one can give at least a psychological warrant to certain claims for discovering *the* marker for history in and among the tangles of joy and terror that make up individual and collective history. Elie Wiesel, for example, has taken his experience as a child in Auschwitz and Buchenwald as the defining experience of his own life. It would be unseemly if not cruel to try to persuade him or any other Holocaust survivor to take some other, happier moment as the historical marker. Suggesting that Wiesel consider balancing the evil of the Holocaust alongside some array of positive goods achieved in art or morality is equally shortsighted: there is something in the nature of *this* suffering that admits no compensation, no balance or deflection through visions of glory or goodness. This view applies as well to the expectation for the future: explanation/compensation in the city of the prince, in heaven. Ivan, in *The Brother's Karamazov*, places cruelty practiced on children at the center of reality. One cannot turn away from the suffering of children to happier vistas; it is for Ivan *the* puzzle of existence and reason enough to reject God, to "turn in his ticket." His experience "on the road" (the suffering of children) is paradigmatic for the whole journey such that he would refuse to enter the city of the great prince were it to be revealed over the final hill.

The situation of Elie Wiesel is not idiosyncratic. The Holocaust has an inescapable effect on the subsequent lives of all those who survived it, an effect that cannot be overcome. Wiesel says in one of his biographical writings that he resisted the very idea of having children, of bringing new life into a world haunted by the guilt and threat of the Holocaust. His love for his wife persuaded him otherwise, but any Holocaust survivor must look on the life of his or her child with a mixture of wonder and fear.

Let us suppose, then, that a community deeply defined by the Holocaust establishes a place of higher learning, a university. As the lives of the survivors' children will be cast under the marker of the Holocaust, so with the university that is established. Just as one would seek to personally educate one's children in "the lessons" of the Holocaust, so one would want the university to know this truth. A Holocaust university would be set within the parameters of a specific history that was destructive and whose threat and meaning perdures.

But what of the scholars within? Could they, like the Stoics of old, look with contempt upon the wreck of history and say that ascent to truth transcends the ruin of fortune. There is something profound and noble in that attitude, as there is in Socrates' transcendence of the executioner's poison cup. Such an attitude, however, is an unacceptable and impossible elitism of intellect. The eminence and depth of their scholarship could no more isolate them from the ravages and threats of that remembered history than it protected earlier scholars from destruction in the death camps. Part of the shock of the Nazis' "solution" for cultural and cultured Jews was that they were regarded by their persecutors to be no better than the meanest refugee from the poorest *shtetl*. If the Holocaust university exists within the lesson of the Holocaust, my supposition would be that it could not regard itself as a retreat from history, an ark of salvation-through-intellect. There would be no physical "salvation" by attested scholarship, and it would be an arrogance of intellect to think that the scholar was granted superiority to history over the ignorant peasant—not to mention the children destined for destruction to whom high learning would never be a possibility.

The Holocaust university would, then, express *the life meaning of scholarship* within the parameters of the Holocaust. The framing lesson of the institution might be stated as "the suffering of the innocent." (As stated, this seems all too cool and bland to muffle the anguish and cries of the slaughtered, but "credal" statements are always lamely insufficient. The believer who recites "I believe in God" passes off the statement as if it could match the agonized spirit of Jeremiah or the transports of St. Theresa.) The practical import of that Holocaust lesson would be to do whatever research and learning might do to guard against the terror of history. Moreover, insofar as the lesson is the suffering of the innocent, it would caution the university against believing either in its physical isolation from destruction or in some spiritual elitism over history.

To be a member of the Holocaust university, one would be expected to accept the framing reality. This would be no place for Holocaust deniers. More complex would be the place within the Holocaust university of those—faculty particularly—who opted for a different historical marker as a framing reality. Even more complicated would be the status of those who opted for no overriding historical marker, regarding history as something like Derrida's array of diverse choreographies. (The last category would, as indicated above, nevertheless reflect a synoptic view of history: a jumble sale.) Just how would a *Holocaust* university deal with deniers, dissenters, and diversity advocates?

The question obviously touches upon the issue of academic freedom, though in a restricted area. There need be no impingement on the obvious work of the academy; physics goes on its way as always. The framing Holocaust assumption only convicts physics (physicists) of sin—and sin says nothing about quarks and the Noble Eight Fold Path (the physics version, not the Buddhist.) But a university founded and sustained by a Holocaust community (survivors, descendants, the larger Jewish community) would legitimately impose certain limitations on the university. The clear case would be the Holocaust denier. It is the easy case since it appears to even "neutral" observers that the Holocaust actually occurred. Appointing a Holocaust denier to the history department would be like appointing an advocate of Creationism to the biology faculty, or a UFO specialist to the astrophysics department. Sheer academic competence would settle that issue.

What about someone who accepts that there is a marker for history, but that the Holocaust is not that marker? Here the issue is tangled. Just what would be involved in such a "dissent"? Is it clear that it really denies the defining character of the Holocaust? Would a Jewish believer in the Exodus as *the* marker be excluded? It might seem so on the face of it, but the Exodus believer may hold that Exodus in some fashion *includes* the event of Holocaust, that one only understands the *miracle* of Exodus against the implacable and inexplicable suffering of the Holocaust—as well as the persecutions and pogroms that have marked diaspora Judaism. The "dissenter" in this case accepts the special marker of suffering, yet holds that within suffering there is still a rescuing hand.

Again, this may seem to be an easy enough case to state, but is is very hard to realize. The Holocaust survivor may well think that any scenario of "rescue" fails. Ivan Karamazov will accept no recompense or rescue for the suffering of children. For the Holocaust victim, there is a defining depth to that suffering that will not be diminished, that resists amelioration. Any attempt to subsume it under an "Exodus" scenario risks softening a shattering past. The "logic" or "psycho-logic" of the Holocaust victim seems impregnable. All one can say is that, within a Holocaust university, the one who offers some *other* paradigmatic history must be cautioned that this new paradigm cannot really diminish or de-center the Holocaust. In the *Brothers Karamazov* there is no "refutation" of Ivan's rejection of God; the saintly Alyosha merely kisses his brother.

Given the special and present historical circumstance of the Jewish community, one might, then, grant special authority to the Holocaust in setting parameters for academic reality. No Holocaust deniers; no alternative paradigms that diminish the remembered anguish of the community. (It should be noted that the "logic" of a paradigm experience could be centered in a wholly opposite fashion: an individual or group may have such an overwhelming experience of "rescue" or life-affirming "joy" that no counterevidence of desperation, suffering, and terror could diminish that marker.)

The most difficult case for the Holocaust university and its "logic" would be that of the "diversity" advocate. Again it depends on how diversity is proclaimed. Take the case of the Derridean dance. One might interpret the diverse dances of history as variations on a theme. In actual present-day universities, diversity is often a variation on the theme of "victim." The diverse experiences brought forward tend to be those of groups who have been excluded or oppressed from mainstream study: women, people of color, gays. There is little interest—well, a negative interest—in studying the folk ways of car sales*men* or corporate CEOs. If, then, diversity is intended to lay claims for the experience of victims, the Holocaust could be arrayed within the diversity. But this solution would be unstable if not wholly unsatisfactory. One can imagine strong claimants asserting that *their* suffering is incomparable and should by no means be arrayed with that of others. Thus there is a significant continuing debate about the *unique* character of the Jewish Holocaust. What about the slaughter of the Armenians, ethnic cleansing in Serbia, genocide in Rwanda? Individual witnesses within a group will testify to the immediacy of an experience that they judge cannot be properly compared and arrayed with that of the others. "You had to have been there!" "You don't *know* what it is like to be a woman/black/gay!"

If, on the other hand, a diversity paradigm only expresses life as a great tumble high and low, up and down, good and bad, *panta rhei* (everything changes), the Holocaust university may overtly and consciously reject it. No, something *has* happened that unalterably colors human experience. Life is not a delightful dance of diversity; like the comic performance of the gatekeeper in *Macbeth*, laughter is enclosed in the final night of tragedy. The diversity advocate lacks the "spirit of seriousness" (or the "spirit of irony") that is the existential framework of the Holocaust university. To be sure, he may be an excellent academic performer, brilliant teacher, and researcher whose work does not apparently impinge upon the existential frame of the university and vice versa: a sense of Holocaust does not control organic chemistry. If, on the other hand, a diversity philosopher speaks directly to the issue of a synoptic view of history, if she rejects the notion that any moment of history can be given overriding and perduring importance, or if she projects some counterparadigm as *the* moment in history, then the issue of "academic freedom" will arise.

Before elaborating on how this confrontation might develop, it is important to note that the quarrel here is not the usual academic dispute. The issue is not whether this or that theory or conjecture can be asserted by marshaling academic warrants. The quarrel is about the character of the university, the *meaning* of history, and the placement of the university in history. To the extent that university argument depends on a certain abstraction, transcendence, or neutrality of the inquirers, this Holocaust "argument" re-places individuals into their historical concreteness. Imagine a diversity advocate elegantly arguing for life as a mix of happy and unhappy—or a dissenter opting for some happy moment in history. (There must be some!) The opponent says, "You can't say that to *me!* I'm a Jew, I saw the camps. There is no 'happy' after Auschwitz." The argument is *ad hominem*—but that is how it must be.

It is quite possible that a Holocaust university would grant wide tolerance to dissenters and "diversityists." If they stick to their physics they are, of course, no great problem. If they actively reject the fundamental existential ground of the university, they may also be admitted—perhaps even encouraged—because their opposition may sharpen the intellectual and emotional development of the dominant paradigm. What would be impossible, however, without abandoning the whole Holocaust university project, would be to accept "diversityism" as *the* framing assumption of the enterprise. The moral of my tale is obvious. Academic freedom is often (almost universally) interpreted as "diversityism" and taken as *the* framing assumption. Only if there is a studied neutrality on *all* issues—particularly religion, it seems—can there be a real climate of academic freedom. In the Holocaust university that framing "dogma" would be rejected. History teaches a lesson that cannot be denied or relegated to academic debate.

The framing reality for a Holocaust university would make a direct claim upon the life of intellect insofar as it would deny intellect's superiority or isolation from the history revealed in the Holocaust. A Holocaust university would fail as a latter-day Platonic academy dedicated to the pursuit of the transcendent world of Form and Beauty. Certainly it would fail as a school of Stoic sages. The Holocaust university would insist that intellect, for all its many values, is embedded in and obligated toward "the real" and that, in the fiery furnaces of historical cataclysm, the scholar and the peasant are in solidarity. The framing reality may not in any way immediately impinge on the integrity of the research and scholarship within. But the Holocaust reality "puts the university in its place"—to use an earlier expression—and that place is not transcendent to the suffering of humankind.

It is crucial (and disturbing to academic assumptions) that the university in this analysis is not the final arbiter of its own meaning. In other words, if the thematic of the university is debate, discussion, always being open to a broad diversity of views, the thematic of the Holocaust runs counter to such an understanding. Something has already happened *outside the university* to define history and the university is therefore embedded in a history that goes beyond it. When the interlocutor above says, "You can't say that to *me*, I'm a Jew!" he is appealing to what lies beyond professional credentials.

I hope a sympathetic reader would accept that in a Holocaust institution there would be a transcending paradigm, an historical "dogma" that defined the existential meaning of the university. A difficult problem for the university, however, would arise over the issue about who or what is the proper guardian of the Holocaust meaning. Put it very concretely. What does it mean to say "I am a Holocaust Jew!"? Who is the "real" Jew? For the radical Rabbi Meier Kahane, the lesson of the Holocaust was paranoid distrust. To be a Jew was to seek the extermination of those who would exterminate Jews. If the university is embedded in *Jewish* reality, how shall it know who speaks for Jews? I have no intention of suggesting how one might go about resolving this problem; I bring up the point because it has such obvious connection to the consideration of the Catholic university later in this chapter. In that case, the church, usually specified as the Roman *magisterium*, claims to be *the authentic* Christian voice. In the Jewish case, the lack of a single hierarchic voice gives a certain "breathing space" for the Holocaust university that would seem to be lacking in the more definitive structure of Catholicism.

SPECIAL INTEREST COLLEGES

Is the character of a Holocaust university capable of extension? We might give special indulgence to such an institution for the Jewish community, but that could be regarded as a "special case" given the frightful history of the twentieth century. There might, however, be other exceptions made: black universities would frame the institution in the memory of slavery, Native American universities in terms of recollected disease, displacement, and defeat. So on across the globe. It is important to recognize that in each case, the *framing* assumption comes from beyond "normal" university modalities. I have emphasized repeatedly the neutrality of the academic or "scientific" mindset. In the abstract, abrogation of that neutrality is regarded as pernicious and destructive, and it often is in the actual instance. The exclusion of Jewish scientists and scholars from the universities in the Nazi period was a *prima facie* case of academic corruption. While there is something deeply correct in this assertion of neutrality and openness across racial, sexual, and ethnic lines, there do seem to be "special situations" in which the framing reality is allowed to encroach on institutional neutrality. If excluding Jewish scientists from Nazi universities was illegitimate, an "affirmative action" practice of appointing Jews to a Holocaust university would seem permissible, even necessary.

Because the framing reality is historically based, individual history reemerges as a factor. Being Jewish is an historical reality which is *per se* irrelevant to the enterprise of science; it is not irrelevant in staffing a Holocaust university. One need not depend on a thought experiment to appreciate the power of historical framing. There was a significant controversy in the recent past at Gallaudet College, a school for the deaf, in which students and faculty strenuously objected to the appointment of a hearing person (who did not even know deaf signage) as president. They demanded that a deaf individual be appointed president, and that eventually occurred. On a purist analysis of academic freedom, it would seem that the *fact* of being deaf is simply irrelevant to science, scholarship, or appointment to university office. Nevertheless, one may suppose that there is something about the lived experience of the deaf that is important not only in appreciating the *teaching* situation of a college for the deaf, but that would give an insight into any historically based scholarship regarding deaf communities. It is not unreasonable to extend the Gallaudet example to other special interest colleges. It would seem odd to have a women's college wholly staffed by males, or a black college wholly staffed by whites.

It is not a simple task to separate off impeccable neutral scholarly credentials and historical embeddedness. A controversy broke out several years ago at one of the CUNY colleges when a Catholic was appointed as chair of the department of Judaic Studies. The individual happens to be a well-attested scholar of Judaism, nevertheless a group of rabbis objected to the appointment. I am inclined to be sympathetic to the rabbis. Insofar as Judaism is in its existential posture a *lived faith*, it may well be that a scholar who does not *live* that faith somehow misses the point. With all the scholarly insight and sympathy that one could bring to the table, in the final analysis one stands outside the experience. Where one so visibly espouses *another* faith, the sense of discordance seems manifest. In this case it was the *chair* position that was bothersome; the rabbis had no objection to the Catholic as a member of the department and a scholar of Judaism.

Special interest colleges, therefore, can welcome and encourage scholars not of the faith or special condition since the"neutrality" (or discordance) of their views could be valuable in checking unthinking, merely visceral response from the special community. What seems unacceptable, however, is that one adopt a *general* neutrality to the issue of faith, gender, race, and so on: the *diversityist* interpretation of academic freedom. There is legitimate concern that those in symbolic positions (presidents, department chairs) be *in* and *of* the special community. There is also a legitimate concern that a significant proportion of the teaching staff reflect the community and, of course, that the curriculum reflect the historical concerns of the special interest (women's studies, black studies, and so on).

How far might one extend the range of special interest colleges? Perhaps every university could be regarded as a "special case" related to a specific community, while ideally the university as such is not obligated to any special history. One might even hold that it is an unhappy necessity that *all* universities are somewhat enmeshed in local history as they are perforce involved in the local language, while the ideal would be something like the world and language of mathematics, which transcends all local embeddedness. Such an "ideal" university would be one whose framing assumption was ahistorical. It might be a "mathematical university" that dealt only with pure science. But even that model is hard to remove from historical influence. A women's "mathematical university" given current historical conditions might be strongly compelled to appoint women as models of scientific competence and to alter teaching and curricular models to conform to "female culture" as it influences modes of learning.

The difficult case would be such an ahistorical university that ranged beyond pure science into the area of social and humanistic studies. There the escape route from some historical framing would be "academically reflexive." University neutrality would itself become the framing assumption and any recognition of special histories (Jews, women, blacks, Catholics) would at best be a curricular concession. Something like this "ideal" is the regnant model at the back of the mind—and the front of the rhetoric—of the contemporary university ethos. A realist about the condition of humanity might well reject such an ideal outright. A university that purported to leap out of history altogether would be not ideal but "fantastic." It would live in a fantasy land beyond the human-all-too-human "faults" of love and tragedy.

I do not wish to suggest that academic freedom/ transcendence-of-the-historic is any less a university demand nor that reconciling its arduous asceticism with the real, historical exigencies of some special framing assumption is a simple task. It is not; it is a matter of ongoing dialogue and negotiation. Perhaps the Catholic really would have been the best chair of the Judaic studies department. Women's colleges have had distinguished male presidents. The only conclusion I wish to draw is that academic-freedom-as-diversity is not necessarily the final word in the construction of a specific college. Academic-freedom-as-diversity *can* be the final word, the reflexive framing assumption. But, in that case, all historically framed institutions will appear as tainted exceptions to the proper rule.

Given the demands of academic freedom and "neutral scholarship" over and against the embeddedness of some special interest college, dialogue between the neutral scholar and the historical framing assumption is essential and the natural condition of the institution. The historical experience that frames the institution (Holocaust, slavery, discrimination against women) is and is not some simple "possession" of historical witnesses. Not every woman speaks for, understands, or expresses the deep current of concern expressed in a feminist college's framing assumption. Scholars legitimately interpret the experience. And yet, insofar as scholars speak of and for *women*, this or that individual woman is to a certain extent a witness not to be neglected. There is a dialogue between academic scholar and actual witness; it is not always clear where authentic speech is found. Still, in any historically framed institution, witnessing has *de jure* final authority. The problem may be *authentic* witness, but it is historical reality and witness to that reality that drives the framing concern.

A CATHOLIC UNIVERSITY

Let that be sufficient for the thought experiment of a Holocaust university and other special interest universities. I trust that the parallels to a Christian/Catholic university are sufficiently clear. For Christians there was/is a paradigmatic historical event, the Crucifixion and Resurrection of Jesus, which serves the role of the Holocaust in present Jewish memory and in my fictional university. The example of the Holocaust university and the sense in which it parallels a Christian/Catholic university offers a framework for understanding the complex relation of the church and the academy buried in the dictates of the papal document *Ex Corde Ecclesiae*. Much as I wish to preserve academic freedom for Catholic colleges and universities, the problems raised by the whole *Ex Corde* discussion cannot be settled by affirming the "normal" *liberal* sense of academic freedom as diversity and sheer neutrality. A Catholic institution insists on framing the world of the university within what it regards as *the* essential and central historical paradigm, the heart of existence and its meaning: the story of Jesus of Nazareth, proclaimed the Christ of God.

There are three marks that differentiate the Catholic university from the special cases cited above: the assertion of universality, the problem of "faith," and the claim for church infallibility. The first issue is relatively easy to deal with in the context of special interest cases, the second is not, and the third will receive full treatment in the next two chapters.

The Catholic university assumption deviates from the cases of special interest discussed above insofar as its framing assumption claims *catholicity*, that is to say, universality. The Holocaust university's claim about the Holocaust as the central paradigmatic event, and the ways that claim impinges on academic freedom, are unique to the history of the Jews. Christianity, on the other hand, claims universal status. The historical event of Jesus is not only for descendants of Palestine, but for all nations: St. Paul's "in Christ there is no slave or free, male or female, Jew or Gentile." Although the Gospel is a lesson within Jewish history, this history lesson is not local, it is universal.

At the beginning of this chapter I pointed out, however, that one can move from a specific history to a universal view. Holocaust, while it is a particular Jewish experience, may be extended as a universal meaning of human history. The Holocaust impinges directly on the life of every Jew: he is a potential participant, she may hear her name called from the darkness of remembered anguish. But every individual, Jew and non-Jew, may be called from within "the real" of the Holocaust to a recognition of history's inexorable destructiveness. The Christian, on the other hand, always universalizes: all humanity is called by name into the drama of Creation, Covenant, and Salvation that constitutes the Christian event in history.

It goes without further argument, then, that a Catholic university following the logic of historically framed institutions may strive for visible "Catholicity" at an institution: a Catholic president, a significant proportion of faculty as Catholic, a Catholic curriculum, Catholic worship services, a Catholic "moral" climate, and so on. All that may seem like a "legitimate" exception—even if grudgingly conceded by the American Association of University Professors and other guardians of academic purity.

A major problem in extending the model of special cases to a Catholic university is the second differentiating mark: "faith." In the case of the Holocaust university and its special relation to the Jewish community, the definition of "Jewish" is fixed in a manner that "Catholic" is not. The Nazis defined "Jewish" racially, by genetic inheritance (the Nuremberg Laws, which ironically are identical to the Israeli Law of Return). Conversion to the Catholic (or any other) faith did not remove one from Jewish designation in the eyes of the Nazis. One can see similar parallels in the other cases of special interest considered above: women, blacks, Native Americans, the deaf are all in some sense "biologically" designated. "Catholic," as faith, seems to have a different logic, since it clearly can range over all such distinctions: Catholic women, Catholic blacks, and so on. The issue of faith presents two problems. Internally, the Catholic institution may have problems deciding whether Professor T is a "faithful" Catholic. The church's history of creating present pariahs who become future saints suggests that finding the faithful is not as easy as checking blood lines. The external problem arises from attempts to solve the dilemma about faithfulness. Authorities decide that one must adhere to certain verbal formulas of faith to be qualify as faithful. But when faith issues in statements about this and that, the conflict with reasoned university beliefs seems to arise.

If Catholicism were to be designated solely in terms of some historically differentiated sect, then individuals who bound themselves to that sect might be seen in the same light as those characterized by biological designations. Catholics in Ulster as a persecuted minority could well make a case similar to that of the other special groups for an historically framed institution of higher learning that would be sensitive to their history of suffering and discrimination. From within the logic of Catholic faith, this sort of historical framing would finally be unacceptable. Even though it is said that the church is founded "on the blood of martyrs," the historical framing of a *catholic* church cannot be in terms of the church's travail or triumphs. Being Catholic cannot mean *our* set or sect as distinguished from some other designated group. The Catholic and Christian claim is not in terms of some special historical experience of the Christian community but in terms of an historical experience that is *the* historical experience of humankind. Creation, Covenant, Crucifixion, Resurrection are not historical markers in the same way that slavery, Jim Crow, and lynching are special markers for black Americans; for Christians the Bible events are everyone's historical marker. That is, of course, a very large claim but it is not logically or psychologically impossible. And it is always possible to extend the experience of black slavery to a universal metaphor of pervasive human oppression.

One can clearly understand the difference between being born a woman or a Jew and choosing a specific religious faith. In the construction of my special interest universities, there is a natural tendency to be concessive toward groups designated by fact, not choice. Special concession is asked for homosexuality because, it is argued, it is a matter of biology, not psychology—it is a given, not a choice. A Catholic university insofar as it is defined by a *set of beliefs* seems to be in a more immediate conflict with normal academic assumptions than a woman's college, where the condition of definition is not a chosen set of beliefs. If the Catholic says, "I believe such and such," then it would seem that belief has to be mixed in with great stew of human beliefs as one argument among many. "Catholic" cannot then be more than a semi-arbitrary dominance of one of the myriad set of beliefs that could exist in any university setting.

There are two qualifications on this observation about the difference between the biologically given and some chosen set of beliefs. In the final analysis, all the cases of special interest depend on beliefs. It is only because societies believe or have a history of belief that women are intellectually inferior or blacks fit for slaves that the biological distinctions lead us to concede special historical framing to their colleges. There is a deep presumption that biological determinants are not themselves the basis of special interest; only historical belief and its consequences create the conditions for permitting special treatment. Thus the day may have passed when special women's colleges are legitimate. (I disagree with such a view, but that is for some other book.)

A second qualification on the difference between chosen faith and given biological characteristic is that, fully understood at its deepest, Christian faith is not something *chosen*, it is a *given*. Faith is a "gift of God," not something that one can chose like a set of philosophical beliefs. This may seem like a mere verbal dodge of difficult problem, but if one follows the logic laid out for the Holocaust university, the claim is understandable. In that university the Holocaust is a given historical marker; it is a fact of history from which, as a Jew, one cannot escape. This *is* Jewish history for Jews. Any individual Jew might turn aside from that history, choose not to pay attention to the Holocaust, decide that the days of destruction are now a thing of a past well forgotten. Presumably something like that occurred with many European Jews in the 1930s who mistakenly thought that by virtue of religious conversion or by being a "good German" they were removed from a history of diaspora and pogrom and racist destruction. There is, indeed, a critical moment of decision about what is to be remembered and what is to be forgotten from history. A British friend witnessing Orangemen's Day in Northern Ireland and the slogan, "Remember the Battle of the Boyne!" observed, "That's what's wrong with that bloody country. They ought to *forget* the Battle of the Boyne." It is not at all clear that Jews *should* forget the Holocaust. The Holocaust declaration is "Lest we forget!"

The Catholic/Christian will say that one cannot *choose* a history for humanity any more than Jews could *choose* some happier past than that of pogrom and Holocaust. To be human is to have *this* (Crucifixion–Resurrection) history. Of course one may choose to forget or to modify that history: there is no marker for history; there is a marker but it isn't Crucifixion; there is a marker—it is Crucifixion but no Resurrection. The question at issue is whether one can choose regarding human history overall any more than a Jew can choose Jewish history. To be Jewish may well be to live under the historically given marker of the Holocaust; the Christian says that to be human is to live under the historically given marker of Crucifixion–Resurrection. Put in theological terms: we live in a world defined by a saving grace.

I do not intend to discuss how someone might be led to believe that she was *already* defined by the Christian historical marker. It is obviously much more complicated than persuading a contemporary Jew to remember the Holocaust as a marker. One can only say that we do "argue" about the meaning of particular histories—and can also argue about the meaning of history overall. Even in the case of biological markers—for example, being female—it may be necessary in any individual case to argue about the meaning of *women's* history. But my point here is only to indicate that when one accepts Christian belief, it is because one comes to think that something is *already* given that makes the story of Jesus a history I cannot choose to forget and one that defines my status in the world.

The three elements of difference between a Catholic university and a fictional Holocaust university are universality, faith, and infalliblity of the church. Universality may be a large claim but it conforms to the logic of special interest cases in the sense that any special case may expand to be definitive of ever larger and finally universal human experience. As for faith, though in one sense it seems to be on a par with a variety of life opinions that one might choose, in its inner core Christian faith is regarded as given in a manner analogous to the way in which to be a Jew is to be already enmeshed with the history of the Holocaust. It is the final differentiating element, namely, infallible *church*, that poses the most troubling problem for a Catholic university—and here it is explicitly a *Catholic* university that is at issue.

Although I intend to deal with this issue at length in the next two chapters, it is necessary to relate the problem of church to the present context of discussion. The examples set forth in this chapter of a fictional Holocaust university and the various actual special interest institutions lend legitimacy to the notion that a powerful history *external* to the university may create a framing assumption that qualifies the normal assumptions about academic neutrality. In such cases, one is inclined to give priority of position to the *witness* of history and to those who are its literal witnesses, for example, Holocaust survivors first, Jews secondarily; women, blacks, and so on as the special case dictates. For all the acumen and scholarship that may be result from the work of the academy, there is authenticity to the one who says, "I was there. I saw it all."

The power and priority of witness remains, however, relatively vague and imprecise. Although the Holocaust scholar finally must defer to Holocaust survivors, there are in fact many witnesses and it may be necessary to sort among them. The scholar makes his or her decision about which witnesses are the most authentic, truly capturing the sense of the event. When applying this logic of scholar-witness to a Catholic university, however, one discovers there an institution that purports to establish in a definitive manner *the* authentic voice of witness. Instead of the voices of many survivors, myriads of women, the complex lives of black families, there is a single voice, the church, *the* witness. Protestants also claim that the church is in some sense the communal body that witnesses to Crucifixion–Resurrection, but Protestantism lacks the institutional mechanisms that purport to arrive at *the* definitive testimony. There is no

Protestant equivalent to the Roman *magisterium* or the Congregation on the Doctrine of Faith or the pope. Protestants look to the Bible as *the* definitive witness, the Word of God; but the Bible is not an institution with an enforcing arm of canon law. Thus when Protestant church members or scholars differ on the matter of authenticity, they often migrate to another denominational church.

The existence of a formal, ongoing, institutional office for "guarding the faith" (the *magisterium*) poses a very different technical and scholarly problem for a Catholic university. There are some analogous situations when the Methodist convention decides that Southern Methodist University has strayed, but such interventions are hardly routine and the formalities leading up to decisions to seek intervention and remedy are much more open to a broad range of denominational viewpoints than the workings of the Roman Catholic Congregations. Finally, of course, there is really nothing like the claim of papal infallibility within Protestantism or Orthodoxy. The *church* may be regarded as in some sense "infallible," but the definition of church is either so open or so mystical that one cannot point to an obvious office or organ of infallible pronouncement.

To sum up, there is significant force to the notion that a university may legitimately stand under the witness of history. What is troublesome about the Catholic university's claim is that witnessing is defined by a fixed institutional office. One may have to search for the authentic Holocaust voice and that gives the Holocaust university significant scholarly openness. For Catholics the authentic Christian voice is apparently specified and enforced, so that the Catholic scholar-theologian may feel (and be) significantly constricted in research. I think that there is no way around this problem except to look more deeply at the Catholic understanding of church.

9

Ex Corde Ecclesiae

The thought experiment in the previous chapter projected a final problem for a *Catholic* university, a problem that does not conform to the "logic" of the other special interest cases considered. That problem is the church or, in the terms discussed in that chapter, an *official* witness, *the* official witness, the *infallible* official witness. While one may believe that there is something between moral demand and reluctant concession for the construction of a university framed by a special history (Holocaust, women's history, black slavery), when that model is applied to a Catholic university there is an apparent difference. The existence of the institutional church as the official infallible witness to the special history deviates from the more open, complex witnessing that occurs in the other cases. It is as if there were an official bureau of Holocaust witness, an institute of *de fide* statements about women. One may believe that there is an overwhelming *problem* presented to the university by the Holocaust, but deny that there is some comprehensive, coherent *answer* (belief) that emerges, not to mention that there might be some institution of official answers. In the case of the Catholic Church it seems one has not just the problem of God-in-history, one has definitive *answers*. Definitive answers—particularly when delivered by external authority—are profoundly disturbing to the spirit and practice of the academy. A *Catholic* university is, then, a peculiarly troubling entity for the open inquiry that marks the academic enterprise.

In order to examine the relation of the university and formal Catholic authority, one need only turn to the most recent papal proclamation on that topic: John Paul II's admonitions in the Apostolic Constitution *Ex Corde Ecclesiae* (1990). The problematics of a Catholic university were not created by this papal document, but *Ex Corde* with its local interpretation in the United States by the National Council of Catholic Bishops has raised anew problems concerning academic freedom that have long plagued Catholic higher education— some of which problems Catholic educators thought had been more or less solved. After the Land O'Lakes statement of 1967 committing the signatory Catholic institutions to "academic freedom," presidents and faculties of those institutions may have thought that vexing problem was put to rest. Not so. One of the principal advisers on the bishop's implementation document on *Ex Corde* grumbled to me about "Land O'Lakes types" and the surface implication of both the papal document and its later interpretation in the United States would certainly suggest that academic freedom is again a contested issue.

Although some of the most troubling issues from *Ex Corde*—for example, how an individual *mandatum* might be granted or denied—remain under review, the overall problems are clear enough (or obscure enough) to cause concern. I hope that by offering some clarification of what can and cannot be accomplished in the presumed interface of church and academy, officials on both sides can come to policies that are legitimate and productive. The task is not simple since confrontation or cooperation is marred by ill-conceived and poorly understood "ideologies" of both church and academy.

A "threat" to academic freedom may not seem obvious in *Ex Corde Ecclesiae* since it is repeatedly stated by both the pope and the bishops that institutions and faculty must have academic freedom:

> Every Catholic university, as a university, is an academic community ... [which] possesses that institutional autonomy necessary to perform its functions effectively and guarantees to its members academic freedom, so long as the rights of the individual person and of

the community are preserved within the confines of the truth and the common good.[1] (*Ex Corde Ecclesiae*, 12)

This statement is then footnoted:

"academic freedom" is the guarantee given to those involved in teaching and research that, within the specific specialized branch of knowledge and according to the methods proper to that specific area, they may search for the truth wherever analysis and evidence lead them, and may teach and publish results of this search. . . .

Such a statement on academic freedom might cheer even the American Association of University Professors (AAUP).

The general statement in *Ex Corde* on academic freedom conforms to the *competence dogma:* academic freedom is guaranteed "within the specific specialized branch of knowledge according to the methods proper to that specific area." The qualifying comment "as long as the rights of the individual person and the community are preserved *within the confines of truth and the common good*" is unclear. It would, however, be one way of expressing what was early identified as the *moral dogma* of the university: the humane demands that qualify "mere" science. Even the AAUP notes that individual faculty members in exercising the right of academic freedom should exercise prudence and recognize their responsibilities as members of the academic community. What worries defenders of academic freedom is *who* establishes "the confines of truth." If it is the Roman *magisterium*, it certainly seems that academic freedom is jeopardized.

One can, perhaps, limit damage by confining the issue of who determines truth to the area of theology. The church could be regarded as having presumptive authority in that area. In my analysis such damage control is doubtful, since I regard theology as "the queen of the sciences" in the sense that the *existential dogma* of the university is perforce theological. The "theology" of the existential dogma can have extensive implications across many fields. Putting aside such broad claims, however, church authority over theology in the university is likely to be rejected on grounds of academic freedom. Or, if there is some church mandate on theology, then "theology" will be regarded with deep suspicion, as something less than a proper academic pursuit. A Catholic university is then caught in a dilemma. It either offers courses in theology and grants them full academic freedom (*pace* Rome), or it offers courses in theology that pacify Rome and offend academic freedom. The Catholic university is either second class, unorthodox-Catholic or second class, unorthodox-academic.

Assuming that academic freedom is a function of competence as *Ex Corde* initially asserts, what is the character of *theological* competence or, more strictly, *Catholic* theological competence? One might assume from the general language of *Ex Corde* that theological competence is like the other specialized disciplines of the university: a tested methodology for the investigation and evaluation of claims to truth and authenticity. But that is not quite so. Over and above the sort of *internal* scholarly attestation of competence, there is an *external* test. *Ex Corde* specifies: "Catholic theology [must be] taught in a manner faithful to Scripture, Tradition and the Church's Magisterium" (*Ex Corde Ecclesiae*, 20). Moreover, a mechanism is specified to ensure that Catholic theology meets these criteria. Theologians are charged to receive a *mandatum* from the local bishop or some other ecclesiastical authority in order to be regarded as genuinely Catholic theologians.[2] In short, competence in Catholic theology is not something internal to an "academic" methodology; it is subject to the judgment of the church as *teacher,* the *magisterium* in the person of the local bishop.

This is a complex issue not amenable to instant condemnation by liberals in or out of the church. Presumably one does not allow anyone to label themselves a "Catholic," "Communist," or "Republican"/"Democrat" theoretician. Formal declarations of heresy and party purges are legitimate means of preserving some reasonable consistency in principles and doctrine. Yet the comparison of Catholic and Communist has a chilling similarity. There were, after all, Communist universities from which faculty were expelled for ideological deviance. It may be one thing to fire a party member, another thing for some *aparatchik* or curial custodian to deny academic competence. Despite the obvious anxiety, it does seem reasonable to insist on some sort of authentication of *Catholic* competence: one can no more be a self-promoted Catholic theologian than a self-declared nuclear physicist.

The Curran case at Catholic University of America (CUA) demonstrates the complexity of such decisions. In that case, the Vatican decided that Fr. Charles Curran was not a proper Catholic theologian and communicated that judgment to the officials at CUA. The issue was then entangled in whether he could teach in the theology faculty at CUA, since students in that faculty were often clerics and other religious. The institution offered him a position in sociology. Curran replied that he was not a sociologist but a theologian—that was the area of his competence and no one had concluded that he was not a competent theologian, even if the Vatican thought he was not a Catholic theologian. ("Catholic theologian" is not a redundancy.)

Curran certainly is a theologian and a highly competent one at that. Moreover, he is, in my judgement, a *Catholic* theologian. He was, after all, at one time the president of the Catholic Theological Society of America, which would seem to indicate that a good number of his fellow Catholic theologians regarded him as competent in that area. If one considers Curran's methodological approach and the "natural law" framework within which he works, he is a *very* Catholic theologian, more like traditional Thomists than many uncensored European "existentialist" theologians. The Vatican's decision seems to have been based on "conclusions" put forward by Curran that do not coincide with with papal pronouncements—for example, on the illegitimacy of contraception.[3]

What the Curran case highlights is that "*Catholic* theologian" apparently does not simply define a learned *methodology* in anything like the usual academic sense. In the ordinary case, one can be regarded as competent, even highly competent, in some academic speciality and still be subject to the judgment that one's conclusions are mistaken. A person does not cease being a competent American historian because he argues for a controversial interpretation of some individual, event, or period. On complex and controverted issues, we admit that there can be differing views from competent scholars and seek to adjudicate the weight of evidence presented. The critical aspect of the academic enterprise would collapse were it not a dialogue of the specially competent. To be sure, enough utterly wrongheaded conclusions may lead to a suspicion about competence, but that is not the first line of consideration. In the Curran case, his prominence in the Catholic Theology Society would seem to suggest that whatever his deviant opinions, the main frame of his work was "orthodox." (Ironically, Curran's specific views on contraception seem to be the majority view among Catholics in the pews, whatever may be the opinion in Rome.)

The problem and concern in the Curran case is that his standing as a Catholic theologian was not decided by other academic or otherwise "professional" Catholic theologians but by church officials in Rome who may or may not have had attested *scholarly* theological credentials. As Catherine Mowry LaCugna has noted, very few bishops are trained as theologians. "Consecration as a bishop does not grant infused scientific or theological knowledge."[4] If the test of academic freedom is competence in a discipline, it would seem that the bishops are on the whole not specially competent and thus should no more be in a position to question the competence of a trained theologian than the average layperson would be prepared to do so in theology or theoretical physics. The issue of competent authority is not settled by escalating the problem to the Roman *magisterium*. When it comes to scholarly assessment, there is no obvious presumptive power granted to the *magisterium* over the work of the university scholar. The scholars of the *magisterium* can present their arguments from philology, archaeology, philosophy, and so on along with the rest of the scholarly community and the decision, if possible at all, will be made on scholarly grounds. Whatever the role of the *magisterium* it does not hold any scholarly trump cards.

It is important here to emphasize that attestation of scholarly competence is not internal to a single institution or a subset of institutions or individuals scholars. Defenders of *Ex Corde* and the *mandatum* frequently point to *external* accrediting agencies for learned specialities—for example, the American Bar Association, ABET (the engineering accreditation body), or the regional accrediting bodies for institutions overall like the Middle States Association. But accreditation by such external review bodies differs from the role of the *magisterium* by virtue of their generally being *peer* reviews. It is members of the bar who review the credentials of law schools, licensed engineers the competency of engineering education, and so on. The reference group for competence, in other words, is not established wholly within an institution's own set of scholars. But when competence is attested, it is within some larger framework capable of offering reasonable warrant for competence. External accreditation is not without controversy, but the quarrels are, on the whole, scholarly disputes among putative experts with some set of plausible credentials in the contested field.

The difference between normal external attestation of scholarly competence and the injunctions of *Ex Corde* are strikingly clear in the very first of the criteria offered for true Catholic theology: faithfulness to the Scripture. The late Raymond E. Brown was perhaps the most distinguished Catholic biblical scholar of our day. He was a member of the Pontifical Commission on Biblical Studies and taught for many years at a very distinguished non-Catholic institution, Union Theological Seminary; his work was widely respected by all students of the New Testament. On one occasion he was invited to speak at a diocesan gathering of Catholic clergy on biblical scholarship. The bishop, in his words of welcome and introduction, remarked on how pleased he was to have Brown speaking on biblical scholarship. The bishop said that he had taken a course in Bible in seminary and didn't understand a thing about it. He looked forward, then, to Brown's instruction. The bishop closed his remarks, however, by reminding Brown that when it came to interpreting Scripture, he, the bishop, was the authority in the diocese. Assume, then, that under the dictates of *Ex Corde* a theologian in said bishop's diocese needed a *mandatum* to be characterized as a Catholic theologian. Who, exactly, would decide whether the theologian had carried out even the first of the qualifications—namely, being faithful to Scripture? Does the ecclesiastic bishop or the scholastic Brown decide?

As a test case of the *Ex Corde* restrictions, Brown's experience would suggest that Catholic theologians could dismiss rulings of the *magisterium* with the same air that astronomers might dismiss ecclesiastical meddling in celestial mechanics. Theologian Richard McBrien of Notre Dame would seem to be correct in steadfastly refusing to seek a *mandatum* since he believes that allowing bishops to pronounce on academic competence is a fundamental violation of the very notion.[5] My sympathies are certainly with Brown, LaCugna, and McBrien on this issue. I believe that the *mandatum* is an ill-conceived instrument that if promoted and put into practice will be a cause of continual mischief. Having said that, the issue of a *Catholic* theologian is not as simple and direct as academic liberalism might hope. If one recalls the model of the Holocaust university, the role of external witness supervenes on scholarly competence. Finally, the Holocaust survivor as witness must authenticate the scholar's interpretation. The church as witness is, in that sense, an indispensable *external* determinant of Catholic theology.

WHERE IS THE "HEART" OF THE CHURCH?

As stated, it seems quite reasonable for a body of believers to set limits on what is believed and believable. One can be a renegade Catholic or Communist and be excluded from the fold. In the case of the church, determining who is and who is not in the fold depends on how one defines "church." If universities are "from the heart of the Church," a first line of clarification is to decide *where* is and *what* is the *heart* of the church. All Christians of every sect and denomination believe in some way that the church is a witness to Jesus' life and message. How "church" is defined in each case determines its nature as a witness and is crucial to the differentiations within Christianity and to the relation of church and university.

Avery Dulles's classic study of "models" of the church outlines five primary types: institutional (juridical), mystical, sacramental, herald (prophetic), and servant.[6] Problems for the Catholic university are heightened or lessened depending on which of these models is chosen for the Catholic Church. Thus Catherine LaCugna objected to *Ex Corde* on the fundamental issue of who speaks for/as the church:

> The critical point seems to be the meaning of the word *church*. As it stands, [*Ex Corde*] very nearly equates the church with the institutional church or with the hierarchical magisterium. But the Church is the whole people of God, all the members of the Body of Christ. While it is impossible to say exactly what the pope has in mind with the word *church*, there is a widespread reflex to read the word, especially as it appears in pontifical documents, as if it means only the hierarchy.... But the institutional church does not control the Spirit....[7]

LaCugna's suspicion is well founded. The institutional model is the one which, as Dulles observed, was dominant in the Catholic world for almost five hundred years—roughly from the Council of Trent to Vatican II. It sees the church as a visible, juridical body whose decisions culminate in Roman magistrates, in the *magisterium*. The model is very close to that of a government in which a "Supreme Court" is the final word in rendering the "law of the land." In terms of our discussion in chapter 8, LaCugna's assertion of the church as the "people of God" shifts the emphasis away from any *official* witness toward the "cloud of witnesses" that might present themselves for a Holocaust university or a women's institution. Yes, witnesses are unsurpassable; but since there are many voices, the university does not face a testimony that is definitive, irreformable, and closed.

The "people of God" scenario has its own problems. These can be highlighted by considering what Dulles identified as the "mystical" model of the church. Rather than a visible institution standing alongside others as a social entity, the church comprises all those who in their hearts face the world with faith and love whatever their verbal affirmations or formal affiliations. Both the institutional and mystical models, however, pose problems for the attempt to resolve the issue of "real Catholic"—and thus real *Catholic* theologian and *Catholic* university. In the institutional model the old formula *ex ecclesia nulla salus*—that outside the institutional Catholic Church of the baptized there is no Salvation—was clear enough but appallingly restrictive. The sad career of Fr. Leonard Feeney, the Catholic chaplain at Harvard in the late 1940s who held that only practicing Roman Catholics in approved official standing could hope for Salvation, was an example of an overinstitutionalized view of the church. Was it really the case that Presbyterians and Buddhists were automatically condemned to eternal fire? Even Rome couldn't accept that and Feeney was officially repudiated.

If the institutional model can be too overt and restrictive, the mystical model seems to set no visible and definable limit to the church. Karl Rahner used the term "anonymous Christians" for those of no ostensible Christian commitment or connection who nevertheless led lives of love and grace. These too are part of "the people of God." There is something profoundly correct about Rahner's view and the extension of Christian Salvation beyond any and all institutional boundaries of Catholicism and Christendom. But while the mystical model may be inherently acceptable for the fundamental "good news" of the Gospel, it is not, unfortunately, much help with the issues surrounding the relation between church and academy. One may be an anonymous Christian, but there is no sense to the notion of an "anonymous Catholic university." (Though some "Catholic" colleges today are pretty anonymous about their Catholicity!) Maybe in their heart of hearts, Nietzsche and Sartre were anonymous Christians, but it would be senseless to claim them as (anonymous) Christian theologians. (Even if, as trenchant critics of apparent orthodoxy, both thinkers revealed issues that often are more important and more fundamental for belief than the standard catechetical manual.) To be a Catholic university it would seem there must be some public allegiance to *something* that would at least sound like "orthodoxy."

The first two of Dulles's models of the church constitute the polar opposites when it comes to determining membership in the church, and thus what may constitute a genuine Catholic institution of higher learning. The mystical model evaporates visible definition and legal restriction; the institutional model offers clear definition, determinative procedure for decision, and the sanctions of canon law. The mystical model evaporates the issue of academic freedom; the institutional freezes it. What about the other models?

The last two models—the heraldic (prophetic) and the servant model— were rightly construed by Dulles as more Protestant than Catholic in their development. I will not explore them in detail. While I am certain that there can be positive constructions of church–university linkages using these models, I also think, however, that there is a natural tendency in these models that make the linkage of church and academy problematic. "Catholic university" for all its worrisome aspects at least makes a claim for a positive link of the two separate jurisdictions. The difficulty of creating a positive link of jurisdictions in these "Protestant" paradigms may explain why the great Protestant-founded institutions in the United States moved inevitably toward secularism pure and simple.

The prophetic model exemplified by a great theologian like Karl Barth can easily come to see the church over and against the university (H. Richard Niebuhr's "Christ against Culture"). The church offers God's prophetic Word against the pride of humanity—in which the university may be especially implicated. A pure Barthian university might engage an official chaplain to caution a community of sinners, but he or she would speak from a pulpit not a professor's podium.

The servant model of the church emphasizes charitable works with diminishing interest in credal truths, and can easily slip into the sort of nineteenth-century Protestant liberalism against which Barth's theology was aimed. George Marsden's study of the secularization of former Protestant institutions demonstrates that many of the presidents and trustees of those institutions identified cultural progress in the university as Christianity at work (Niebuhr's "Christ in Culture"). Eventually one comes to think that just "culture" will do. Good works in and out of the university are understood to be the substance of religion; there is no need for doctrine and odd beliefs. It was just this sort of liberal Protestantism at the beginning of the twentieth century that propelled the Protestant colleges and universities in their slide away from specific *Christian* dogma. The herald and servant models of the church drift toward making the role of a Christian university either impossible or unnecessary. Prophets stand over against the pretense of intellect: one does not study to acquire prophetic competence, and prophets do not get tenure. Culture, on the other hand, dissolves doctrine, leaving the Christian academic nothing special to profess.

Four of Dulles's models, then, pose what may be insuperable problems for the claims of a Catholic university: the institutional model is highly restrictive and violates internal norms for academic freedom; the mystical model is vaporous; the church as herald would not want to be *in* the university at all; and the church as servant would just as soon be in the culture doing good works. That leaves Dulles's final model of the church: the sacramental. It is the one I would adopt and it seems closest to the actual ongoing life of Catholicism (the Roman Curia is *not* the church). *Sacramental* is a complex notion that I consider in the following chapter. Before turning to that task, I want to expand on the problems of the institutional model since that has been the dominant Roman

Catholic understanding and, as LaCugna has suggested, is the implicit model in *Ex Corde*.

THE INSTITUTIONAL JURIDICAL MODEL

Catherine LaCugna objects to *Ex Corde*'s unstated assumption that "church" means "official hierarchy." Using the terminology of Vatican II, she allows that there is church determination of belief, but contends nevertheless that the church is the whole "people of God" (even including theologians), not the Roman establishment. That observation is helpful as far as it goes—as far as it goes in checking peremptory dictation from above; but it does not settle how the people of God comes to any sense or consensus of faith. Moreover, if the reach of the church as the people of God extends far enough to encompass even "anonymous" Christians, then no distinctive belief would distinguish the pope from the Dalai Lama. For there to be a *problem* of Christian *belief*, there must be some distinguishable beliefs that mark a *Christian* people of God.

But even if one restricts "people of God" to those who at least claim some allegiance to the Gospels and then goes on to those who at least "claim" that they are Catholic Christians, one might still be tempted to accept a "democratic" determination of belief: put it to the "[Catholic] people of God!" A democratic determination would be in its way no less puzzling than the most pretentious papal claims. On the issue of "true" belief, if it is difficult to believe that the pope speaks infallibly on faith, it is no less extraordinary to believe *vox populi, vox dei*. For myself, as bothersome as many pronouncements from Rome may be, I daresay that a democratic consensus on belief would probably be even more objectionable. Nor is it clear that scholarly theologians should be given power to settle matters of faith. There have been official councils of the Catholic Church where the theologians sat as "voters" in numbers well in excess of the bishops in attendance. But learned theological consensus has often been as wrongheaded as the most obnoxious clauses from the Syllabus of Errors. It is fashionable today to reject manual scholasticism, but it was in one way or another the consensus theology of the past century.

A democratic referendum or a consensus of theologians (or an ecumenical council for that matter) are all defective means of settling belief, if these instruments are conceived as *juridical*. The problem of true belief is not solved by changing the judges from popes to people, or bishops to scholars. If the belief attested is said to be definitive, necessary, "infallible," then one must claim—as the church does—that the real judge is the Holy Spirit. This view is undoubtedly correct, but again, by adopting the juridical model, the Holy Spirit is introduced as a *deus ex machina*. I believe that the Holy Spirit works through the church more intimately than as a rescuer of last resort. (In grammar school we were given conundrums about what the Holy Spirit might do if the pope were about to declare false doctrine. Strike him dead? Twist his speech? Ventriloquize?)

The attraction of a judicial model is, however, obvious. In the practical life, both personal and political, one wants to avoid endless discussion and diffusion of topics; there must be some point at which a decision is finally reached. Church apologists for the authority of the *magisterium* often analogize its role to that of a Supreme Court, in which a specific body is authorized to render a final judgment. There is no appeal from the Supreme Court, it is *the* authority. This model is implicit in *Ex Corde* and in the final implementation document. The American bishops' original notion was that bishops and universities should "dialogue" (the academic model?). Rome rejected that model and insisted on a *juridical* model that would incorporate canon law. The local bishop backed by the Roman *magisterium* would then be in the juridical position of a Supreme Court, able to define and decide. My supposition is that if and when faith is "defined"—and recall that one is *defining* a mystery (however that is possible)— neither dialogue (academy) or judicial models (law) will work. One needs a methodology peculiar to the sense of "church." As I suggest in chapter 10, my preferred sacramental model of church fits neither university nor legal decision.

A Supreme Court analogy fails to support an infallible *magisterium* for two obvious reasons. First, political Supreme Courts are not infallible and they do reverse themselves. The *Dred Scott* decision (1857), which upheld the ownership rights of slave holders, was as decisive as it was wrong. But Lincoln noted at the time that the Court did not "issue Holy Writ." And, of course, the decision was eventually reversed. Second, and more important in weighing the judicial analogy, is that political courts do not declare on matters of *belief.* The state and its courts are concerned with *actions,* not beliefs, while the *magisterium* is, it seems, concerned with beliefs. Courts operate in the world of the practical, which, as Aristotle points out, concludes with a *decision to act.* Aristotle contrasts the world of the practical with the world of theory and truth. In the world of theory the end of the effort is a proven statement that has been demonstrated. Scientists must wait patiently for proof; practical people are charged to act, even if it must be on less than complete knowledge—as it usually is. Either way the *magisterium* seems to make an impossible claim: if it purports to rule on the *Truth* it violates the patience and methodological skepticism of proper knowledge (the academic assumption); if it rests on the juridical model it must admit that decisions to act often are based on less than perfect knowledge and hence are eminently reformable.

If the *magisterium* rules on the truth of belief, the Supreme Court analogy fails. No court would think of adjudicating on cold fusion not to mention the doctrine of the Trinity. The canon law model embedded in *Ex Corde* and the statement by the National Council of Catholic Bishops (NCCB) seems on its face to have the fatal defect of a juridical determination of truth—a category mistake. On the other hand, if it is really like the judicial model, its rulings are subject to alteration. *Dred Scott* was reversed on a better understanding of the social consequences of slavery and a greater appreciation of the status of blacks. On that model, our better understanding of the status of women should affect such matters as the all-male priesthood. (Aquinas, like practically all thinkers of his time, regarded females as biologically defective males. If anything is the case biologically, it is the opposite.)

Having said all that, one can have some sympathy with Rome in its tussle with the universities. Faith is not something that can be parked in the limbo of academic dialogue. All well and good that university theologians and bishops should dialogue about faith and theological interpretation, but there is a hovering sense of a need for the definitive that must be acknowledged. Faith involves a commitment that goes beyond the proper skeptical review of scientific research and the reformable policies proper to the practical world. Faith commitments are "infallible" at least in the sense that they do not fall under Peirce's prudent "fallibilism," which places all knowledge under a canopy of tentativeness. As was discussed earlier, faiths may collapse and be utterly undermined, but because they are at the heart and center of the believer, the lover, the passionately committed, one does not *in principle* stand aside and above them assessing and reviewing their worth. The two models we have been discussing for arriving at truth—the academic model of dialogue and the *magisterium* model of juridical decision—are both flawed. The former rejects "faith" or definitive commitment in principle as a violation of open discussion; the latter arrives at definitive commitment by a humanly defective method rescued by the Holy Spirit *ex machina*.

THE RULES OF THE GAME

The juridical model does, however, have the virtue of emphasizing the definitive character of faith. Just as the Supreme Court ruling defines the "law of the land," so in some analogous sense the believer's faith, the lover's commitment, is a "final" word that is not under the review of methodological skepticism (the academic mode). The lover regards his faith in the beloved as "infallible"; this commitment is "beyond question." The issue for the church is whether juridical structure is the only or appropriate model for expressing the essential character of unfailing faith and commitment. As it stands, the juridical structure is certainly discordant to the academy's sense of how truth may be ascertained.

It seems absolutely necessary for a *Christian* theologian to accept at least some of the "orthodox" beliefs, certain *givens* that are the "data" to be studied. I have no idea exactly what to say about the death-of-God thinkers as *Christian* theologians since they seem to hold that there is no God at all. "I believe in God" is how the whole credal recital takes off. That a Christian theologian must accept some more or less central "data" may seem no different than the scientist who has to accept specific data as the basis of theory. A scientist who deals in factual data might even be willing to accept a constraint on theologians, not as a constraint of *fact*, but as the *rules* of a game. So, it might be argued, while there are *givens* to Christian belief they are like chess rules. If you want to play chess, then you have to regard this piece as moving only diagonally, this piece only one square at a time, and so on. A Christian theologian has to "play" by the Christian rules, but there is no more "truth" to those rules than there is to the fact that chess pieces move in specific directions.

Giving the Roman *magisterium* ultimate authority analogous to the International Lawn Tennis Association—it sets the rules of the game—is hardly a satisfactory solution. Believers obviously think that there is more to faith than an elaborate game—though not a few sermons delivered and theological tomes printed seem to be not much more than a set of linguistic changes on a set of "facts," as essentially irrelevant to life as the rules of chess. Christian theology as "rules of the game" would be a university study only in the field of anthropology. There one studies the taboos, customs, and rules of tribes and peoples to discover their intrinsic structure, without in any way assuming that the rules have any relation to reality as such. It is fascinating that the *X* tribe has a taboo against eating goats, but there is no presumption that such an injunction has any general truth value.

The Catholic understanding of the Christian "givens," however, is that they are in some sense truths to be affirmed, not moves in a game. Further, in the Catholic understanding—and that of mainline Christianity—Christian belief is also not a *metaphorical* game that points to activities of "real life," as one might regard chess as a metaphorical game reflecting the real-life power of hierarchy (the queen attacks the hapless pawns). The reduction of belief statements to life-metaphor is a special temptation of the servant model of the church, under which the stories of the Bible are expressions of love, tools of prophetic caution, or spurs to social amelioration. For the church understood as social servant, the Bible and Aesop teach vital moral messages, but one need no more regard them as true than one need believe in talking animals to get the point.

AUTHORITY AND TRADITION:
A MUSEOLOGICAL MODEL

The virtue of the institutional/juridical model is that it retains a sense that there is something decisive to be believed. The model presents enormous methodological problems, however, when it comes to establishing the *truth* of any belief, as is acutely revealed in the interface between the *magisterium* and the normal academic model of truth. If there is any solution for the problematic relationship between academic pursuit and church *magisterium*, one has to return to the nature of Catholic "truth" and the "methodology" of that truth. The methodology of church truth is "authority," which, as has been indicated often enough, seems on its face to be wholly unacceptable to the academic freedom granted to disciplinary competence. The underlying problem with accepting a method of authority is that it also gets cast in the juridical model. But the juridical is not the only, or in this case the appropriate, lodging for authority. One might suggest instead a "museological" method of authority. Though in the final analysis a museological context for authority fails religious discourse, it is a much closer approximation than the juridical.

The museological model is derived from the earlier discussion of the truth of art and the role of exemplars. We can only "know" good and bad art, truthful and sentimental art, by fitting the work at hand into a history of art. The dialogue between past masterpieces and present offerings illuminates the values in both works—sometimes to the detriment of past works. (The history of art is littered with forgotten masters!) The validity of art depends, then, on some means of maintaining a tradition of exemplars. Lacking a continuing tradition of art, every creation would be an utter novelty and we would lack appraisive capacity.

Understanding church authority as museological acknowledges that there must be a tradition of exemplars: revelations and interpretations. Jesus makes sense and is evaluated from the perspective of a long-standing Jewish tradition.

(Christians accept Jesus as the long-awaited Messiah; Jews reject that claim. Both rely on biblical tradition as warrant.) *Ex Corde's* insistence on faithfulness to tradition is appropriate since only through tradition can exemplars/revelations be assessed. One could, then, give significant weight to the Roman *magisterium* as the guardian of a tradition of assessed revelations as well as commentaries on their value and import. Without an authoritative tradition, one could no more assess or even understand doctrine, true Revelation, than one could ascertain true art without an authoritative tradition. The *magisterium* can legitimately insist that Christian doctrine is not something made up on the spot but must of necessity come to terms with centuries of tradition from apostolic days through the Fathers and so on. Thus Raymond Brown's comment on Episcopal bishop John Spong's version of Jesus' life and message: "I do not think that a single NT author would recognize Spong's Jesus as the figure proclaimed and written about."[8] Utter failure to deal with New Testament witness would fairly disqualify an opinion as *true* Christian belief.

There are two flaws with a museological *magisterium*. First, insofar as the model is adopted from the realm of art, it can easily become a matter of simply following the "rules of the game." For example, to understand certain poses and figures in art, one has to know the iconographic and artistic "rules." The lion represents the Gospel writer Mark and that is why the lion is floating over this figure's head; it is not proto-surrealism. Again, we are able to explain, understand, and appraise art because it follows the "rules" of the genre. Even when the rules are broken—as they are by the most creative artists—we come to appreciate the daring and insight of the creator against the previous and extant conventions. In the long run, a museological interpretation—based as it is on the arts—fails to remove the "veil" that separates art from life, art from religion.

The second flaw in the museological model is that for Christians, certainly for Catholics, some of the exemplars are definitive, *de fide*, "infallible"—they are not subject to the back-and-forth appraisive dialogue that exists in the realm of art. Holy Scripture is in some sense unsurpassable; thus the importance of "faithfulness to the Scripture." In art there must be a *canon*, but it is a relative canon. Works thought to be canonic may not withstand the test of time as they are reappraised in the light of later creations. Even Shakespeare may be cast into shadow. In sum: while for art there must be *a* canon, for Christianity there must be *the* canon—namely, the canonic writings of the Old and New Testaments. Bishop Spong's New Testament (really "new"!) might in an artistic canon outstrip the older version, but that won't do for doctrine. This is the difference between art and religion, the difference between religion and the religion of art.

Religions in general—Catholic Christianity for sure—purport to tell us *the* truth about ultimate reality. Buddhism is based on the Four Noble Truths, and Christians have not been utterly wrongheaded to wrangle over dogmas. As I have developed the notion of truth, there are three quite different modes in play: scientific, artistic, and religious. Because of the oddity of the religious claim to truth—at least the Christian religious claim to truth—there is an apologetic temptation to legitimate religion by analogizing, if not downright conflating, Christian truth (Jesus' statement, "I am the Truth) with the truths appropriate to science or art. But neither scientific or artistic models can accomplish the religious task. The scientific model fails because it rests on the condition of neutral spectatorship, the world seen *sub specie aeternitatis:* under the aspect of eternity. In contrast to science, art sees the world *sub specie temporis, historicae.* When it comes to assessing the truth of human existence as temporal, the arts are indispensable. The great *omnium gatherum* of sensibilities contained in the arts allows us to survey the range and depth of the human. Yet for all the necessary instruction of the arts in the ways of humanity, there seems to be something missing. The arts stand on a boundary between learning about life and living life. One can *live a life* of relishing and refining sensibility across the ever-expanding canvas of the arts. It would be a "sentimental education" in the best sense of that expression: an education of the sentiments. But such a life may be *only* sentimental.

It is vastly important to educate the sentiments, and artists are prime pedagogues for the task, yet it is not clear whether art ends in aesthetics or "reality." There is a necessary moment of "abstraction" in art that is as important in its way as the transcendence of the scientist. Poetry is more or less as Wordsworth said—"emotion recollected in tranquility." It is the dominance of a "retreat to recollection," an *aesthetic* life, which is rejected by the anti-artists, who aim to prevent aesthetic distancing by making the viewer/reader a participant—sometimes a guilty participant—in the reality "depicted." Not exactly *depicted,* but rather *presented* as a chaotic happening of the moment. The children's art from the Holocaust in its very naïveté, its *un*artiness, is participatory. It demands our participation in grief. Wittgenstein: "Things are placed right in front of our eyes, not covered by a veil.—This is where religion and art part company."9

The church's role is to present "infallible" truth. But what does it *present?* It is not a "topic for discussion" nor "the law of the land." Even if a topic for discussion proved to embody impregnable truth, it would still be an "arms-length" truth. Even if the "law of the land" proved to be wholly just and fair, it would still only govern action, not constrain belief or position us toward "the real." When the church presents its truth, it presents something iconic. Something is "placed right in front of our eyes . . . where religion and art part company." In presenting "the real," the iconic participates in the reality depicted. In this sense, opening to "the real" certainly sounds like opening to truth, rather than to what only may be the comforting, inspiring, educating, and appraising modes of the merely aesthetic.

Iconic presentation is at the heart of the "sacramental" and the sacramental model of church. In the classic Catholic definition, "sacrament" is an outward and visible sign of an inward grace; it is iconic. The Eucharist, for example, is not just a sign of something wholly external to it, a memorial of the Last Supper. Rather it participates in the reality it signifies. As Catholics say, the Eucharist is the *real* presence of Jesus. The Eucharistic bread does not merely signify the holy, as the word "holy" signifies the holy. It is an icon/sacrament that participates in the holy, is in some sense itself holy. In the following chapter, I further develop the notion of "sacramental church" and consider how its presentation of the truth concerning "the real" relates to the university.

10

Lex Orandi, Lex Credendi

Christian belief is claimed as true and definitively so—at least by Catholics and various shades of orthodoxy. In the Roman Catholic version of Christianity, the claim for infallible truth is more than a mystic aspiration; it is an officially proclaimed prerogative that comes with a sanctioned bureaucracy more than willing to pronounce, denounce, defend, and deny. It is the claim for *official* truth that vexes the academy, which assumes that the university is the proper instrument for attaining truth; its methods of patient investigation and proper tentativeness seem fundamentally contradictory to the decrees and definitiveness of Catholic Rome. This issue has been the underlying concern of the book: is a "Catholic university" a contradiction? My final claim will be that it is not, but that it offers a contrarian position to some of the fundamental—though largely unexpressed—"dogmas" of the university. To confirm the legitimacy, perhaps even the desirability of a Catholic university, I must now address just what sort of claims to truth a church might make. The Catholic claim is, properly, for *sacramental* truth, and explicating that notion is the focus of this chapter.

As discussed earlier, one might allow "special interest" universities in which some powerful external witness frames the institution in terms of an historical truth of experience. Such constraint runs counter to the "diversityist" interpretation that is often regarded as the essence of academic freedom. The difference between various special interest universities constrained by witness and a Catholic university is that in the latter there is an "office of Truth" believed to have been delegated by Jesus to Peter and his successors. While there are many witnesses for the Holocaust whose assessments of the past and advice for the future differ, thus opening some space for academic debate, the Roman Church claims that through Peter it speaks with a single, consistent voice. An "office of Truth" closes discussion.

Despite occasional nods toward diversity in faith and tradition, the history of the Catholic church shows a consistent claim for consistency (real or imagined). The fact that papal teaching has in many instances—for example, usury, slavery, capital punishment, antisemitism—been inconsistent is often blandly or elaborately denied; it was not *the* church which erred, only individuals (even popes). The claim of consistent, infallible teaching continues to define the Roman *magisterium*, thus creating a drive for conformity in verbal formulation, ritual, and moral teaching. As noted earlier, at the opening of Vatican II the bishops of the council were enjoined to take the Anti-Modernist Oath. True, the fathers of the council demurred and, following the lead of John XXIII, opened the windows of the church to the modern world. The pontificate of John Paul II has, in the eyes of many within and without the church, closed many of those windows, battening the hatches against much of the modern world and its "isms." *Ex Corde Ecclesiae* seems one clear example of a trend toward shutting down—and shutting up, as in the injunction forbidding even *discussion* of women's ordination.

Declaring truth and shutting down discussion are anathema to the university's way; it is no wonder then that the papal demand in *Ex Corde Ecclesiae* for "Catholicity" in Catholic universities has caused widespread concern—particularly in the United States, which has a large number of Catholic colleges and universities and where the tradition of open university discussion is so firmly embedded. In the discussion of *Ex Corde* in chapter 9, I suggested that before one could decide whether universities were "from the heart of the church" one should decide just *what* church one had in mind. Avery Dulles's five models of church pose quite different problems for the university, from juridical constriction to prophetic denunciation. I rejected four of the models on the basis of their incoherency in the context of a Catholic university, though that judgment is, I would admit, somewhat high handed. I might be persuaded to agree with Dulles that a plausible and acceptable model of church could be created starting with any of the options, and that perhaps one might be able to stretch each of these models into an appropriate construction for church + university. But I am nevertheless inclined to reject the four models discussed because they involve too many *ad hoc* adjustments to accommodate the genuine authority of the university—not to mention the danger of straying into quite awkward, limited, and often unpalatable views of church. Ptolemaic astronomy with its epicycles did describe the heavens, but it was awkward and subject to the sort of tinkering that finally led to its complete collapse. The rejected models have an inherent tendency toward misleading or truncated understandings of church, and as a consequence fail to accommodate both church and university.

The juridical model tends to compromise academic freedom thus violating *university* assumptions; the mystical model makes the notion of "Christian/ Catholic" so interior that one could not be certain what "Catholic" means in "*Catholic* university." Under the prophetic model, the prophet's pervasive sense of sin rejects the pretensions of intellect and wants no part of the university; in its most extreme expression, prophetism also rejects the notion of "church." *The* church is never established or visible; it is always *semper reformanda.* The basic Reformation view is that God relates directly to the individual soul without mediation of church, priest, or sacrament. Given the "sinfulness" of the university and the fragility of "church," whatever species of "church university" might be constructed using the prophetic model would be highly unstable, which might explain why the Protestant "church university" in its Calvinist form has all but disappeared. Finally, the servant model of church embraces the university's commitment to the advancement of human culture and to social welfare, and would just as soon avoid difficult and distracting "dogma." For the servant church, "Christian/Catholic university" is redundant since the university may be all the church one needs. There is an almost Hegelian dialectical reversal in the historical movement from the Protestant prophetic colleges to the servant university. Place God's Word sufficiently high, utterly removed from a sinful world, and pretty soon one may just give up on the unattainable Word, and seize on the admittedly fallible word at hand—with the falliblist university as the best we can expect.

Having rejected four of Dulles's models as flawed, I now turn to a consideration of his fifth model: the sacramental model of church.[1] What is the sacramental model and how does it relate to the world of the university? What is a "sacramental truth"? How does "truth" function within a set of "sacramental" assumptions? In what way would a view of sacramental truth fully affirm the legitimacy of university truth, the sciences and arts? How does sacramental truth *add* anything to the university task such that a Catholic university could be more than a concession and become a desideratum? If the sacramental model works it must somehow manage to give legitimacy to both Christian truth and university truth and then regard them as appropriately linked.

"THE REAL" AND TRUTH

If truth is the final and fundamental area of contestation between church and university, the Roman Catholic *juridical* model at least has the considerable virtue of thinking that some sort of *expressible* truth is important. But while a hard-line, Catholic theory of religious truth is troublesome for academics, issues of religious truth can be a bother for the other models of church. Mystics may believe in truth, but it cannot be expressed. Prophetic and servant models of church aren't sure that religion is into truths at all. All is mystery, obedience, or good deeds; let the university do what it wants with "truth" since religion is in some sense beyond it, "beyond truth." In an important sense these latter positions would seem to overstate the case. Like classical skepticism that proclaims the truth that there is no truth, these various religious options cling to the "truth" of their particular model of church. However uneasy they may be about some specific dogma or dogma generally, they all use "truth" as a metaphor to express an utter conviction about proper religious consciousness. In short and at minimum, each option holds to the unshakeable meta-truth of its preferred model even if the consequence of the model is that there are no truths that can be uttered. The mystic, for example, is utterly convinced about the absoluteness of the Spirit; that conviction reduces all mundane truth (and even religious sayings) to distortion.

The Roman Catholic juridical model differentiates itself from the mystical, prophetic and servant models by its claim to offer specific, stateable dogmas— which certainly look like ordinary statements claiming to be verifiable. In John Paul II's *Fides et Ratio*, there is a sturdy defense of truth claims in both the supernatural and natural realm. Richard Bernstein's comment excerpted in chapter 2 about the multiple, ambiguous uses of "truth" in *Fides et Ratio* points, however, to the defect in the pope's presentation. Not only is there the serious question about whether a juridical church model can be understood to *adjudi-*

cate truth (à la the Supreme Court), there is a fundamental confusion, or conflation, of supernatural and natural types of truth. It is as if "truth" was used with only one sense so that the division between natural (scientific) truth and supernatural truth is a division of *subject matter*, like a distinction between the geological description of an area and an historical description. To describe an area geologically and in terms of its human history are clearly different enterprises, but the notion of truth is the same. On some occasions there may be a correction of one by the other. The claim that there is a geological mound near the river, for example, is corrected by information that it is the remains of ancient quarrying. Thus Rome in the past has derived natural truth from supernatural (the Galileo scandal); sometimes it seems to derive supernatural truth from natural (the presumed proofs of the existence of God from natural causality).

The Roman juridical model in practice shares the flaw of biblical fundamentalism in seeking to move back and forth between biblical "facts" and scientific facts. It is only in the last fifty years that Rome has warily accepted higher biblical criticism, and it continues to show manifest capacity to be literal and fundamentalist when challenged—as in the issues surrounding the ordination of women or the claim to papal supremacy, based on literal or unsophisticated reading of the injunction to Peter. If there is to be an adequate account of church in a manner compatible with the university, it must be one that does not confuse or conflate the truths appropriate to each. I believe that a sacramental model of church avoids this dilemma, granting legitimacy both to religious truth and the mundane, natural truths that are the normal ken of the university.

AN EPISTEMOLOGY OF RELIGIOUS TRUTH

I assume that the nature and place of natural truth in scientific and scholarly work within the university is well understood. The issue then is to locate religious, or supernatural, truth in such a manner as not to compromise the integrity of natural truth. What is needed is a clear and differentiating "epistemology of religious truth." "Epistemology" is a fancy philosophical term for the study of "how we come to know," and thus I am interested in *how we come to know Christian truth?* (I suspect that the epistemology of Christian belief is analogously present in all *religious* claims, but that is not my present concern.)

How we come to know x is an essential factor in the *meaning* of what we know. As the modern philosophical slogan states it: the meaning of a statement is the method of its verification. The *meaning* of "$2 + 2 = 4$" and "the cat is on the mat"—two of the most deeply analyzed phrases in modern philosophy!— are different not because one is about integers and the other about tabbies, but because the first statement is verified through the interior meaning of the concepts "2," "4," "+," and "=." The second statement is verified by checking the mat for cats. The first is an analytic statement, the second empirical. What we know in mathematical statements is radically different from what we know via empirical claims because of the different methods of verification. In terms of either of these two well-accepted methods of verification, however—methods that are the mainstay of university science—one would find it impossible not merely to *verify* Christian belief statements, one would quite fail to *understand what they mean.* "Jesus is the Son of God" baffles the empirical method on so many levels that it is not worth discussing. As an analytic statement, "Jesus is the Son of God" would establish truth at the expense of sending Christianity off into the realm of linguistic rules governing assorted "language games." In the Christian language game, Jesus is the Son of God, but one is not at all compelled to "play" that game. If there is to be any meaning and truth for Christian claims, any supernatural truth that compels assent, there must be some different methodology, an epistemology for religious faith.

The ancient church principle that heads this chapter—*lex orandi, lex credendi*, the law of prayer is the law of belief—captures the fundamental epistemology for supernatural truth. Prayer is "raising the heart and mind to God" and only in that "mental/spiritual" modality can one access the meaning and truth of belief. *Lex orandi* says that we do not first have a set of beliefs as "facts" and then proceed to pray; rather we pray, *then* we fashion statements of "belief." Belief statements are essentially "prayer language" while also serving as our "description" of what is going on in the act of prayer. Supernatural truth is accessed in the mode of prayer.

J. N. Findlay offered an elegant account of the order of prayer and belief in an article intended to prove the nonexistence of God. Starting from the obviously religious attitude of *worship*, Findlay asked what would be the necessary conditions for worship, which he rightly described as utter devotion, abasement, "bending the knee." It would be bizarre or irrational to worship something that one regarded as defective or imperfect. Building on an analysis of the attitude of worship, Findlay concluded that an object of worship, not merely one that is respected or revered, would have to be supremely perfect and, in addition, could not just *happen* to exist. It would have to be beyond happenstance, it would have to exist necessarily. That is the conventional definition of God: a being whose essence is to exist. In the act and attitude of prayer/worship, one introduces the word "God" as an expression of what must exist for worship to occur. There is no prayer/worship without the use of a "God-word" and only the assumption that there is some "God" addressed makes worship "rational." (For Findlay worship leads to a logical contradiction, a "necessary existent" that he holds to be a logical contradiction like "round-square.")[2]

A similar argument to Findlay's (but with a positive theological outcome) can be found in the work of the Catholic existentialist Gabriel Marcel:

> [S]ide by side with faith we posit love. . . . [L]ove is the condition of faith. . . . I believe that in reality love and faith cannot be dissociated. When faith ceases to be love it congeals into objective belief in a power that is conceived more or less physically. And love which is not faith (which does not posit the transcendence of the God who is loved) is only a sort of abstract game. . . . I cease to believe in God the moment I cease to love him; an imperfect God cannot be real.[3]

Findlay and Marcel both made a profoundly important and crucial point. There is no appropriation of the truth of faith, the reality of God, except through the attitude of worship, prayer, or love. If one says in a "neutral" fashion that God exists, then for Marcel that is not God but "an objective belief in a power . . . conceived . . . physically." *Empirical* verification that equates "God is in his heaven" to "the cat is on her mat" could only end up with a god-object. God conceived *objectively* (empirically) would only be an *object*, what Martin Buber called an "it" in contrast to a "Thou." Conversely, love that has no aim, no relation to a real other (I am avoiding "object"), is an "abstract game." One might regard such "love" as a "free-floating sentimentality." The whole argument can be restated somewhat crudely: for a blind person there is simply no reality for the notion "visual object." Lacking the necessary receptive capacity, the idea of a visual object is empty. For Findlay and Marcel, the individual who is not positioned in the mode of worship or love cannot know the proper object of worship or love. There is no belief in the religious "facts" except through the "perception" of prayer, worship, or love. As Wittgenstein put it: "only *love* can believe the resurrection."[4]

To repeat: there can be no belief in religious "facts"/ "truths" in the mode of the empirical observer or the dispassionate constructor of linguistic rules. The essential demand of scientific *observation* is neutrality to the facts as they just happen to turn out. The empirical observer passionately committed to cats on mats is suspect. More soberly, Sir Arthur Evans's passionate belief in the existence of a high Minoan civilization led him to "discover" elegances in the Palace at Knossos that were just not there. If the empirical investigator is constrained to neutrality, the constructor of linguistic rules may certainly regard the language game as only a "game"—hardly the attitude of genuine religiosity. In the case of religion we only reach the object "known" in and through "passion," which is to say worship or love. One must first be positioned in the mode of worship and *then* the object is manifest. The God reached in worship is, as Findlay noted, not the empirical observer's "By Jove, He happens to exist!"—like actually discovering the cat on the mat. God, if worth anything, if actually "met," exists "necessarily."[5] For Marcel, a "neutrally" discovered God would be an object, an "it," and not a fit locus for love and worship. For Catholicism, faith is established within the world of worship, most pointedly in the sacramental act, the central ritual of worship.

Making prayer or worship necessary conditions for apprehending belief may seem like special pleading for religion, but the argument applies in varying degrees to the special interest institutions discussed in chapter 8. In the prime case of the Holocaust university, the injunction is "lest we forget." But this should not be taken as an injunction for archival memory. To *remember* the Holocaust requires remembering the *Holocaust,* that is, precisely *not* to take it as a "neutral" object. Someone who with an air of "objectivity" says, "I know all about the Holocaust" does *not* know about the Holocaust. Some things are only known or named with a prayer. "The Holocaust, God have mercy on us!" "The Holy One, blessed be He!" The truth of the Holocaust is uttered in a mode (the shudder of prayer?) that is not part of the academic repertoire of impartial inquiry and appraisal. If there is to be a Holocaust university that "knows" the truth of the Holocaust, there must be recognition of a sense of truth beyond the academic mode of objectivity. There is something *in the nature of the reality* addressed in prayer, worship, and love that demands those spiritual attitudes and postures as a condition for understanding the *reality* of what is presented. Thus a reflexive relationship exists in which the reality encountered demands a certain attitude in reponse, but at the same time one must first come to that reality with a certain emotional commitment for the reality to be opened.

If the Holocaust were a fiction, it would not command the attitude demanded. We have emotional reactions to fiction, but do not grieve forever over Little Nell. If there is no factual basis at all to the New Testament—if it were an early novel by St. Paul—we might sympathize with the protagonist but not create a church to worship him. And yet, while there is a "reality" necessary to religion, it is not a reality that can arise from simple factual veracity.

The epistemology of prayer has a further and more radical difference with respect to the dominant and accepted academic disciplines already discussed—

scientific proof and artistic evaluation. For different reasons, scientific inquiry and artistic appraisal conform to the open assumptions normally associated with academic freedom. Science in its modern Peircean, fallibilist interpretation is obviously committed to academic freedom. In art, while there is a canon of exemplars that in one sense predetermines value, the canon is regarded as open (the modern anticlassicist assumption.) In the course of my argument, I have gone on to suggest that in the phenomenon of "anti-art" there is an urge toward a realm—"the real"—which cannot be captured by science or art. It is Henry James's "splendid waste" that is "life"itself. It is in the category of "the real" and in the mode of apprehension of "the real" that religious truth is located. Falling into "the real"—*the* real—carries a sense of "infallibility" that the distanced and diffident (literally: without *faith*) academic mind avoids or rejects. Put most baldly, the real reveals the final, absolute, infallible truth.

To locate the truth of religion in "the real" immediately results—plausibly enough—in a confusion between religious claims and university investigation. If one claims to present *the* real or to be present to *the* real, it sounds as if one is offering something quite "objective" that anyone could apprehend: the real truth! But it turns out that "the real" can only be apprehended within some mode of personal participation. Ivan Ilych's death is "the real" for Ivan Ilych. Individuals who fail to participate (in their own death, in prayer, in being "shocked" by anti-art) do not understand what is going on, do not reach "the real" that is revealed. In short, apprehending "the real" violates the studied asceticism of science and the distancing of artistic appraisal. Kenneth Clark made a careful distinction between the "nude" and the "naked." The nude of classical art is a study in form and sensibility, it is not the naked erotic. Much of anti-art, despite the arch attitudes of aesthetes, is naked and intended to be erotic. Erotic arousal affects the viewer; it changes the nature of the object viewed and the subject viewing from neutral to engaged. A God loved (worshiped in prayer) is a different "reality" than a God viewed. A naked Christ on the cross is not nude; he is an object of revulsion or, as Christians think, worship.

If the epistemology of belief is worship, prayer, and love, is there any more reason for a praying community, the church, to urge attention to the locus of prayer (God) than for the individual lover to demand academic attention to his Juliet or her Romeo? If one emphasizes the sense of *individual* participation necessary for accessing "the real" and hence religious truth, one can well understand the university's view that religious belief is merely subjective, personal opinion. However, while it may seem illegitimate on its face that the university pay attention to my specific love life—Juliet or Jesus—there would seem to be quite general truths that stem from the human experiences of love and death, anti-art, and religion. Such experiences are certainly participatory and individual but for all that not idiosyncratic. *Everyone* faces death though each death is personal. As the old black hymn says, "You got to cross that lonesome valley by yourself"; but everyone crosses that valley. Varied experiences of "the real" escape scholastic measurement and yet are universal—that certainly is the claim of religions.

To assert the meta-truth: "the real" exists, either *extends* the university's domain of "truth" or it *limits* the area of university studies by pointing to ranges of reality beyond the scholar's capacity. To locate "the real" in the sort of deep experiences already indicated can either extend the university's range of "reality" or sharply delimit university scope. "The quad's a fine and studious place, but none I think do there embrace." Acknowledgment of "the real" provides a horizon for scholarly study—setting the limit of vision and, perhaps, indicating a "beyond" worthy of thoughtful attention.

I would expect sobriety to follow and accept this chain of argument. Yes, there is "the real" beyond the ken of science and art. (I note that a scrupulous Platonist would regard my notion of "the real" as "the *un*real," preferring the clarity of knowledge and art to the confusion of "life." Plato "knows" existence as a chaos to be transcended in the tranquility of the ideal.) The crucial question for a Catholic university is whether the necessary relation to "the real" undermines the university or reinforces it. I believe it does the latter: the sacramental relation to "the real" that is characteristic of Catholicism demands the assertion of "ordinary" truth and reality.

THE UNIVERSITY AND "THE REAL"

When people come to a sense of "the real" it is through some powerful experience that shatters our normal appraisive abstraction. The reason that there is no bridge from *Death in Venice* to death in Auschwitz is that the chaotic destructiveness of the latter resists artistic shape and remains a dark puzzle for the rational mind. As I have suggested throughout, it would be salutary for the university to come to a self-consciousness about its relation to "the real." The university may, of course, take up the *existential* stance of neutrality, abstraction, and distance; one moves to the grove of academe and abandons the tumult of the marketplace. The value of such appraisive distance hardly needs defense. But, on the other hand, an institution existentially committed to "neutrality" may well be shunned by those upon whom history has impressed its deeper hopes and fears. The grove of academe and the ivory tower become "false" retreats. Lovers abandon such ordered precincts. The Holocaust witness cannot abide a *de jure* retreat from what he regards as life's urgent and enduring meaning and task. The university that takes academic abstraction *as* existential reality may well be regarded as inherently defective and even dangerous. It damages the individual soul, leading it to an arid place away from life, paralyzing the will to deal with the "splendid"(!) waste of history.

In this regard, with respect to the earlier discussion of the various models of church, it should be clear that whatever model for church is adopted only instantiates or institutionalizes a certain *general* mode for dealing with "the real." The church is a self-conscious, institutional mode of dealing with "the real," just as the university is a self-conscious, institutional mode of apprehending truth through science and art. (That is a first approximation of the university, since in my judgement the university also comes to terms with "the real" whether positively or negatively.) The first consideration for the individual and the university beyond the meta-truth that "the real" exists is whether one flees from chaotic life or embraces it. Is one to be Da Vinci with his ordered composition of a serene Mona Lisa in muted tones, or Duchamp gleefully painting a moustache on that classical figure and plopping the disfigured *donna* next to a found urinal?

Insofar as there is an issue about "the real" for the university, one can completely bracket out all considerations about church and religion, and concentrate solely on how the university might position itself *vis-à-vis* " the real" and any of the "secular" philosophies that speak about it. There are "mystical" views of "the real" that are by no means religious—or at least they are not at all "churchy." In Sartre's *Nausea*, the protagonist has a mystical vision of the sheer density of existence that he judges to utterly subvert science and scholarship. For Sartre, it is because there is no God that sheer existence is impossibly dense and incomprehensible. One can only plunge off into the world of action and commitment with no hope for avoiding the ambiguity and confusion of life. In the case of anti-art one does not fly to the monastery; one embraces the chaos of drugs, sex, and destruction as the only "measure" of the unmeasurable "real." A Duchampian (anti-art) university would be as much a contradiction on its face as a Catholic university. For the Duchampian it is the *university* that is "dogmatic." The anti-artist is the one who acknowledges the true freedom and fluidity of life—a reality that always escapes the confines of scientific concept and ordered art. Mysticism, then—whether saintly, Sartrean, or Duchampian—

offers no ground for the university. Given the abyss between academic order and "the real," the academy may well retreat to the Platonic model, seeking safety in the conviction that it is the world of Ideas that is *really* real, that the chaos of life is to be transcended toward knowledge and order. The anti-artist, the mystic, and Sartre want no part of the academic philosopher's tidy world, and the university philosopher will judge "good riddance."

The models of church so far discussed embody general claims about how one might regard "the real." In various ways, the rejected models of church avoid ordinary truth and thus the instrument of ordinary truth: the university. For the religious mystic ordinary truth is evaporated in the "wilderness beyond Being" (Meister Eckhart); for the prophet, the ordinary fades before the sinfulness of humanity; for the servant churchperson, the university is the best truth there is—although it is inherently "fallible" because one can never know "the God's truth." The juridical model seems to equate the truth of faith and the truth of fact, which can be fatal either to the church or the university, depending on who presumably commands the facts. What stance does the last model, the *sacramental* model, take toward ordinary scientific and artistic truth as it may relate to what "the real" reveals?

If there is a mystical (religious or nonreligious) attitude toward "the real," there is also a sacramental attitude, upon which Roman Catholicism properly rests. It is not necessary to argue at great length about the historical centrality of the sacramental within Catholicism. One need only recall such incidents as Zwingli's claiming "thus is the sacrament overthrown" as a way of distinguishing the new faith from what he perceived to be the superstitious adulation of the Eucharist in Roman Catholic practice. It is my general contention, however, that the sacramental model of church preserves the given reality as detailed in science and art while at the same time opening up a supernatural dimension of human life and perception.

It will certainly seem a wayward digression to discuss the university via the notion of sacrament. But if I am correct in asserting the centrality of the sacramental for Catholicism, then a *Catholic* university would be a conjunction of the sacramental and the scientific. Catholic university = sacrament + science. To make any sense of such an odd equation, one must first understand what is meant by "sacrament." The standard Catholic definition is "an outward and visible sign of an inward grace."[6] What is critical but also puzzling about this formulation is its conjoining of the reality of the sign *and* the reality of the inward grace.

The traditional Catholic interpretation of the Eucharistic Sacrament is that in the ritual the bread and wine are "transformed" (transubstantiated) into the body and blood of Jesus Christ. The claim is utterly counterempirical; to any sensible observer or empirical test, this is just bread, just wine. Countering the weird realism of the Catholic view, it seems much more sensible to speak of the Eucharist as a *symbol*, which is basically the position taken under the other church models. The assault of the sacramental on common sense poses no special problems for the mystic. Appearances are *always* deceptive; thus it is not strange that the appearance of bread deceives. Spirit is omnipresent, the wilderness beyond the Being of all beings. Language and ritual are more or less arbitrary symbols for an overflowing reality. Just as mystical writings struggle to find expression for overwhelming visions, finally attesting to the futility of language, so the bread and wine are "mere" symbols for the inexpressible closeness of God. As mentioned above, the Eucharist as "symbol" is characteristic of the other notions of church. It is certainly the position of mainline Calvinism— a clear example of the prophetic model.[7] Because the church-as-servant refuses to accept anything supernatural and miraculous, under that model the Eucharist is nothing but an ordinary symbol of human fellowship.

The Catholic sacramental view suggests that there is some sort of radical repositioning of the bread and wine: it is "transubstantiated," which certainly sounds like a profound change of some sort. But in contrast to the mystic, the traditional Roman Catholic view of the Eucharist retains a sober grasp on common sense. A common characterization of realism is that it "saves the appearances"—there is no greater grasp on reality available by going *behind* the appearance. But this is just what mysticism seeks, the reality *behind* the appearances. Thus a mystical interpretation of *real* presence is that Jesus is *disguised* as bread! The Eucharistic Sacrament is akin to servants in enchanted castles who are converted into teacups and mice that are converted into coachman. The real servant or mouse exists *behind* the enchanted disguise. In the traditional Catholic doctrine of "real presence," however, the appearance (bread and wine) is not a disguise. There is nothing hidden *inside* or *beyond* the ordinary.[8]

If the Eucharist as "real presence" is not Jesus disguised, what is being asserted in the traditional doctrine? I recall a pious Catholic bishop congratulating his fellow Catholics on the fact that in the Roman Church Jesus was *physically* present in the Eucharist. But it would be some sort of wild miracle (or nonsense) to say that this real bread is the real Jesus who preached in Galilee. "Jesus is a real presence in the Eucharist" is a *sacramental* truth and as such is in no way comparable to the straightforward (or mystical) interpretation "the bread is Jesus in disguise" or the absurdity/miracle "this real bread is this real Jesus." Jesus is present but *sacramentally* present; that is the sacramental claim and sacramental truth.

The sense of sacramental *real* presence (not disguise or miracle) can be understood as a denial of *symbolic* presence. I return to the difference discussed earlier between icons and symbols. Symbols are just symbols; the symbol "c-a-t" has no feline characteristics. Icons, however, participate in the reality that they signify. The children's art of the Holocaust was said to be iconic because it did not simply depict the reality; it was, in some sense, a part of the reality. Children's art makes the reality present and makes us present to the reality. Similarly, the impetus of anti-art is iconic in its desire to make present the reality signified. In a sacramental view, the Eucharist is more than symbolic, it is iconic and participates in the reality (the Body of Christ) that it signifies.

Rosemary Houghton offered a splendid explication of this sense of "sacrament" in a discussion of Jasper Johns's flag paintings,[9] in each of which the artist filled his canvas with a painting (in various media) of an American flag. What the viewer of the painting is presented with is *both* a flag and a symbol/representation of the flag. The painting is not *the* flag (the star-spangled banner that still waves), it is a representation of the flag on canvas, hanging on the wall of the art gallery—but it is also a *flag*. The flag painting both presents and symbolizes at the same time. There is both a present reality and yet an absence of the real thing in its full experiential density. While the children's art makes the Holocaust present in one sense—unmediated and colored by the sophisticated technique of the mature artist—in another sense it only "symbolizes" the Holocaust. To view the children's picture is not to actually experience Auschwitz, not to be cast into that hellish place. Viewing Jasper Johns's flag is not " a call to the colors" with the emotional density of a patriotic occasion. It is only a "symbol" in a gallery after all. And yet it is also a flag and thus *directly* linked to the attitudinal density that the *real* flag commands.

A complex way of stating what is happening in the flag painting is that "the real presents itself in the mode of absence": it's only a *painting* of a flag. Conversely, one could say that the flag painting expresses "the absence of the real flag in the mode of presence": the painting is *only* a flag. (The same ambiguity infects pop art: "This is *only* a Brillo box.") The presence/absence of the real flag from Johns's "painting" commands an attitude or relation that a "mere" symbol cannot. We are troubled by this re-presentation of the thing itself. Are we to react as we would to "the real thing"—salute, say the pledge of allegiance? That doesn't seem right, but this is not just a symbol like the word "flag," which is utterly other than then reality itself. Holy icons of the Eastern Church present the same confused mode of apprehension. Are they themselves holy objects that command a religious reverence or merely a *symbol* of a saint and thus not to be revered. Holy icons were traditionally only painted by "holy" monks; like the children's art they witnessed or *issued from* holiness as much as they symbolized it.

In the Catholic Eucharist, the actual species of bread and wine are invested with holiness. They are not merely symbols of the holy. The Eucharistic Sacrament—bread and wine—is not the real, physical Jesus of Nazareth any more than the painting by Jasper Johns is the *real* flag. However, in the sacramental ritual of the Eucharist, the bread and wine become Jesus present (in the mode of absence), or Jesus absent (in the mode of presence.) The point is that the bread and wine have the ambivalent character of the Jasper Johns flag. They both make the respective realities "present"—though, of course, not with the fullness of the real flag and not the real, "physical" Jesus.

Asserting "real presence" in this iconic sense is not something that occurs by magic; it depends on creating a proper "iconic" context. In the case of pop art, one shifts the context from the A&P to the art gallery; the soup can is represented in the context of a museum. The essential condition for the sacramental/iconic revelation is that there be a context of worship, without which the bread is just bread. I agree with those Catholic theologians who argue that "transubstantiation" depends on the existence of a present, worshiping community. The juridical view of church often suggests that the mere formulary of consecration, with or without a context of worship, transubstantiates. But that is magic! The context of museum or worship is essential. We venerate Rembrandt and worship God. The shock of pop art is that we are asked to "venerate" the mundane when it reappears in a museum; the shock of Eucharist is that we "worship" bread!

The attitude we bring to the context and what is demanded within that context are crucial. The children's art makes the Holocaust present so one is not allowed the luxury of artistic judgment: one must weep, pray, or curse. Concomitantly one cannot come to the children's art with the fixed attitude of an aesthete. For the work to have its iconic power, one must be in some sense already open emotionally to the reality depicted. The example in chapter 7 of the Jewish girl who heard her named called at Yad Vashem illustrates that point.

Catherine Pickstock delineates with great care St. Thomas's view that in the worship structure (prayer) of the Mass, the attitude of the congregation is shaped in such a manner that the people are led to desire and accept the *real* presence of Jesus. One begins with a confession of unworthiness (*Confiteor*), moves to a recognition of the utter worthiness of God (*Gloria*), and proceeds on through a series of prayers, readings, and petitions that prepare one "emotionally" for the sacramental real presence. The aim of the liturgy is to shape the emotion of the congregation toward a special "desire" for the "Body of Christ," which is understood as the desire that God should be truly *with* human reality, *in* human reality. Recalling from chapter 5 L'Heureux's "expert on God," the desire is to be held in a loving presence.

Is there a *real presence* that holds us in love? The Eucharistic Sacrament is the answer to that desire generated by the ritual. Pickstock is careful to say that the Eucharist is not the *fulfillment* of such a desire. As the culmination of the attitudinal shaping of the Mass, it is only a *promise* that the desire for "the body of Christ" is real and not vain. The congregation worships in faith and hope, not in knowledge and present fact. A nonbeliever will think that the desire for the Body of Christ is empty. The Christian believer thinks the desire is not absurd because of the promise in Jesus. Resurrection says that the reality of God present did not vanish with the death of Jesus. We do not yearn for a past God.

The flag case outlines the ambivalent character of sacramental presence, but it may seem an easy case because Jasper Johns's flag is a flag—even if it is not a flag. What are we to make of bread and wine as Jesus? In the Eucharist, *remembrance* replaces *resemblance*. Jesus commands the disciples to repeat the meal of bread and wine "in remembrance of me." I have a teacup that belonged to my sainted grandmother; it has always reminded me of her. Now, suppose that in her last days she gave me this special cup specifically as a remembrance. While I would not hesitate to discard any other cracked cup, to throw this cup out would be an insult to the giver whom I venerate. The cup is invested with grandmother "present" in the poignant mode of her absence. Of course, grandmother is definitively gone, not here. Veneration of the cup is nostalgia.

In the Christian case, the Eucharistic Sacrament stems from Jesus giving the bread and wine to his disciples at his last meal. In giving the bread and wine, he says remember me. I am the one who *gives* this bread and wine, I am the one who gives his life for his friends. The bread and wine are my present to you and will remain as my being present to you in remembrance. Resurrection, then, proclaims Jesus alive and with the promise that he will come again. The teacup is venerated in poignancy and nostalgia; the bread is revered in hope. As one commentator says, "The sacrament is a nostalgia for the future." The ritual of the Eucharist makes this clear: immediately after the consecration of the bread and wine, the congregation acclaims "Christ has died, Christ is risen, Christ will come again."

Real bread and real wine remain quite firmly anchored in our ordinary meaning of bread and wine. (This is a real teacup.) In the sacramental words of worship they become Jesus (sacramentally) present in the mode of his real absence. Just as remembering the Holocaust is not a feat of memory but the command of an attitude, so in remembering Jesus we are commanded to the attitude of veneration unto worship. Remembering Jesus is believing in God's love "as it was in the beginning, is now, and ever shall be." The Eucharist is an icon of hope. It is because "the real" of the Holocaust is not over and done with that we recall it in care, with care; it is because Jesus is not over and done with that we recall him in prayer, with prayer.

THE REALISM OF SACRAMENT

In contrast to the mystic take on "the real," the sacramental mode holds that signs can, in the right circumstance, open to "the real" while retaining their determinate meaning and status. Grandmother's teacup is just a cup, but it is made "holy," more than a teacup, by her gift and my affection for her. The Brillo box fails to be effective as an "art" object if I refuse to grant its reality as a Brillo box. Access to the holy is "sacramental" insofar as the real item at hand is deepened but not obliterated or dissolved into the wilderness of God. The Catholic theologian John Dunne is fond of quoting the following four phrases from Tolkien: "Things are meant." "There are signs." "The heart speaks." "There is a way."[10] For the sacramental view of life and reality, "things are meant" in the sense that ordinary reality, things, can be deepened as the heart speaks. "I give you this in remembrance of me." Things become signs; there is a tangible way into "the real" of life and love and gift. Entrance into "the real" does not obliterate the visible thing.

Not only does the Jewish/Christian sense of religion and Revelation not obliterate ordinary reality in some mystic transcendence, it demands the reality of actual life and history. Strange, miraculous, mythologized, and theologized as it may be, the Scripture has a mundane meaning and presence as sure as bread and wine. But just as ordinary bread and wine are transubstantiated into the sacred, so Jewish history, the Jewish people, and the Jew Jesus are transubstantiated into sacred history. The Bible is not a *wisdom* book, it is a sacred *history* book. Christians do not fall into mystic silence or ecstatic cries; they tell and retell a story of God in our quite real history. Surely in Christianity the centrality of Incarnation suggests that the story of Jesus is a thoroughly real, ordinary story of suffering and death, even if that history is also an icon of God, God's real presence. The Brillo box has to be in one sense *just* a Brillo box in order to shock us when it is placed in a museum; Jesus of Nazareth must be *just* a fragile human like all of us for all that it "shocks" us in the mode of worship that he is proclaimed the Christ of God.

My conclusion is that a sacramental view of reality affirms the ordinary with all the gusto of robust realism, but then says that if taken up in the mode of the heart, there is a way in which things are deepened into the reality of a Creation and a God of Creation. I can relate to the teacup as a scientist understanding the importance of glazing to its function, as an artist appreciating its delicacy and shape, or in thankfulness, venerating the one who presented it to me. One knows the teacup but also appropriates it with thankfulness. One knows the world but appropriates it as a Creation such that we thank the Creator. My analysis has come full circle from the argument in chapter 1 that the biblical doctrine of Creation legitimates the realism of science and knowledge. The truths proclaimed by a sacramental model of church—which would certainly seem to be the actual heart of the Roman Catholic Church—are what we can know in the mode of sacramental prayer and worship.

To the extent that truth is a contested issue between church and university, this chapter has attempted to outline the special epistemology of religious truth, which is open to us through prayer, in worship. To be more precise, "positive" religious truth is accessed in worship. One may be "religious" in a negative mode: "the real" is accessed and felt in cursing and bitterness, not in gratitude and blessing. The issue for the university is what it should do with the whole range of unique attitudes that open to "the real." A Sartrean or a Duchampian will utterly reject the university because of the chaotic inexpressibility of "the real," preferring to plunge into chaotic life. A Catholic university, in contrast, holds that "the real" tells a tale. Life is more than "a tale told by an idiot, full of sound and fury, / Signifying nothing." For Catholics/Christians access to "the real" is not, as with various mysticisms, a fall into the Absolute, the Wilderness of Being. These are hyperbolic metaphors that may be used to express the "mystery" of God, but there is a more "commonsensical" access to "the real" in the story of the Bible culminating in the "historical" tale of Jesus of

Nazareth. God is not just the ineffable mystery, somehow he is present in the specific, concrete history of the Jewish people and—if one is Christian—finally in the actual history of Jesus who, for all that he is a wandering preacher and human victim, is the icon of God.

The *definitiveness* of an actual history (deepened though it may be into God's presence) radically separates Judaism and Christianity from the mystical turn of many if not most other great religious traditions. Definitiveness is the root of the *institutionalization* of the Roman Catholic *Church*. The final formulization of *Catholic* university is a relation of the *institution* of church to the *institution* of the university. In the following chapter I turn directly to a consideration of what it means to say that the Catholic Church is a *sacramental* institution, which I hope to differentiate from the traditional notion of a judicial institution.

11

A Contrarian University

A complex theology of the Eucharist may seem utterly irrelevant to the sober work of the academy, but in the confrontation with the university, "church" (in all the models previously discussed) simply instantiates one of the claims about "the real" with which the university has to deal whether pressed by specific religious, anti-art, or general philosophical (for example, existentialist) considerations. How will a claim about "the real" (God, "splendid waste," chaos) impinge upon university science and art? A response that the university will not make is to reduce its own academic effort to mystic or prophetic straw. My argument in this book is that the university could adopt a sacramental view of "the real"—a view that I believe legitimates science and art while also opening up a realm from which these worthy endeavors are methodologically barred. I would go further and say that a sacramental approach to "the real" *requires* the legitimacy of science and art, of "ordinary" reality. Sacramental perception deepens ordinary reality, it does not destroy it. Jesus is a figure of ordinary history not myth; only in that way can our experience of him be deepened into an icon of God.

A Catholic (sacramental) university "solves" the relation of the university and "the real" in a manner that preserves the integrity of science and the sacred. In the other church models of "the real," there is either a threat of encroachment (judicial model), abandonment (mystical), irrelevance (prophetic), or absorption (servant). In the juridical (and fundamentalist) model, one fancies that natural truth can be corrected by Revelation. The mystic abandons prosaic truth for the All. The prophet holds learning infected with sin and irrelevant to the of divine demand for justice and mercy. The servant accepts ordinary truth to be all that is available, turning the university into the "church" of cultural eclecticism.

SACRAMENT VERSUS CHURCH

The point has been made several times that some of the church models are not only antithetic to the university's way of truth, they are deeply suspicious of the institutional church. The mystic bypasses the institution for direct communion with the All; the prophet sees the church as *semper reformanda*—barely and usually badly institutionalized. The servant may regard the institutional church as either unnecessary or only a gloss on the cultural work of the university. Catholicism's historical assertion of the juridical-institutional model of church at least has the virtue of creating a definitive entity that does not fade into private rapture, dubious structure, or the unnecessary. An *institutional* Catholic Church (and its "truth") stands over against the university as institution. It is the *institutional* assumption of Catholicism that makes a *Catholic* university problematic for the university.

In the previous chapters I have outlined what I consider to be the failure of the traditional Catholic institutional model. That model confuses Christian truth and university truth by constructing a judicial hierarchy of truths that fails to grant autonomy to the university while also being an inappropriate model for the Christian community. Having said that, I do not think that the notion of "institution" can be wholly abandoned, as seems to occur in the other models. If, as I claim, the proper model for church is sacramental, it is necessary to see in what sense a sacramental church is an institutional church. How does a sacramental *institution* relate to the university?

Sacramentalism shares with all the church models a relation to "the real." Any relation to "the real" poses a problem for the more prosaic truths of science, art, and common sense. Some modes of sacramentalism may also reject church. It is important to understand such a position as a means of reintroducing the importance of *institution* in the discussion of church.

A possible example of sacramentalism rejecting church is described by Tom

Beaudoin in *Virtual Faith: the Irreverent Spiritual Quest of Generation X*.[1] He suggests that X'ers are strong on sacramentality but defiantly antichurch. X'ers in Beaudoin's analysis are everywhere "religious" in dress, drugs, sex, and rock music. Body piercing, baseball caps, hair styles, and tatoos all become signs of an inward "grace." Piercing is a stigmata in which the person's very body is signed as a theater of special revelation. In the flux of appearance, one anchors the vaporous self to "the real" of body with a nose ring. Beaudoin regards these outward and very visible signs as indications of a spiritual quest—something deeper than conformity to fad and fashion. Let us accept the X'er's odd gestures as sacramental. Body piercing does not just *say* "I am a free spirit, a rebel, my own self," it makes that reality present in the ultimate real of body. X'er fashions are like anti-art presentations: the thing itself is not just a symbol but iconic, that is to say, sacramental.

To the extent X'ers are into iconic presentation they are engaged in *participatory* experiences: sex, body piercing, drugs, and heavy metal. But such participatory experience is not sought in the pews of Sunday service. The church as institution is seen as a principal barrier to the sort of participatory access to life ("the real") that has been at the core of my explication of "the religious." Can there be an "institution" of "participation"? In a hierarchy of contradictions, these might be thought to rank higher than "Catholic university."

From the standpoint of Catholic Christianity, X'ers express free-floating sacramentality. What X'ers value is the *fact* of participatory experience, entrance into "the real" that the "sacraments" of their culture promise or permit. Given the antiseptic, anesthetic, analytic culture they identify with some combination of bourgeois values, pious religiosity, and—I fear—academic culture, the young want to seize or be seized by life. Any break into "the real" is valued. The historic church should understand the absolute importance of breaking through to "the real." Where it differs from the Generation X sensibility is in the belief that there is some *definitive* lesson within the realm of "the real." The Holocaust survivor points toward participation in "the real," but that experience—the Holocaust—is a defining experience: it is "*the* real." By centering on a definitive experience, the Holocaust survivor or the Jerusalem Traditions (in Exodus or Resurrection) take on an "institutional" cast.

The connection between fashion and X'er spirituality is more than accidental. X'ers live in a world of evanescent sacramentality. X'er spirituality and church spirituality can be analogized to the difference between seduction and marriage. Sexual seduction carries the special thrill of revealing the strange and novel other. Life is directed to such moments of "breakthrough," which by definition cannot be repeated. One who is obsessed with "breakthrough" becomes a Don Juan engaged in the ceaseless and "heroic" quest for new "revelations." Marriage "institutionalizes" breakthrough by centering on a definitive other. Sex in marriage is not a novel revelation but a sacramental evocation of the original moment of opening to the other. The church calls itself "the bride of Christ," and one might say that the community of the faithful is *married* to the life, death, and resurrection of Jesus—it is not spiritual Don Juanism always seeking a new Lord.

The urge to "institutionalize" is expressed in the formula *Lex orandi, lex credendi*. There is, after all, a "law" of prayer that creates the "law" of belief. That around which one organizes life and meaning is some *critical* moment of presence and participation among the many contestants for revelations of "the real." The Holocaust, the Exodus, the Cross, or the torture of the innocent is *the* crisis event of history to which one turns for meaning—or the event that drains all meaning from life and history. There is a "belief" entailed in the event toward which one turns in worship or overwhelming despair.

In the end, then, one cannot avoid the sense in which Judaism and Christianity "institutionalize," write creeds, set up codes of behavior, and form rituals because they hold that there is something definitive in the core experience of "the real." In the idea of a Catholic university, we are faced with connecting two institutions: the Catholic Church and the university. This church is *sacramental*, and the sacrament carries a special message beyond the *frisson* of connecting to "the real." The church has a fixed gaze, a loving commitment, a "marriage" (institution) to what it judges to be "*the* real."

There are many experiences of "the real," other claimants to the centrality of the experience of "*the* real," from high religion to simple sex. Claims about "*the* real" are like so many exemplars in the artistic tradition—except that because they press upon us as "*the* real" we do not have the luxury of an ever-open canon against which they may be judged. But the mode of artistic appraisal approximates the approach to this array of claimants. One aligns experiences and evaluates the proffered incursion of "*the* real" in the context of other exemplars. And in those varied "breakthroughs" one may seize upon—or be seized by—an experience that defines "*the* real." For Ivan Karamazov, "*the* real" is the torture of children and all else falls under that transcendent judgment. For the Holocaust victim it is Auschwitz that shadows life. For the Jerusalem Tradition it is Exodus or Crucifixion/Resurrection. It is in this sense that one *institutes* "*the* real."

Being pressed by a definitive experience as "*the* real" creates a continuing community: the Holocaust community, the Exodus community, the Crucifixion community, the Resurrection community. Organized around the memory of a central, determinitive opening of "*the* real," the community becomes a "worshiping" community. It insists that only the posture of "worship" measures and opens up the character of the definitive experience. I have placed "worship" in quotation marks. The attitude may be worship or "anti-worship": gratitude or bitter rejection, prayer or cursing. The essential point is that the attitude is essential to the truth of the "*the* real." The danger for the religious believer is that one will confuse the sense in which the core experience is *definitive* with the notion that one can *define* it. But the very fact that the definitive opening to "the real" can only be appropriated in prayer, love, worship, despair, or cursing means that it cannot be held at a distance, circumscribed in the manner of ordinary definition. The poet asks "How do I love thee? Let me count the ways. . . ." and there seems to be no end to the metaphorical expressions of love's meaning. It is only appropriate that there be a thousand names for God.

In a Catholic university, then, there is a conjunction between a community organized around a *defining* experience (Crucifixion/Resurrection) that resists definition, and an intellectual community that seeks clear definitions and prescinds from defining experiences in favor of intellectual distancing and appraisal. In the dynamic of Catholic + university, when church moves from the defining experience to a *once-and-for-all definition*, it misunderstands its own inner life as a worshiping community and improperly interferes with the task of the university. This is not to say that church talk is free floating. Because of the definitive character of the core experience of "*the* real," church talk always circles about that core in the manner of the lover trying to grasp the sense of this love at this time in these words and images. Gabriel Marcel's "mystery of the self" is paradigmatic for the dilemma of church talk: I sense (know) myself as something *definitive*, I am not a blank slate on which one may inscribe any set of properties that come to mind. But every ascription partly misses the mark because the self "described" is not "out there" but that within which I live and breathe. In the church, one can no more define the central mystery than one can define one's own personal mystery. Paradoxical as it may sound, the inability to define the mystery not only does not make it less *definitive*, it is the compelling involvement at the heart of mystery.

A CONTRARIAN UNIVERSITY

I have throughout contrasted university and church. Both terms are subject to significantly differing interpretations. I have outlined several contrasting models of church; one can do the same for the university. The philosophical assumptions of nineteenth-century American colleges embedded in the classical curriculum of Greek, Latin, and the Bible were radically different from those that prevail in the contemporary American research-oriented universities and colleges. The earlier institutions were much closer to "church" than their contemporary descendants. Conforming closer to the church modalities did little to advance the academic quality of these institutions. In this final summation contrasting a Catholic contrarian model of the university with the prevailing secular model, it is critical that the latter be understood along the lines of the contemporary research model derived at whatever remove from the philosophical assumptions of the Enlightenment.

The defining marks of a Catholic contrarian view are as follows: acknowledgment of "the real"; the importance of the participatory; participation not only in "the real" but "*the* real; that "*the* real" is revelatory (positive); and that "*the* real" is historical. The contrasting positions of the secular university are: "the real" is "unreal" (for university purposes); participatory experience is private and outside university scope; nothing can be judged to be "*the* real"; whatever "*the* real" may be it is not revelatory (it is negative to the work of intellect); history does not provide an opening to any universal reality. I expand on these contrasts more fully below, drawing on discussions throughout the earlier chapters of the book.

Acknowledging "the Real"

Catholic University: "The real" must be acknowledged as that which is beyond the appraisive distancing of science and art. There is at least *life*, in the sense of Henry James's "splendid waste," to be made sense of. The university must make a conscious philosophical decision about how its normal modes of thought relate to "the real."

Secular University: What is pointed to as "the real" is indeed "waste," a chaos that utterly eludes comprehension. Plato was correct to regard the "real" as the "unreal" precisely because it cannot be understood, made an object of order in science or art. However one juggles the metaphysical terms, the university has no interest in "the real" except as "the Ideal."

Participatory Knowledge

Catholic University: "The real" is opened only through personal participation. Because the Catholic university holds that opening to "the real" is an essential task for a university, it considers that presumed accounts of such participatory moments are an essential subject for understanding and appraisal within the curriculum. It seeks opportunities to further moments of participatory experience for students both in terms of direct confrontation with those life experiences commonly associated with the participatory—life decisions such as love, vocation, and loss—as well as through the ritual and sacramental moments that invoke "the real." The Catholic university can accept the Socratic notion that "the unexamined life is not worth living," but its emphasis is on *living* a life.

Secular University: Apprehensive about participatory experience, the secular university advocates a studied critical distance. Whatever the value of participatory experience, it is not as such a matter that falls within any academic competencies. Thus, one may *study* religion, for example, but any decision for this or that "faith" is personal and subjective in a negative or dismissive sense. The critical impulse says that "the examining life is the *only* life worth living." Life is held at a critical distance lest one succumb to passion, prejudice, or fanaticism—inveterate faults of religion.

"The Real" Is Revelatory

Catholic University: Contrary to those who revel in "the real," the Catholic university proclaims revelation. There is not only love, but love's *knowledge;* there are "reasons of the heart." There is more than the somatic thrill of sex, drugs, and heavy metal—or whatever more "refined" excitements may come from Bach or constructing high theory. The fact and possibility of passion and participation reveal a truth about human being. The Catholic university accepts and depends on art and science in their normal modes, but it is also concerned with the human passions that are invested in art and science for good and for ill. What does it say about a human life if one *lives* science or art? On the one hand, there is a lesson of dedication; on the other the temptation of abstraction, the life of the "mad scientist" or the ruthless artist.

Secular University: While admitting the undoubted pleasures of a variety of participatory experiences, the secular university is hard pressed to find something there that is akin to "knowledge." In what sense are there "reasons" of the heart—it seems the most quixotic and irrational of human organs. The dedicated scientist, the one whose *life* is science, may actually conform to the formal demands of the university. What she may be in private life, in extracurricular passions, is irrelevant to the university's mission. Descartes's motto "I am a thinking thing" is the only demand made or expected.

"The Real" Is Universal: There Is "the Real"

Catholic University: This is perhaps the most contrarian of the claims that could be made by a Catholic university; it is the source of the dogmatism for which the Catholic institution is taxed by its secular confreres. A secular institution might admit that there are experiences of the density of life that qualify as "the real," but as the varied religions, philosophies, and artistic expressions would suggest, these experiences are highly varied and do not offer any single vision of what might count as *"the* real." The Catholic university claims on the contrary that the core of the biblical story, climaxing in the life and death of Jesus, is somehow the paradigm story of humanity, of life, of *"the* real." Since this is the most contrarian of Catholic claims, it carries with it a special burden for pedagogy and argument *vis-à-vis* other moments (non-Christian) of "revelation."

She who has come face to face with "the real" in the dense participation of life will inevitably conjure that moment as *the* mark of human reality. The Holocaust is not a reality only for the one who endured the persecution; for the Jew it can become *the* life metaphor for humanity in its cruelty and despair. There is a demand for the universal in experiences of "the real." The Catholic/Christian claim is that in the Jesus story one can enfold all the varied claims. To show that "truth," to establish the universal in the Christian story, is not something that can be accomplished by dogmatic declaration or demonstration. One must move inside the participatory moment of the other and then return to one's first story prepared to alter, enrich, and restate.[2] Because the religious claim engages the totality of the believer at the deepest levels of his life participation, interreligious dialogue is inherently as difficult as it is risky. What seemingly cannot be laid aside is the universal demand within claims upon "the real."

Secular University: Given its wariness over participatory experience and its strong allegiance to appraisive distance, the secular university will, if it admits "religion" at all, do so under a "multiculturalist" banner. Religious interests will be regarded more or less like varieties of artistic expression. Just as it would seem foolish to ask whether Western art or Far Eastern art is "superior," so it would be equally inappropriate to rank the virtues of Judaism and Buddhism. The secular view values an "arm's length" dealing with religions that—so it is argued in this text—results in an inability to grasp religions on their own terms. The "arm's length" approach is often expressed as respect for diversity, but when further analyzed "diversity" often degenerates into "diversityism"—an approach that misses the very depth of participation and commitment that makes us value diversity in the first place. Secular universities have departments of religion; they do not have departments of theology.

"The Real" Is Historical

Catholic University: Human beings are finally defined within their historical individuality: the individual is more than an instance of a type. The truth of this claim is linked to the participatory nature of "the real." Only when we seize upon the particular moments of life with all their uncertainties, risks, joys, and threats do we encounter the final reality, Henry James's life as "splendid waste." If "the real" is specially caught up in the historical particularity of the individual, then whatever "universal" revelation there may be will perforce be within the historical. Finally it is history that marks *the* meaning of life; the historical reality of the Holocaust can become the life marker. Life markers may assert a "meaning of life" or they may drain away all meaning, as in the case of Ivan Karamazov or the many who have contemplated the genocidal ways of humankind. For Judaism and Christianity, life is encased in "sacred history."

Secular University: Insofar as the secular university conforms to the Platonic search for the universal, for the Ideal (which it regards as "the real"), it will make no sense of "sacred history." At best, history might be understood as the enactment and reenactment of myth, just as the individual is an instance of a general type. What exists on "the other side" of the general type are the innumerable choreographies (Derrida's expression) of human subjectivity. One may revel and delight in the dance, but no special value, priority, or depth can be assigned to such an infinite array of turns and twists. If there is any meaning to life it will be either in the transcendence of particularity (caught in the universal human myth) or a blissful *carpe diem* where life's lesson is in the vibrancy and passion of the dance.

TYPE AND FACT

Is the above an accurate contrast drawn between our current institutions of higher education? I certainly hope not. The contrast is between "ideal" types that probably exist nowhere in actuality. The analysis is particularly distorted on the side of the secular university. This is to be expected since the secular university is in so many ways an *omnium gatherum* not only of all sorts of specific academic disciplines but also of philosophies about higher education. I have in my construction of the secular university categorically ruled out demands from and upon "the real" and the knowledge peculiar to participation. That is hardly fair. There are scores of deeply engaged faculty at secular universities who ardently wish their students to engage religiously with life—and they teach with that end in mind. It is also the case that many students will awaken to the religious dimension through confrontation in class with some revealing account of "the real." Reading Kierkegaard when I was an undergraduate was such an experience for me. But for all that there are dedicated teachers and earnestly seeking students, there is an overall cast within the secular institution which has a very difficult time discriminating between wariness and withdrawal.

The secular university's caution about commitment needs to be honored. Fundamental life commitments—religion not the least—are not to be entered into just because they give a certain density to life. In a Sartre short story, "Childhood of a Leader," the protagonist decides to become an antisemite because it gives him an instant solidity in society that a more free-floating, uncertain self lacks. "One does not ask Jules to parties with the Levinsons because he is so anti-semitic!" Sartre saw the temptation to solidity as the root danger of religion. One solution to solidity, fanaticism, and the temptations of the religious is to "stay loose," accept nothing except as a probative hypothesis. In many ways, this fallibilist approach to any and all belief is the framing assumption of the secular university. Of course there is a value of caution, but such a framing assumption can turn life into merely a "topic for discussion." To be sure, one needs to discuss deep commitments, wariness is in order, the risks are extreme—but everlasting discussion leaves one Hamlet-like: "the native hue of resolution /Is sicklied o'er with the pale cast of thought,/And enterprises of great pith and moment/ . . . their currents turn awry."

Given a framing assumption of everlasting fallibilism, whatever the earnest efforts of "religiously" oriented faculty or curricula within a secular university, there will be an incoherence between specific teaching and the framing reality. The problem for a Catholic university will be to assert a framing assumption *for* faith that is everywhere sensitive to the riskiness of faith. Dogmatic demands and assertions may be no more than the temptations to solidity that Sartre so rightly warns against.

I have suggested that the secular university is more complex than the typologies outlined. This is no less true of Catholic universities. If one took actual examples, it would seem that putative Catholic institutions exist across a spectrum. There are highly dogmatic institutions like Steubenville, where oaths of fidelity and conformity to the letter of the *magisterium* are the rule of the day. At the other end are "liberal" Catholic institutions that seem indistinguishable from secular institutions in their framing assumptions—Catholic faith is one of the topics for discussion. The dogmatic institution makes the religious task all too simple and bereft of risk; the liberal institutions have great problems discovering why they are Catholic or faith-directed in any clear sense.

Admitting that probably all secular and Catholic institutions fall somewhere along the spectrum between the ideal types set forth, I still want to assert that there is a legitimate and important distinction to be drawn between the two, a distinction comprising intellectual, moral, and spiritual differences about the nature of learning and the life of learning. Henry James's distinction between life and art points to an intellectual problem the university must face in one fashion or another. Locating reality in a Platonic Form and Ideal or in the existential density of lived life is not a matter of taste. It involves complex intellectual assessment no less intricate than Plato's dialogues or Sartre's *Being and Nothing*. Following Plato, one ends up in the Platonic academy; agree with Sartre and one abandons the classroom for the café. The Catholic university has a further intellectual alternative to argue.

Making a judgment about the life of learning leads to judgments about life in its moral and spiritual dimensions as well. A Stoic–Platonic attitude toward life seeks to avoid the cruel shocks of history by the practice of discipline and contemplation. A Sartrean dares the tragic engagement with fragmentary existence. Christians believe against the grain that the shocks of history are to be engaged because they are encompassed in Resurrection. The acceptance or rejection of these three options—and more that could be outlined—are all worth pondering.

12

Practical/Praxis Postscript

In this final chapter I turn to some "practical" expressions of the idea of a Catholic university. That these are no more than a postscript will, no doubt, be frustrating to faculty and administration "on the ground" wrestling with having to construct a specific curriculum, set up a system of governance, establish codes of behavior in the residence halls, and so on. It is also something of a personal embarrassment that in a previous book[1] I sharply criticized works bearing the title "The *Idea* of a . . . University." The argument of that book was that most treatments of higher education are defective since they talk about intellectual life in general while the university is only one possible, historically conditioned, *institution* of intellectual life. I offered the example of early modern science, an intellectual activity of the highest order, which developed wholly outside of and often in opposition to the universities of the day. Using my earlier argument, then, I might criticize this effort as irrelevant to the institutional problems of a Catholic university. Interesting, perhaps, about Catholic/Christian thought patterns, but not specifically applicable to the problems of constructing a university committed to such modes of thought.

In the book's introduction, I noted that my original intention was to be more "institutional-directed," but that as the work progressed it seemed more and more necessary to clarify central ideas like "academic freedom," "dogma," and "church." Unless those ideas are clarified philosophically and theologically, any actual construction of a Catholic university would be something of a patch job: enough rhetoric about academic freedom to satisfy the American Association of University Professors (AAUP), cobbled together with sufficient ritual and good works to mollify the Congregation for the Doctrine of the Faith.

One of the conclusions of my earlier book was that universities must finally act in terms of their *mission*. The mission of many contemporary universities seems to be, either explicitly or by default, replication of faculty disciplines. That is *a* mission and surely not an unworthy one. It underlies the assumption that faculty determine the curriculum and appoint teaching staff. In the earlier book the point was expressed by quoting the claim that "the faculty *is* the university," which was I. I. Rabi's reply to Dwight Eisenhower's statement at a faculty meeting that he was pleased to meet the "employees" of Columbia Universty. As such, "the faculty is the university" was the fundamental, central, or governing half-truth about the university. The real and full truth is that "mission is the university"—even if the mission is the replication of faculty! Any mission other than "faculty replication" directs, frames, or (if regarded negatively) compromises the disciplines. In the case of a Catholic university, it would seem obvious that it requires a mission that is driven by something over and above the often conflicting ideologies of the varied disciplines at hand. One of the aims of this book, then, is to articulate a mission for a Catholic university within which curriculum, governance, extracurricular matters, and so on are understood and "constrained." Such constraint is, I believe, the proper price to be paid for any explicitly mission-driven institution, such as a women's college or a black college.

The argument of this book has been that "Catholic" in "Catholic university" is a term that *frames* the institution. Various terms have been utilized to exploit this metaphor. Christianity exists in a region *beyond* the "normal" capacity of the academy; it is directed at what we have called "the real" beyond science and art. The fact of something beyond establishes a *horizon* for the university. Because Christian theology asserts and characterizes that horizon, one can say that theology exists at the *margins* of normal academic study. When "margin" is construed negatively, theology is "marginalized," no longer considered essential to or even welcome within the core life of the academy, as is so often the case at secular universities. Prophetic or mystical Christianity may return that disdain by viewing the academy and all its works as arrogance and pride. As Tertullian put it: "What indeed has Athens to do with Jerusalem? What concord is there between Academy and Church? . . . Our instruction comes from the porch of Solomon. . . . Away with all attempts to produce a mottled Christianity of Stoic, Platonic and dialectic composition."[2]

The notion of theology at or over the margin of the university, positively or negatively, expresses the practical and pedagogical dilemma of the Catholic university. Is Christian theology *in* the curriculum—in which case how does religious revelation or Christian theology intersect with the usual critical, sceptical, and open stance of the normal academic researcher and scholar? Or should religion be placed only in the extracurriculum in works of social justice—in which case what is the difference between a Catholic university's connection to good works and the social urges of secular campus activists who probably would share none of the beliefs of their Catholic counterparts?

Given the marginalization of religion/theology argued for in my analysis, one can easily see why there has been the slide to secularism in the institutions of higher education and why many putatively Catholic colleges have located their Christian commitment outside the curriculum in campus ministry and social good works. My own construction of theology-at-the-horizon rejects these exclusionary solutions. Theology is, I contend, a necessary study *within* the genuine work of the university.

THEOLOGY: DEFENDER OF THE UNIVERSITY

Insofar as theology is directed at "the real" it may seem (or seek) to undermine academic pursuit. "The real" impinges on us in a "totalizing" fashion that dissolves the clarity of science and the order of art. Since "the real" emerges only with participation by the individual—I alone realize *my* death—there is a constraint placed upon the neutral, distanced, open inquiry of science and the open canon of the arts. The Holocaust opens "the real" as a totalizing defining experience; it "closes" the canon of life and constrains academic freedom as mere diversity.

If the academy with all its virtues and high arts is bounded by a reality beyond its capacity to analyze, and if religion points to and resides in that beyond, does religion have some *positive* role to play for the academy or does it stand only as a theological signpost on the academic wall? Within the Catholic tradition at least, it seems clear that theology is intended to be more than a warning sign or, worse yet, a condemnation notice posted outside the science building. In the record of history, Catholic theology has had a more positive attitude toward the university enterprise than the demands of "the real" might suggest. The elaborate scholastic theologies of the Middle Ages are, if nothing else, draped in the rational subtleties that are a delight to the academic mind. Thomas Aquinas's mystical insight that his own massive work was "straw" is powerful because his philosophical work is *not* straw. There is no great revelation in dismissing real trivia. Anti-art is shocking, effective, and important because conventional art is so significant. Rejecting the utterly rejectable is no revolutionary turn.

Without withdrawing from the fundamental notion that religion and Christian theology should not in any way be cast in the mold of science or art, it is critical to the idea of a Catholic university that theology be *inside* the university, in the curriculum, part of the "proper" academic life. A Catholic theology that approaches "the real" as *sacramental* protects the university from destructive encroachment by a chaotic or mystic view of "the real." One does not allow the Creator to absorb His Creation reducing it to illusion, and one does not allow the modes of understanding proper to Creation (the academic mindset) to reduce the Creator to illusion. (Note: a materialist "theology" may also reduce truth to the illusory motion of unknowable ultimate matter.) The theological issue *for* the university and *in* the university arises whenever one seeks to defend the integrity of science and art from subversion by "the real."

Placed into the range of university studies, theology is a "meta-discipline." It asks how university work is possible given the nature of ultimate reality. Since this chapter is intended to be "practical," however, it should be pointed out that in one sense studying and teaching theology is not practical. In *practice*, the professor in the lab or study need have no care or concern over theology, and simply assumes the value of the research at hand. In *practice* the university may sail on without a theological care or department thereof. However, in the larger scheme of things, especially when the problem of academic freedom and the legitimacy of truth is broached, any university may find theology valuable to justify its claim to truth.

The nature of argument in theology is highly complex, however. Because theology rests on some "intuition" about the chaos, density, "splendid waste,"

utter givenness of life and "the real"—and about how all this relates to our ordinary sense of reality—one cannot expect or require the sort of neat abstracted
demonstrations that characterize less messy academic fields. Nevertheless,
there are considerations that must be taken into account if one advances some
mystical or skeptical view of truth and the real. At the meta-level of argument,
the very notion of offering argument is, however, reflexive. A determined skeptic will not be convinced by any refutation. Since there is no truth at all, there is
no argument, refutation, or convincing. Dealing with an obdurate skeptic is, as
Aristotle says, like arguing with a vegetable.

I believe that there are considerations beyond vegetable vituperation that
can be brought to bear in considering the validity of the university enterprise,
but that is not my primary concern here. As noted above, there is a practical
sense in which the university will sail on grandly without self-consciously won-
dering about its own legitimacy for truth. I am more concerned with the more
"positive" role of theology for faith, and to that I now turn.

THEOLOGY: DEFENDER OF THE FAITH

If theology is taken only as a rarefied, reflexive meta-discipline that grounds the
ongoing work of the university, it may be granted a place in the academy—an
important place in fact—but it is not likely to be part of the core curriculum.
The eager freshman is no less convinced than the advanced chemist that there
are "truths" to be acquired and searched for, and is prepared to get on with it
without worrying for a nanosecond about the nature of truth. Theology, while
it can serve as a protection for university truth, has another function. Insofar as
it studies and establishes a "horizon" for the university, a positive theology
posits something about "the other side." Certainly that is the case with Christian Revelation. Opening "the real" within the curriculum is a demand by life
upon the university.

If theology is given a place within the core curriculum, there will be no
shortage of claimants for the truth about "the real" beyond the walls. In the
course of this book, I have outlined several high philosophies—like Platonism,
Stoicism, and Sartrean existentialism—whose powerful theological claims vitally affect the nature of academic study and set forth quite specific "ways of
life." Freshmen who know nothing of these elegant theories come drenched
with the "pop" philosophies of popular culture that often constitute the "theological" *lingua franca* of everyday student life. (The most elaborate and insight-
ful columns in the student newspaper are reviews of the latest rock recordings.)

Pop theology is pervasive on the quad, willy-nilly, so let me turn to the specifics of constructing a theological curriculum in a Catholic university.

The most immediate practical problem facing a Catholic university is setting the curriculum and finding the place for theology within the course of study. It is also the most difficult, if not well-nigh impossible, task. The problems with inserting Christian claims about "the real" within the university are varied, and beset with counterclaims as well. First is the sheer complexity if not mystery of these claims. Whether one proclaims a Christ or a Nietzschean "overman," there is a definite sense that the crisp confines of academic discourse have been irreparably breached: too much passion, too much conjecture, too much hope, despair, dismay to fit polite discourse. Passion and rhetoric reflect the priority of participation, praxis, and prayer as the "investigative tools" of this arena of "the real." The tweedy professor lecturing on Nietzsche from 9:00 to 10:00 three mornings a week seems a comic figure.

The presence of passion and prayer may be thought bad enough, but also the unconscious ideological assumptions of the contemporary university resist a hierarchical ordering of the curriculum such that any arena of study or truth is considered more important than any other. The curriculum seems, as its critics maintain, a sort of department store of goods of equal value to be chosen by the student customer according to her needs and desires. It is increasingly hard these days to argue that you *must* know physics or French or anything specific—even about the meaning of life!

The modern egalitarian array of academic goods is, one should recall, a very recent pedagogical development. The nineteenth-century denominational colleges in the United States had a determinedly hierarchic curriculum of "classical" studies that culminated in the senior required course on morality and theology. To underline its importance, this course was normally taught by the college president. (College presidents presumably knew about *real* life!) These hierarchized and structured curricula eventually gave way before the need to insert natural science into the course of study, which was accomplished by the introduction of electives. Opening the course of study through varied electives made it very difficult to compare educational outcomes in different programs and colleges.

The Carnegie Foundation for the Advancement of Teaching (founded in 1905) introduced the "Carnegie Unit," which is a point system granting credits for various courses on the basis of hours and effort. Although initially intended as a way of assessing high school performance, the credit system soon became the rule in higher education. Instead of an ordered hierarchy of study with a culminating course, all you had to do was count course units. The credit system "quantified" education by turning it into a process of mere accumulation of value-neutral units. For Catholic educators, the Carnegie initiative was doubly disastrous since the foundation had a direct policy forbidding grants to church-related schools. When Timothy Brosnahan, S.J., the then president of Boston College, declared about the Carnegie Foundation that "[i]f it had been designated . . . 'the Carnegie Foundation for the Secularization of Education' its purpose and ultimate aim would have been manifested,"[3] he was probably irked about lack of financial assistance. But his words could also carry a deeper philosophical meaning about the effect of quantitizing the course of study.

Brosnahan's comment reflects the Jesuit theory of higher education, the *ratio studiorum*, which was an ordered, hierarchized curriculum ending in the overviews of philosophy and theology. Theology was the traditional queen of the sciences; it was the study of Charles Taylor's "hypergoods," which are those actions in life that are superior to the "domestic" goods of everyday life: the monk abjures sex and the soldier risks his very life, both in search of a hypergood. Abandoning hierarchy in a course of study implicitly raises the question whether there are any *hyper*goods at all. If the answer given is no, then all goods are domestic, "economic" goods, and the choice among economic goods is largely on the basis of the desires of the consumer and the needs of the economic system—a fair description of the current state of higher education and its student customers. Quantification of the curriculum leads to commodification. It should be clear that at a minimum *Catholic* higher education would have to attend to hypergoods. Allegiance to hypergoods—any sort of hypergoods—creates academic dissonance since it imposes a hierarchy upon the democratic ethos of equally valued disciplines. Academic freedom can contribute to de-hierarchization since any claim that *A* is more important than *B* is matter of unending dispute. Settling the issue by asserting "*A is* more important than *B* and *must* be taught" sounds utterly dogmatic.[4]

The primary hurdle to be overcome, then, in constructing a Catholic curriculum is the lack of general academic belief in hypergoods. Lacking such a belief, all subjects are considered to be inherently of equal value; if there is to be a choice among them, it should be left to the student-consumer or to the vagaries of departmental politics. In any university marked by definitive historical memory such as our imagined Holocaust university, there would, however, be an *external* determinant establishing curricular priority. It would be unthinkable that students at the Holocaust university should drift through the curriculum without confronting the historical memory of the camps and genocide. Remembering the Holocaust in this institution would not be merely an "academic" interest similar to the value of learning about the culture of late imperial Rome or the Trobriand islands. The latter are worthy and legitimate academic tasks, but recalling the Holocaust creates, should create, a life attitude and commitment. "The real" of history impinges upon academic equanimity and creates "practical" priority.

Whether and how history impinges upon the egalitarianism of disciplines is a fundamental decision that cannot be avoided. As discussed in chapter 6, every university instantiates an "existential" dogma whether self-consciously or not. In shaping the curriculum, that existential dogma will be expressed. If history is final nightmare and chaos, that "real" may well be rejected and ignored in order to exploit the fragile light of intellect within. The existential dogma will be "expressed" by exclusion of chaos. On the other hand, if history has some deep, pervasive lesson such as the Holocaust, the curriculum will be shaped to open that lesson for the community. Prioritizing to Holocaust study will be self-recognition of the existential dogma that defines the institution.

A university—Catholic, Holocaust, Exodus Judaic—formed around a definitive historical memory will embed that paradigm experience within its curriculum. I believe that there are two parts to such a curricular formation: fundamental theology and dogmatic theology. Both should be part of the curriculum—and, in the undergraduate curriculum, the sooner the better.

FUNDAMENTAL AND DOGMATIC THEOLOGY
Assuming a "positive" take on "the real" of history—that it is not chaos to be ignored—the university's existential dogma should lead to a course in "fundamental theology." What is fundamental theology? The last thing would be some elaborate proofs for the existence of God. *Fundamental* theology explores the "logic" or "grammar" of "the real" with or without "the real" that contains or is a *theos*. Fundamental theology follows the comment that I attributed to Wittgenstein: "You can't hear God speak to someone else, you can hear him only if you are being addressed—that is a grammatical remark." Fundamental theology deals with the *grammar of being addressed*. To put it in terms used earlier, fundamental "theology" addresses the status of love, commitment, and decision. Marcel's comment quoted in chapter 10 suggests why these realities are fundamental for theology. Any "god" who is not the object of love, not discovered through love, is no God. Conversely, any God worthy of religious attention must *address* us—and one is properly addressed only when there is a loving

bond. I can "address" my children, call upon them in their depths, because they are my children. The tax department cannot "address" me; I am only a tax ID number to that bureaucracy.

I realize that it may embarrass the normal academic "cool," but I suggest that there be a fundamental theology course for freshmen on "Love, Commitment, and Decision (LCD)." A course with such a subject matter breaches academic proprieties in the sense that it speaks to attitudes that move beyond open inquiry. Love closes options and "inquiry." A course on love points beyond academic review to life choice, to participation beyond appraisal. There are manifold issues for such a course. Is love possible? Is love a reality? The course should consider the cynics and the Stoics, for whom love and its attendant commitments and decisions are either illusion or spiritual dangers. What about love as an illusion of the selfish gene? If love etc. is a reality, what is the grammar of love? What is life without love and decision?

I have made the point that prioritizing the curriculum occurs because of an incursion of history, "the real" of history, into academic equanimity. How would LCD fit the historical condition of present students? Is this "the real" of their history? Would they be "addressed" by such a course? Are they *within* some participatory story? That may be a genuine problem. In Nick Hornby's novel, *High Fidelity*, we meet Rob, the owner of a failing record shop that specializes in the half-forgotten, but sensational, singles that Bobby Bland recorded for the Stax label.[5] Rob's life is a record collection. Friends and lovers are sorted by consonance of record favorites. Like Barry Manilow and you are out! At the beginning of the novel Rob has just broken with Laura, his latest in a succession of girl friends. Later, Laura's father dies and, quite unexpectedly, Rob is asked to attend the funeral. Rob "freaks out" at the cremation and flees before the ceremony is finished. It turns out to be the turning point in the novel and his life:

> What happened to me during the funeral was something like this: I saw, for the first time, how scared I am of dying, and of other people dying, and how this fear has prevented me from doing all sorts of things, like giving up smoking (because if you take death too seriously or not seriously enough, as I have been doing up til now, what's the point?), and thinking about my life, especially my job, in a way that contains a concept of the future (too scary because the future ends in death). But most of all it has prevented me from sticking with a relationship, because if you stick to a relationship, and your life be-

> comes dependent on that person's life, and then they die, as they are
> bound to do, unless there are exceptional circumstances, e.g., they
> are a character from a science fiction novel . . . well, you are up the
> creek without a paddle, aren't you? . . . To me, it makes more sense
> to hop from woman to woman until you are too old to do it any-
> more, and then you live alone. . . . He sleeps with other women be-
> cause he has a fear of death!—well, I'm sorry but that's the way
> things are.[6]

The problem with Rob—and the irony of the title—is that he is a record
collector who lacks "high fidelity." Life, the novel says, is not a record collection—of "Louie, Louie" by the Kingsmen and "Little Red Corvette" by
Prince, *or* the recollection of ex-girlfriends that Rob reviews in the course of
the novel. Rob decides that he needs to become an "adult,"to see that there is a
future even all the way to death, and that he should reach for the high fidelity of
love and even marriage to Laura.

Rob's journey from adolescence to adulthood, from collecting records to
high fidelity, strikes me as "the real" for the late adolescents clustered in our
current classrooms. Rob is a comical and basically good-natured fellow caught
up in a show of cynicism. Not a bad description of lots of rock music and the
souls of youth. Hornby makes my required reading list as an illustration of life
with or without high fidelity. That may be the fundamental lesson that must be
learned before *any* theology makes sense. I leave it to the inspiration and inge-
nuity of faculty on the ground to fill out the syllabus for LCD, but the aim of
the course should be clear: exploration of the fundamental reality and grammar
of "life participation." If this is a course in a Catholic university, presumably
part of the depth grammar of high fidelity will reveal the grammar of "God."
"God" becomes a possible concept—Christians will say a necessary part of the
grammar of love, commitment, and decision.

I would make the LCD course in fundamental theology a required course
for every student at a Catholic university, lest the ultimate existential meaning
and base of the university's fundamental enterprise be distorted or go unrecog-
nized. Whether a second course on "dogmatic theology" is required would
depend on how it is actually constructed. The simplest model for a Catholic
university would be to use the grammar of fundamental theology to expand and
articulate traditional Catholic orthodoxy. There exists an enormous body of
liturgy, theology, dogmatic pronouncements, meditations, catechisms, moral
instructions, spiritual guidance, and so on that constitutes the language of

Catholicism. That "language," however, is untranslatable, like ancient Etrus-
can, until one knows the grammar. And learning the wrong grammar will lead
to profound mistranslation. If there is a fundamental and pervasive mistake in
the teaching of Catholicism in higher education, it seems to me to be drilling in
the orthodox language or rational scholasticism (however updated) without
first ensuring the grammer is understood. Unless one understands that orthodoxy rests on a fundamental grammar of love, commitment, and decision, one
distorts the meaning—often with disastrous results intellectually, institution-
ally, and personally.

The course in dogmatic theology must minimally read Catholicism according to the proper grammar. It is possible and, I believe, desirable that the course
also examine other religious traditions from the grammar of fundamental theology, whereupon it will likely be discovered that not all religions use the same
grammer. If the grammer of Buddhism is quite different, does the Buddhist rejection of "desire" entail rejection of love, commitment, and decision?

Fundamental theology in the core curriculum insists on the importance of
participation in life and goes forward to characterize in dogmatic theology
what attitude and life stance emerges from confrontation with the density of
"the real." At this point, however, one is faced with a true dilemma. The *sense* of
"the real"—the participant reality of the Holocaust survivor, of the black minority, of the Exodus Jew, of the devout Hindu—differs markedly and yet for
each it is ultimate and defining. What do we do with the counterclaims about
"the real" that emerge in dogmatic theologies? We are dealing with participant-
knowledge in the palace of abstract truth and open canons, so that normal pedagogy for dogmatic theology will seem highly problematic. (Not a "topic for
discussion.") After the Holocaust, not all options and opinions are open. Coming to accept "the real" as love, horror, or waste is not a matter for clever argument or elegant proof. What is universal, however, is the epistemology of "the
real," how we come to know "the real" and whether some claim about "the real"
has standing.

Claims about "the real" emerge from deep "experience," which should not
be taken in the sense in which we use experience to verify specific scientific or
factual claims. The experience in question comes not from observation but
from participation—particularly with those who in some fashion seem to have
"drained life to the dregs." One finds in such deep, participatory experience
that "the real" is manifest—this is the truth about life, the meaning of life. In
assessing claims about life and "the real," we use different categories than ordi-

nary "true" and "false." Views are assessed as "deep" or "shallow," "rich" or "re-strictive." In any conflict over characterization of "the real," mere judicious and tolerant diversity is unsatisfactory. This is an issue of "*the* real." If there is to be dialogue, any coming together among claimants on "the real," it will be as I have suggested in the "conflict" between a Holocaust survivor and traditional Jewish belief in the Exodus. To the extent that each view emerges from a par-ticipatory encounter with "the real," any "resolution" cannot de-center the ex-perience of the other. In the Christian story, Resurrection cannot de-center Crucifixion or vice versa. In ecumenical and transreligious dialogue, the reach to "the real" of other insights cannot be negated or de-centered. If there is a "geometry" for such discussions, it is one of concentric circles where all in-sights converge on a common center.

Does reading about love, commitment, and decision "connect" students to those realities? It may be more important to move students out of the class-room and the library into life situations that demand love, commitment, and decision. I read with approbation about a course in basic ethics at Boston Col-lege in which part of the curriculum involved work in a social service agency. In such a setting, ethical decisions are demanded by *life*, not discussed inter-minably. The reality of decision was made present. There is much to be said for the experiential dimension, but there is no mechanical connection between ex-perience and developing the insight that changes Rob's life toward "high fi-delity." It is not cyncical to observe that people may do good works because it is fashionable—every movie star has to have a "cause" these days. One may be motivated by guilt, aesthetic distaste of the conditions of the poor, or covert de-sire to impose more orderly (bourgeois values) on the wayward life of happy peasants. The pedagogical problem for instruction in love, commitment, and decision is how to move from reading or experiential practicums to the *reality* of love, commitment, and decision. Experience is not self-interpreting and lan-guage may stray from the reality it purports to comprehend. Students may miss the point in or out of the curriculum.

Neither reading about commitment or evenings in a soup kitchen may awaken one to the importance and reality of love, commitment, or "high fi-delity" in life. One may *practice* without entering into a praxis that anchors ac-tion to fundamental belief. Still, if one does not at least practice, the possibility of deep insight is diminished. Thus Pascal's infamous instruction about praying in the hope of belief. One can see, then, why in the actual construction of Catholic colleges, one places "faith" in the extracurriculum of "good works."

The only mistake would be failure to understand that such practice is vital to the academic curriculum. Following the liberation theologians, one would only expect theology and belief to take off after the Jesuit Volunteers return from the *barrios*.

Good works may be performed without any "faith" at all or with quite different "faiths." It can't be just the helping hand that is involved. Praxis is not merely the act, it is the structure from within which beliefs are to be articulated and then judged appropriate. I recall reading many years ago the account of a secular sociologist who spent a year with the Catholic Worker in New York. The Worker's "house of hospitality" day in and day out acts as a refuge for the derelicts of the street. No effort is made to convert those who seek its shelter—though help of whatever form will be offered. Recidivism is the rule as the same destroyed faces appear each day at the soup line. Ruminating on his personal experience at the Worker, the sociologist commented that he did not see how one could do what these people did without having the beliefs which they had. There had to be a "hope beyond hope" to minister to this continuing pathos.

Faith follows from prayer: *lex orandi, lex credendi*. Return to compulsory chapel is more unbelievable than that story of Joshua and the sun, but a direction from practice to praxis to prayer is essential to the "academic" exercise of Christian faith and theology. "Good works" practicums are not, then, mere uplifting add-ons to the curriculum; they are necessary epistemological moments in the development of theology.

THE EXTRACURRICULUM

Critics of Catholic higher education are more likely to be exercised about the extracurricular life of the Catholic campus than with the curriculum. Dot in some courses on theology or religion and one could be led to believe that Catholicity is being attended to. (My own take is that some "theologies" are more damaging to faith than no courses on theology. Give people a bad argument for a good position and they may reject the whole thing.) What really causes a disturbance are events outside the classroom. Should there be a gay and lesbian organization officially recognized on campus? Can one have a pro-choice speaker on campus? Is it proper for a Catholic college to give an honorary degree to a senator who voted to sustain the veto on partial birth abortions? Presidents of Catholic colleges get very few letters complaining that St. Bonaventure's *De reductione artium ad theologiam* has been dropped from the curriculum, but if President Clinton (the wrong politician) shows up on campus or the gay rights committee meets in the chapel, the telephone won't stop ringing.

If the Catholic institution in the light of its moral beliefs rejects a speaker, refuses to recognize an advocacy group, or censures certain behaviors, it is subject to criticism from traditional "liberal" sources within and without the academy. The grounds for such critique are not entirely clear. At times it seems that the criticism rests on an extension of the notion of "academic freedom." Given the vast uncertainty about proper life and conduct, it seems arbitrary and repressive to restrict advocacy and behavior. Uncertainty about morals seems, however, to be only the most superficial flourish from liberalism. Not only is there the obvious *moral* imperative in liberalism, "Thou shalt not restrict conduct or advocacy," liberalism in its current incarnation has a variety of special causes it favors and sanctions with fervor. The *New York Times*, a cynosure of liberal opinion, commenting on John Paul II's millennium apologia for the sins of the church, sniffed that the pope should have gone on to ask forgiveness for condemning abortion and homosexuality. The *Times* obviously thinks that the rights and wrongs of these contested behaviors are clear enough despite the supposed murkiness of morals. At the time of this writing, liberalism of conduct *cum* academic freedom is tied in an interesting knot at several colleges on the issue of whether student organizations of conservative Christians (not Catholics in this case) must admit homosexuals to positions of leadership. Do the Christians have the freedom (academic?, moral?) to exclude from leadership those who espouse moral positions that the organization rejects? The initial response of the colleges seems to be that the Christians do not have the right to exclude. One can only wonder what the reaction would be if the situation were reversed and a conservative Christian wanted to run for leadership of the gay and lesbian alliance, a white supremacist for head of the black students organization. These are only anecdotes from the current campus "culture wars," but they do suggest that when it comes to moral *restriction*, it is often Christian views that are restricted on the liberal campus. Moral "dogmatism" is not a Catholic exclusive.

My assumption is that all campuses are rife with morality and moralisms. Open advocacy and open conduct are not present in almost any collegiate setting. During the Vietnam War it was impossible for members of the Johnson administration to speak on most campuses. The National Abortion Rights League will be shunned at St. Mary's, the National Rifle Association at Antioch. Pick your cause, pick your campus. In short, I do not think that Catholic campuses are *de facto* different than most campuses in having a pervasive moral cast.

The problem is that Catholic moral directions do not necessarily agree with prevailing academic liberalism that sees the restrictive mote in the Catholic eye and ignores the beam in its own.

If it is the case that moralism abounds on college campuses, then advice on how to deal with opposing moral positions has application beyond the Catholic setting. As with many free speech issues (not academic freedom issues, see chapter seven), there is a distinction between advocacy and action. It seems to me appropriate to be as permissive as possible where advocacy is concerned, with two restrictions—restrictions that in a sense rest on the same principle. Advocates of racial or ethnic supremacy, purveyors of "hate"speech, may, I believe, be legitimately banned from the *academic* campus. The root assumption of supremacists is that some "other" is below discussion. No use conversing with blacks or whites, men or women, straights or gays—whatever may be the ill-favored group. The claim to moral supremacy *beyond discussion* controverts the essential spirit of the university as a place of dialogue. One might, of course, throw that accusation back on the Catholic campus itself. Does the Catholic campus open itself to dialogue to those with whom its disagrees? While there may be Catholic supremacists—I worry about Mother Angelica!—that is certainly not the normative or fundamental theological stance. Paul VI put the point in French. The church's aim is *pas vaincu, mais convaincu:* not to vanquish, but to convince. Theologically, no one is beyond redemption and we are all sinners anyhow. When it comes to actual practice in the classroom and on the public lecture platform, the presentation of Catholic points of view at Catholic institutions is inevitably and invariably contested either by self-conscious academic design or just the sheer scepticism of student audiences.

The second restriction on open advocacy is related to the first. If a controversial speaker is to appear on campus, the college may, as the shrine of dialogue, require that the speaker put forward his position in formal discussion. Such a restriction would harken back to the medieval *disputatio*, open debates in which the most unorthodox theses, for example, that God does not exist, could be argued pro and con. This restriction would, I think, only apply to issues clearly contrary to the prevailing moral position on campus. Thus by all means the generals should have had their say on campus during the Vietnam War, but only if counterarguments would have been offered in the same forum. If—a very big "if"—either side had actually *listened* to the opposing point of view, it might have ended the war sooner or prevented rather pointless campus mayhem. As it happens, there is for most issues no formal or informal campus concensus one way or the other, so the resort to the *disputatio* is likely to be unnecessary. But in the event an outside advocate refused the mode of *disputatio*, that would be equivalent to a speaker who refused to take questions. Neither figure should be welcome on campus.

There may well be exceptional cases where the appearance need not be framed in the mode of disputation because the experience or presence of the individual is what is valued. I have had occasion twice to deal with the appearance on campus of a U.S. president: Ronald Reagan and Bill Clinton. In the case of Reagan, a concerted group of left-wing faculty were outraged at the very idea of his appearance; in the second instance, a group of right-wing trustees were similarly outraged. Left or Right, they were both wrong. Whatever your political leanings, when the president of the United States comes to campus, it is the *president* and the *office* that is honored, not the views of the current incumbent. One need not—and probably cannot—demand that the president enter into disputation on Star Wars or partial birth abortion.

A similar exception may be made when the individual is not so much an advocate as an exemplar of a position. This is not an easy distinction to make, but it is worth having in one's administrative decision kit. Take the easy case. Not every individual should be expected to argue their position. A victim of racial apartheid speaks out of that experience; the victim is a "witness" in the sense discussed earlier, and it may be impossible or immoral to engage him in disputation. More difficult is the case of an exemplar of some morally loathsome position. Maybe there is some reason that the academic audience should experience a neo-Nazi at his most raving moments. But here the issue of commitment and decision discussed above comes to the fore. Does an institution truly *committed* to racial justice have to open itself to skin-heads just to show how broadminded it is? A touch of "dogmatism" here could be salutary: "No, that position is beyond permission; it is not tolerated in advocacy or deed." That sounds like the death of academic freedom and openness, but in the long run academic freedom that tolerates political pornography (the other stuff seems to be already well inside the permissible) may have surrendered all interest in moral truth.

"Advocacy" in the area of the extracurricular, as informed by issues of "freedom," is relatively easy to deal with. "Action" can be more difficult. A typical problem for a Catholic university is the activity of an on-campus abortion advocacy group or a gay and lesbian association. The Catholic Church takes such strong stands in opposition to abortion and active homosexuality that the active presence of these organizations certainly seems contrary to the institution's fundamental beliefs. One can well imagine dismay on the part of church officials at tolerance of such activities within the Catholic institution. Again it is useful to be reminded that Catholic institutions are not unique in adopting restrictive attitudes toward on-campus activities. As noted above, liberal campuses can be as wary of conservative Christian organizations as Catholic colleges are about a local branch of Queer Nation or Act-Up. Presumably no campus will tolerate a white supremacist student organization. A Holocaust university should not be required to have an organization for Holocaust-deniers out of some abstract allegiance to academic freedom or, worse yet, a defeatist attitude about the uncertainty of all claims to truth and morality.

Because of its general allegiance to freedom, the liberal campus is likely to give wide latitude even to moral positions that the general campus culture finds wrong or distasteful. That freedom permits some downright noxious notions to be expressed is a price worth paying. Banning activity might be legitimated only when the organization appears to violate the principle of freedom—thus the dilemma of whether a Christian organization violates freedom of association by excluding homosexuals. I suggest that the Catholic institution start from a different principle than freedom—namely, love or compassion that has its theological backing in the Augustinian dictum about the human heart: "Thou hast created us for thyself, and our hearts are restless until they rest in thee." At the deepest level, *all* human activity is motivated by desire to "rest in God." The drama of human life is structured around sin and conversion. Sin seeks the love of God but in the wrong direction; the sinner must be "turned around," converted. The spiritual attitude toward the sinner starts from acknowledging the yearning of the heart buried in the sinful course. In the specific hard cases at Catholic colleges one should start, at least, by acknowledging the residuum of love and compassion in the activity advocated. Surely there is a genuine compassion for the distraught, pregnant fourteen year old, for the exhausted mother living in the slums, for the victim of rape. Surely there is genuine love between members of the same sex that may extend to the final solace of bodily embrace. If these life positions are to be controverted by church teaching, it is not without recognizing the complex and conflicted conditions that are at issue.

The initial response to controversial claims by a Catholic university should be compassion based on a belief that there is a core or aspect of love and concern in the position rejected. This seems to be the actual reality. Although opponents of abortion like to classify it as murder and to compare its widespread practice to Nazi genocide, that cannot be a proper description. No matter how firmly one may oppose liberal abortion laws and practices, these are not comparable to the Nuremberg laws that singled out the Jews for persecution and eventual death. John Paul II has preached against abortion repeatedly on his trips to America. If America were comparable to a Nazi state, determined to eliminate a whole class of people, would a pope dignify such a wicked nation by his presence? When pro-life advocates debate their position with pro-choice supporters, do they debate the pros and cons of murder? Or, to put things back on the campus, would any college tolerate an organization advocating murder or genocide? Hardly. In short, at some level such contested issues as abortion and homosexuality involve genuine and positive moral interests. There is love and compassion there.

From the standpoint of the Catholic college, however, one can say "love is not enough," or, more accurately, love requires thoughtful action and policy, not the immediate pulse of feeling and compassion. One may feel that the quick and easy death of a loved one in terminal illness would be a blessing, but not therefore assist their suicide or become an advocate for euthanasia. Private acts and personal compassion have public meanings. The fullness of moral decision involves public weight. It *always* involves something larger if one accepts any version of the Kantian imperative that we should act so that the maxim of our action could be taken as a universal law for humankind. Offhand liberalism sometimes says that what people do *privately* is of no public concern. That may well do as a philosophy for the bedroom, but not as a general principle. If the neighbor down the street is beating his children, that is more than a private concern.

The burden of these considerations for a Catholic university is that there be an institutional imperative to discover whatever exists of genuine moral interest, love, and compassion in the contested position. This means that the interest is not to be rejected *tout court*, out of hand, not-to-be-discussed. In taking that position, the university has the right to demand a parallel response from the other side. Failure occurs on the parts of both institution and advocacy organization when absolutism is asserted and dilemma denied. Unhappily that is the common case. If, then, some campus organization sets itself up to advocate a course contrary to church teaching, the critical question is whether it is willing to take that case to the institution in a nonabsolutist fashion. Does the advocacy group admit the reality of moral complexity? (One has the impression that the rhetoric in the abortion debate has little taste for moral complexity.) Can the institution acknowledge the dilemma within which the advocacy group is enmeshed and from which its advocacy has some legitimacy? As argued above, if there is really no moral core at all to a position, racial supremacy, for example, then there is no dilemma of good and bad, no possibility of dialogue, and such advocacy has no place on the university campus.[7]

For on-campus advocacy groups, the suggestions made above about external advocates could be applied as well. It is fair to assume that the campus organization that opposes "official" positions seeks to change those positions. If so, then it should be prepared to engage in an orderly and formal discussion about the grounds for its advocacy. On the other hand, if the organization only plans to agitate, it strays from the institution's dialogic assumptions and, in essence, rejects its own interest in effecting change by refusing to muster convincing argument for its position. Paul VI's *pas vaincus, mais convaincus* is a maxim for both church and demonstrators.

Again, the really difficult issue is not advocacy, but action. Say there is a demand for providing abortion referrals at the student health service. At that point, the institution has every right to say, "Sorry, that is not a policy conclusion to which we have come. We cannot permit that action." This may seem to violate the spirit of freedom, but freedom means nothing to individuals or institutions if it prevents decision. There are good reasons for having racially segregated residence halls, but there are also strong counter considerations. A very liberal institution may forbid racial segregation or allow it, in either case on the basis of a conclusion it has reached given the complexity of the issue. For Catholics, sexual morality (which is the area that attracts the most attention) is complex. On a number of issues and conclusions, I think the official church positions are poorly argued and finally quite wrong—contraception being a clear case in point. However, the church is correct in seeing sex as a complex issue as against the simplifiers who see it as a pleasant romp with whomever, with no unalterable consequences.

The reasons for blocking certain actions go back to the complex relation between private actions and private motives and their public meaning. If condom machines are placed in the student lavatories, one can take the position that it says nothing as such about premarital sexuality but, given the age of the student population, such a position seems naïve in the extreme. Kant said correctly, he who wills the end, wills the means. I cannot really *will* to be a violin virtuoso, but decide never to practice. There is a reverse logic, he who wills the means, cannot be ignorant about the ends. There are many reasons to be understanding, tolerant, and forgiving about premarital sexuality; but certain university policies shade into the permissive. Perhaps that is the correct moral position, but it is not clear that it is so, and a Catholic institution may legitimately attempt to draw a line between being understanding and being permissive.

I do not pretend by the above to suggest that making the distinctions between advocacy and action are easy. Nor is it simple to locate and define the dilemmas involved in any significant moral position put forward. It is even more difficult and complex to persuade opposing sides on a moral issue to recognize and acknowledge the social, cultural, and political ramifications of the positions they advocate with such great enthusiasm and commitment. Recognizing the line where action becomes public permissiveness is hardly an exact science. Nevertheless, one can well advise a Catholic university to view counterpositions in advocacy and action with love and compassion. Catholic compassion can create an arena of freedom aimed at commitment; the freedom of an unchecked liberalism, however, can create an arena where nothing finally matters.

A CONTRARIAN CONCLUSION

The Catholic university distinguishes itself from its grand secular counterparts insofar as it opens its life and study to the realm of "the real," the participatory immersion within which love, commitment, and decision have lodging. The "revelation" at the heart of Christianity places it wholly within the density of human existence. This revelation says that if you move into "the real" with the lens of prayer, the eye of love, the demand for decision, this move toward life is not an illusion, a mistake, a sheer absurdity. "The real" is encompassed by a God of love, a God who is fully in the chaos, confusion, waste, destruction of human experience. This God makes "all things new" beyond the palpable terrors of history. For the Catholic university, this faith supports the work of science and art, the high truths of the university. At the same time, the Catholic university says that the academic stance is not all. Socrates was right enough: the unexamined life is not worth living (good academic slogan), but living a life is not an exercise in perpetual examination (love intervenes).

The position stated is not meant as pious sentiment for the college catalogue. If the Catholic university accepts its own faith, there are concrete decisions to be made in shaping the life and study of the institution so that the full reality of life is not masked or hidden in service of academic fastidiousness. I had a course in college from a theologically inclined faculty member who always wrote "God" in quotation marks. Perhaps the ultimate aim of this book has been to remove the quotation marks.

In these times when all universities and colleges are pressured by students, their parents, and the needs of a changing economy to provide a *practical* education, the recommendation that institutions place theology in the core of their curricula is certainly contrarian and utterly dot-com countercultural. This may be particularly the case for many Catholic institutions struggling along with limited endowments and facing aggressive competition from high-prestige privates and low-price publics. Commend "the real"? Get real! So be it. But especially to those of a strongly practical interest, I would emphasize that higher education should prepare students for three things: job, career, and vocation. These are definitely not the same idea. Students should receive skills sufficient for a job—the first job. But *higher* education should look beyond a job to a career. What is the second job, what pathway of positions can one hope for across a working life (and even study in college)? That is one's career. Finally, one may land a good job, have a successful career, yet lack a vocation. To what should we be called in the depth and richness of life? The question of vocation resonates across many of the curricular and extracurricular issues that define college life. Does the curriculum offer narratives of vocation? Does the extra-curriculum intersect with individuals with deep callings? Even the puzzling issues of campus morality can be better understood under the banner of vocation. We would all be much wiser if we were to stop asking about the "morality" of this or that sexual inclination or act and ask about sexual vocation. To what are we called in our sexuality and deep desires?

While it is admittedly a great oversimplification, it seems that secular education has abandoned vocation. Vocation is a personal choice, a subjective interest. The secular university will give you the tools for a job and a career. One learns the skills of a doctor, lawyer, or professor of poetry. But should one go further and invest one's *being* in medicine, law, or teaching? In the past it seems, for better and for worse, individuals identified their person with their job and career. One had the vocation of a being a doctor. Today there seems to be a dissociation—a job is just a job, and one seeks to find a sense of self away from the workplace. But where? Family? Families seem to be drifting into "meaningful relationships." When the meaning attenuates, one seeks a new edition. I do not wish to end with a jeremiad on the "lostness" of contemporary—particularly American—culture. But as Nick Hornby's novel *High Fidelity* might be understood to say, we have come to substitute collecting experiences for being "called." Catholic education that attends to student's vocations can help us recover "high fidelity" to a calling. That is its vocation.

Notes

1   Judge Weisberg concluded: "The university may choose for itself on which side of the conflict [between academic freedom and un-wavering fealty to the Holy See] it wants to come down on and nothing in the contract of Professor Curran . . . promises that it will always come down on the side of academic freedom." In Larry Whitman, *Curran vs. Catholic University: A Study of Authority and Freedom in Conflict* (Riverdale, Md.: Edington-Rand, 1991), p. 268.

2   Mary Burgan, "Scholarly Ideals and Changing Reality," *Academic Questions* 10, no. 4: 22–25.

3   In the earlier drafts this was translated as "mandate," a term that was strenuously objected to by the universities. Leaving the Latin original presumably lessens the threat.

4   Edmund Malloy and Donald Monan, "'*Ex Corde Ecclesiae*' Creates an Impasse," *America* 180, no. 3 (1999): 6–11.

5   Peter Steinfels, "A Journalist's View: Does Rome Have the Best Answer?" *Commonweal* 126, no. 7 (1999): 14.

6   This "slide from grace" is exhaustively chronicled in George Marsden, *The Soul of the American University* (New York: Oxford University Press, 1994).

7 For an extended discussion of the philosophical assumptions of the research university, see George Dennis O'Brien, *All the Essential Half-Truths about Higher Education*
   (Chicago: University of Chicago Press, 1997).

8 Alisdair MacIntyre, "Reconceiving the University and the Lecture," in *Three Rival
   Versions of Moral Enquiry: Encyclopaedia, Genealogy, and Tradition* (Notre Dame: University of Notre Dame Press, 1990), p. 221.

9 Simon Schwartzman, "The Focus on Scientific Activity," in *Perspectives on Higher
   Education*, ed. Burton R. Clark (Berkeley: University of California Press, 1984),
   p. 201.

10 The philosophers lurking behind the text are ones on whom I have spent the most
   time during my teaching and publishing career: Wittgenstein, Hegel, and Sartre.
   The theologian in the wings is Karl Rahner. All of them are notoriously obscure
   even by philosophic and theological standards. If I feel constrained to use their arguments, I hope to do so in as intelligible a fashion as possible. No doubt that will involve the distortion of simplification, but to pursue any of these thinkers in depth
   would produce a work impossibly long and probably as obscure as the original.

11 Dennis O'Brien, "Living by the Loopholes," *America* 181, no. 3 (1999): 18.

12 George Dennis O'Brien, *God and the New Haven Railway: and Why Neither One Is
   Doing Very Well* (Boston: Beacon Press, 1986).

CHAPTER ONE

1 For an extensive and rather gloomy assessment of the demise of Catholic (and all
   Christian) colleges, see James Burtchaell, *The Dying of the Light* (Grand Rapids:
   Eerdmanns, 1998).

2 The text of the Land O'Lakes statement is contained in *American Catholic Higher
   Education: Essential Documents, 1967–1990*, ed. Alice Gallin, O.S.U. (Notre Dame:
   University of Notre Dame, 1992), pp. 7–12.

3 Herbert McCabe, *God Matters* (London: Geoffrey Chapman, 1987), p. 8.

4 Stephen C. Ferrulo, *The Origins of the University: The Schools of Paris and Their Critics*
   (Stanford: Stanford University Press, 1985), p. 307.

5 The epigraph to Moore's *Principia Ethica* (Cambridge: Cambridge University Press,
   1903).

6 Pierre Bourdieu notes that the prominent deconstructionists—Foucault, Derrida,
   and Barthes—were or are all marginal to the French academic establishment. If they
   held academic appointment at all, they were often not permitted to supervise students for the *aggregation*. Life as illusion, power play, and social construction is an interesting synoptic view of the university from the outside, at the margins, but it
   evidently doesn't serve the daily curriculum. See Pierre Bourdieu, *Homo Academicus*,
   trans. Peter Collier (Stanford: Stanford University Press, 1984), p. xviii.

7   Roger Scruton, *Sexual Desire: A Moral Philosophy of the Erotic* (New York: Free Press, 1986), p. 59.
8   Mary Douglas, *Purity and Danger* (London: Routledge, 1966), pp. 42–58.
9   A Talmudic story retold by Edmund Cahn, *The Moral Decision: Right and Wrong in the Light of the American Law* (Bloomington: Indiana University Press, 1956), p. 310.
10 Raymond E. Brown, *An Introduction to the New Testament* (New York: Doubleday, 1997), p. xxiii.

CHAPTER TWO

1   C. N. Cochrane, *Christianity and Classical Culture* (New York: Oxford University Press, 1957), p. 266, summarizing from Julian's *In Galileos*.
2   John Paul II, *Fides et Ratio*, 4 (available at <www.vatican.va>).
3   Richard Bernstein, *Books & Culture* (July/August 1999): 32.
4   Walker Percy, *The Message in the Bottle* (New York: Farrar, Straus & Giroux, 1954), p. 141.
5   Franz Rosenzweig, *The Star of Redemption* (Notre Dame: University of Notre Dame Press, 1970), p. 342.
6   One might qualify this statement in two ways, neither of which are fundamental to the essential contrast. There is the fascination with certain quantum phenomena in which it is postulated that interaction with the observer qualifies what is observed. However one wants to understand this claim, it seems to do nothing to the basic "neutrality" of scientific observation. Quantum physicists do not publish their results like poets manifesting and seeking the personal voice. The second qualification is that science is itself a human artifact. To be sure, and many cultures have been as uninterested in science as Byzantine artists were in landscape painting. But the *culture* of science when it is practiced aims at the personal neutrality of the observer that is commensurate to the sheer givenness of empirical fact. Not all scientific researchers may be up to the asceticism of the neutral observer, but that is the ideal.
7   Alvin Plantinga, *Books & Culture* (July/August 1999): 33.

CHAPTER THREE

1   I have written more extensively on the problem of the authentic voice in an article on Richard McKeon in *Pluralism in Theory and Practice: Richard McKeon and American Philosophy*, ed. Eugene Garver and Richard Buchanan (Nashville: Vanderbilt University Press, 2000).
2   I have singled out the fine arts as essentially signatured. One can and in some cases should extend signature to works of history, philosophy, literary criticism—whatever gets classed in the modern "humanities." Gibbon is a unique literary stylist, thus it has been said that his *Decline and Fall*, while it has been superceded by more exact

accounts, has never been surpassed. Pierre Bourdieu (in *Homo Academicus*, trans. Peter Colllier [Stanford: Stanford University Press, 1984], p. 29) makes the interesting comment that the naturalist Buffon has not been given his proper respect within science because he was such an elegant writer. To be scientific, one is expected to present work in a deliberately flat, impersonal style. The obverse of Buffon is found in some of the social sciences where an "air" of science is given by masking mere opinion in flat jargon and elaborate statistics of the obvious. I have chosen to concentrate on the fine arts because the signatured character is presented there with special clarity.

3   Of course there is a merely descriptive sense of art that is used to distinguish works of nature from works of human hands. Barring an explosion in a cheese factory, dripped cheese is likely to be a work of human hands. Not all Art-done is Art-valuable. A reverse confusion of art and nature occurs in Pliny the Elder's natural history. Discussing the nature of rocks, Pliny offers a chapter on ancient statuary: a particular formation of rocks.

4   Shakespeare may or may not be the best example for a universal artist of humanity. Wittgenstein did not much like Shakespeare. "People stare at him in wonderment, almost as at a spectacular natural phenomenon. They do not feel that this brings them into contact with a great *human being*" (quoted by Iris Murdoch, *Metaphysics as a Guide to Morals* [New York: Viking, 1993], p. 112). On the other hand, Harold Bloom, in *Shakespeare: the Invention of the Human* (New York: Riverhead, 1998), asserts that Shakespeare *defines* what it is to be human. The *universality* of Shakespeare can, it seems, be taken as if he lacked a *personal* core (like a natural phenomenon) or as if he defined *all* that is human.

5   It is not possible to say ahead of time how much differentiation is necessary to fall out of family resemblance. If one plays *Macbeth* as comedy, does it fail of family resemblance? If I paint a large canvas in black and label it "Macbeth," am I relating to the play? Would it relate better in blue? I suspect that the contour of *Macbeth* is so strong and powerful that we would be tempted to find or conjure a family resemblance between the play and anything—anything!—that was labeled "Macbeth." But the more *outré* the examples, the less I am likely to regard the object as a reading of *Macbeth*.

6   The argument offered on the role of the arts in moral instruction is necessarily brief. Given the interest in moral "universality" expressed in *Fides et Ratio* and in Catholic moral teaching overall, it seems necessary to offer some comment on the subject. Placing art and its "intuition" of human inwardness as fundamental may seem to undermine universality—and in a sense it does. The argument offered, however, has roots in Aristotle's notion that in making ethical decisions it is the guidance of the "man of practical wisdom" who determines the mean. This person (man or woman,

obviously) has a sort of direct perception based on experience. The analogy to the connoisseur is obvious. For an extensive and richly detailed argument, which I believe parallels my own, see Paul Ricoeur, *Oneself as Another*, trans. Kathleen Blamey (Chicago: University of Chicago Press, 1992). Ricoeur finds the ultimate core of ethical goods in narrative. There is a necessary moment for Kantian universality in ethical argument, but finally ethics must be contextualized within a life narrative.

CHAPTER FOUR

1   In this regard, it is important that nowhere in the Gospel narratives does Jesus proclaim himself to be the Son of God/Messiah/Lord/etc. He asks "Who do *you* say that I am?" but offers no interpretation himself.

2   Quoted in *The Modern Theologians*, ed. David F. Ford (Oxford: Blackwell, 1997), p. 149.

3   A comment made by Frost at poetry reading at Dartmouth College.

4   "The real . . . is the mystery of the speaking body . . . ." Jacques Lacan, *On Feminine Sexuality, the Limits of Love and Knowledge 1972–1973*, trans. Bruce Fink (New York: Norton, 1975), p. 131. In my use, "the real" is both mystery *of* and mystery *to* the speaking body.

5   Henry James, *The Spoils of Poynton* (New York: Scribner's, 1908), pp. v–vi.

6   Karl Rahner uses the term "symbol" in a manner similar to my notion of the iconic. I think that "icon" is a better term. In the first place, it already carries the special sense of the religious from the tradition of holy icons in the Orthodox Church. Second, "symbol" can be used in a variety of ways and often means "*only* a symbol" as against the real thing. For example, saying it was a "symbolic protest" suggests that it did not engage the question directly. Roger Haight might have conveyed the presence of the divine in Jesus better had he titled his book *Jesus: Icon of God*. See Haight, *Jesus: Symbol of God* (Maryknoll, N.Y.: Orbis Books, 1998).

7   W. B. Yeats, *Autobiographies* (London: MacMillan, 1955), p. 5.

8   The notion that Duchamp's art is "iconic" in any sense similar to Christian icons may be enhanced by the suggestion that *The Bride and the Bachelors* is an inversion of the traditional Annunciation themes of Christian painting. The upper panel offers the Bride while down below the Bachelors angels exude a spiritual erotic essence. *The Bride and the Bachelors* is to a traditional Annunciation what the mustached *Mona Lisa* is to the original.

9   Ernest Hemingway, *A Farewell to Arms* (New York: Scribner's, 1949), p. 191.

10 Richard Kalina, "The Rutgers Group: Garden State Avant Garde," in *Art in America* (December 1999): 55. He goes on to say of Roy Lichtenstein's "comic strip" art: "Lichtenstein was much taken with . . . [the] belief that art does not have to look like art . . . ." Ibid., p. 57.

11 Wittgenstein did modify this early restrictive view of "what could be said" in his later work, but his religious views remained "mystical," hinted at in asides and aphorisms penned in the margins of his more conventional work. The quotations are from the famous last propositions in the *Tractatus*. Many of his apothegms about ethics, religion, and art are collected in Ludwig Wittgenstein, *Culture and Value*, ed. G. H. von Wright, trans. Peter Winch (Chicago: University of Chicago Press, 1980).

12 Jean Paul Sartre, *Nausea*, trans. Lloyd Alexander (New York: New Directions, 1964), p. 174.

13 Ibid., p. 127.

CHAPTER FIVE

1 Gabriel Marcel, *The Philosophy of Existence* (London: Harvill Press, 1948), p. 7.

2 Charles Taylor, *A Catholic Modernity?* ed. James L. Heft, S.M. (New York: Oxford University Press, 1999).

3 Andy Warhol, *A. A Novel* (Grove Press, 1998). To underline the ambiguity between "the real" (chaos) and the encompassing by signature, the "novel" was constructed from audio tapes of a day at the factory.

4 *Ludwig Wittgenstein, Personal Recollections*, ed. Rush Rhees (Totowa, N.J.: Rowan and Littlefield, 1981), p. 146.

5 Ludwig Wittgenstein, *Remarks on Frazer's Golden Bough*, ed. Rush Rhees (Norfolk, England: Brynmill, 1979), pp. 2–3.

6 Leo Tolstoy, *The Death of Ivan Ilych and Other Stories* (New York: Signet Classics, 1960), p. 104.

7 John L'Heureux, *The Expert on God*, in *Celestial Omnibus: Short Fiction on Faith*, ed. J. P. Maney and Tom Hazuka (Boston: Beacon Press, 1997).

8 Ludwig Wittgenstein, *Culture and Value* (Oxford: Blackwell, 1980), p. 33.

CHAPTER SIX

1 Not that there are no "true believers" in cold fusion. One need only surf the Internet to find them. A typical entry speaks of the "war" against cold fusion, an unholy alliance of the fossil fuel industry and the mainstream physics community. Skullduggery, fraud, and deceit are charged. The promises of cold fusion have an apocalyptic cast: a magazine touts the claims under the title *Infinite Energy*; a video proclaims *Fire from Water*.

2 Lawrence L. Langer, *Admitting the Holocaust: Collected Essays* (New York: Oxford University Press, 1995). Langer notes in his preface that he quotes Améry so often that it is like an "epiphany."

3 Pierre Hadot, *Philosophy as a Way of Life: Spiritual Exercises from Socrates to Foucault*, ed. Arnold I. Davidson, trans. Michael Chase (Oxford: Blackwell, 1995), p. 309.

4   Richard Dawkins, *The Blind Watchmaker: Why Evidence of Evolution Reveals a Universe without Design* (New York: Norton, 1986). Dawkins's overall notion that human behavior can be fully understood as the activity of "the selfish gene" leads directly to "atheism." From the standpoint of the argument in this book, Dawkins scarcely can give reality to human being—we are the ephemera of the gene—not to mention God.

CHAPTER SEVEN

1   The terms are Peirce's, quoted in Julie A. Reuben, *The Making of the Modern University: Intellectual Transformation and the Marginalization of Morality* (Chicago: University of Chicago Press, 1996), p. 55. Reuben's study is invaluable in understanding the ideological transformations that created the contemporary academic mindset.

2   Ibid., p. 50.

3   Ibid., p. 40.

4   For the historically concerned, I am not here asserting the sort of "two-truths" doctrine that was such a matter of contention in medieval theology. As I understand that controversy, a two-truths doctrine would create a kind of moral and intellectual schizophrenia in which one could alternate descriptions of the world between, for example, Darwinism and biblical Creationism. My view is that there is one world and one array of truth. The truth of art or the truth of religion are not alternate scientific descriptions, they are enrichments in some "total" characterization of the world and humans in that world.

5   David Tracy, *The Analogical Imagination* (New York: Crossroad, 1986), p. 67.

6   Epictetus, *Discourses*, bk. 3, chap. 24, in *The Stoic and Epicurean Philosophers: The Complete Extant Writings of Epictetus, Lucretius, Marcus Aurelius*, ed. Whitney J. Oates (New York: Random House, 1940), pp. 397–98.

7   Raymond E. Brown, *An Introduction to New Testament Christology* (New York: Paulist Press, 1994), p. 28.

CHAPTER EIGHT

1   For Hick, religious faith is like any empirical claim except that it is confirmed "eschatologcally." See John Hick, *Faith and Knowledge* (Ithaca: Cornell University Press, 1957). The argument of this book is that faith arises within present history.

CHAPTER NINE

1   Apostolic Constitution on Catholic Universities (*Ex Corde Ecclesiae*), part I, A.1 (available at <www.vatican.va>).

2   The actual situation in the implementation document from the National Council of Catholic Bishops is much more complex if not hopelessly murky. It is up to the indi-

vidual theologian to seek a *mandatum;* it does not appear to be required that he do so or that failing to make such a request would threaten his status as a Catholic theologian in good standing. Confusion such as that surrounding the *mandatum* are what suggested to me that the bishop's document was a tissue of "loopholes." See Dennis O'Brien, "Living by the Loopholes," *America* 181, no. 3 (1999): 18.

3   Curran suffered because of two "defects." First he wrote in a manner that Rome could understand, unlike many of the "existentialist" theologians, who are so deep in phenomenological jargon that it is not always clear what they are up to. Second, he has a taste for the public arena. Had he published in small-circulation, learned tractates, no one might have paid any attention to his views. However, since the sexual issues he addressed (contraception, masturbation) were fraught with concern and controversy, they deserved the sort of public airing he generated.

4   Catherine Mowry LaCugna, "Some Theological Reflections on *Ex Corde Ecclesiae,*" in *The Challenge and Promise of a Catholic University,* ed. Theodore M. Hesburgh (South Bend, Ind.: University of Notre Dame Press, 1994), p. 124.

5   Richard McBrien, "Why I Shall Not Seek the *Mandatum,*" *America* 182, no. 4 (2000): 14–16.

6   Avery Dulles, *Models of the Church* (New York: Doubleday, 1978).

7   Ibid., p. 121.

8   Raymond E. Brown, *An Introduction to the New Testament* (New York: Paulist Press, 1994), p. 11.

9   Ludwig Wittgenstein, *Culture and Value,* ed. G. H. Von Wright, trans. Peter Winch (Chicago: University of Chicago Press, 1984), p. 6e.

CHAPTER TEN

1   In a later expanded edition—*Models of the Church* (New York: Doubleday, 1987)—Dulles added a sixth model: the church as community of disciples. This model comports well with my earlier emphasis of the centrality of the Teacher–disciple relation compared with the teaching–student relation. For this reason I have chosen not to discuss the disciple model in any detail here. Moreover, I believe that the disciple model requires interpretation *within* the context of the sacramental model, for only in the sacramental sense can Jesus remain present as Teacher-Savior.

2   J. N. Findlay, "Can God's Existence be Disproved," in *New Essays in Philosophical Theology,* ed. Antony Flew and Alasdair MacIntyre (London: SCM Press, 1955), pp. 47–56.

3   Gabriel Marcel, *Metaphysical Journal,* trans. Bernard Wall (Chicago: Henry Regnery, 1952), p. 58.

4   Ludwig Wittgenstein, *Culture and Value* (Oxford: Blackwell, 1980), p. 33.

5   Findlay is correct in holding that in terms of the primary epistemologies of empiricism and analytic logic, the phrase "necessary existent" is incoherent. No existent

thing can exist necessarily. The sense in which God is necessary for the religious believer is that God is the everlasting, imperishable ground for the attitude of prayer and worship. Having "fallen into" prayer, one makes no sense of it except as it is directed toward and grounded by God. If worship makes sense, then God as "necessary" makes sense. Findlay should conclude not only that "God—necessary existent" is nonsense, so is worship since it is directed at nonsense. The fundamental question for religion may well be: does worship *ever* make sense?

6   This discussion of the sacramental owes a great deal to the work of Catherine Pickstock. See "Thomas Aquinas and the Eucharist," in *Catholicism and Catholicity: Eucharistic Communities in Historical and Contemporary Perspectives*, ed. Sarah Beckwith (Oxford: Blackwell, 1999), pp. 47–68. The close relation between academic and religious modes of thought under the structure of sacramentality is expressed in the title of her book, *After Writing—On the Liturgical Consummation of Philosophy* (Oxford: Blackwell, 1998).

7   For a detailed discussion of Protestant "symbolic" versus Catholic "real" presence, see Denys Turner, "The Darkness of God and the Light of Christ: Negative Theology and Eucharistic Presence," in *Catholicism and Catholicity: Eucharistic Communities in Historical and Contemporary Perspectives*, ed. Sarah Beckwith (Oxford: Blackwell, 1999), pp. 31–46.

8   The technical doctrine of Transubstantiation, rather than suggesting that Jesus has *changed* into bread or that bread has *changed* into Jesus (the disguises scenario), should be understood only in a "spiritual" or "sacramental" sense. In the Aristotelian/Thomistic metaphysics of substance, *substance* is never transformable. Substance is what remains the *same* through change: the rock (substance) becomes hot. Thomas's introduction of trans-substance "change" is denial of any "real" change such as would occur if I disguise (change) myself by putting on a mustache. The subsequent paragraphs in the text attempt to give a sense of "real" change and "real" presence in the sacramental mode.

9   Rosemary Luling Houghton, "Converting Symbols," *Religion and the Arts* 1, no. 1 (1996): 58–73.

10 To offer only one citation. John S. Dunne, *Reading the Gospel* (South Bend, Ind.: University of Notre Dame Press, 2000), p. 3.

CHAPTER ELEVEN

1   Tom Beaudoin, *Virtual Faith: The Irreverent Spiritual Quest of Generation X* (San Francisco: Jossey-Bass, 1998).

2   An example of this sort of dialogue is contained in several works by Hans Kung and partners in the area of Islam and Chinese religions. Hans Kung and Julia Ching, *Christianity and Chinese Religions* (New York: Doubleday, 1989).

CHAPTER TWELVE

1   George Dennis O'Brien, *All the Essential Half-Truths about Higher Education* (Chicago: University of Chicago Press, 1997).

2   *De Praescriptione Hereticorum* 7, quoted in Harry A. Wolfson, *The Philosophy of the Church Fathers*, vol. 1, *Faith, Trinity, Incarnation* (Cambridge: Harvard University Press, 1956), p. 102.

3   Quoted in Philip Gleason, *Contending with Modernity: Catholic Higher Education in the Twentieth Century* (New York: Oxford, 1995), p. 35.

4   There is, of course, logical hierarchization in the academy. You can't do thermodynamics until you know calculus; you can't study Proust in the original until you master French. But whether French or thermodynamics is more important for the life of the student depends on customer interest.

5   Nick Hornby, *High Fidelity* (New York: Riverhead, 1995). A film version of the book was released in 2000, shifting the locale from London to Chicago.

6   Ibid., pp. 247–48.

7   On general theological grounds, no position is without some moral content, but it may be so perversely expressed that it blinds one to anything short of radical conversion. Racial supremacists usually speak from a profound spiritual poverty, a sense of victimization, that is compensated in their false doctrine. The church can well recognize the spiritual poverty and the hidden cry of the victim while utterly rejecting his proposed solution.

Index

A: A Novel (Warhol), 68

abortion, 206, 209, 210–11, 212

academic freedom: AAUP exemption for religious colleges, 25, 141; as academic dogma, 88; and advocacy on campus, 207, 209; and Catholic universities, 1–2, 13, 88–107; competence as basis of, 90, 91–94, 148; diversity interpretation of, 135–36, 138, 139, 165, 196; Enlightenment rationality in interpretations of, 13; and *Ex Corde Ecclesiae*, 147–63; free speech contrasted with, 89–91; in Gallaudet College controversy, 137; and a Holocaust university, 133, 135–36; Land O'Lakes statement on, 13, 147; in natural science, 90–91; science and art as conforming to assumptions of, 172; Statutes of Paris of 1215 as charter for, 14–15

academy, the. *See* universities

accreditation, 151

advocacy, 207–13

African art, 38, 39

American Association of University Professors (AAUP): on academic freedom, 25, 89, 148, 195; Catholic University of America on censure list of, 1; on religious colleges, 25, 141; and Statutes of Paris of 1215, 14–15

Améry, Jean, 96

analytic statements, 169

Annunciation theme, 219n. 8

anti-art: Catholic anti-artists, 107; conventional art's significance in effectiveness of, 197; eroticism in, 56, 57, 172; as giving only a slice of actual life, 77; as going beyond art, 56, 57, 64, 65, 96; happenings, 68, 71; as iconic, 57–58, 86; installation art, 56; on intransigence of existence, 79; pop art, 56, 119, 178; presence in, 56, 64; "the real" in, 55, 57, 64, 172, 174; as signatured, 64–66; urge to order resisted by, 97